A MOSAIC
OF BELIEVERS

A MOSAIC OF BELIEVERS

DIVERSITY AND INNOVATION IN A MULTIETHNIC CHURCH

Gerardo Marti

INDIANA UNIVERSITY PRESS
BLOOMINGTON · INDIANAPOLIS

This book is a publication of

Indiana University Press
601 North Morton Street
Bloomington, Indiana 47404-3797 USA

www.iupress.indiana.edu

Telephone orders 800-842-6796
Fax orders 812-855-7931
Orders by e-mail iuporder@indiana.edu

First paperback edition 2009,
with a new preface
© 2005 by Gerardo Marti

MANUFACTURED IN THE UNITED STATES OF AMERICA

The Library of Congress has cataloged the hardcover edition as follows:

Marti, Gerardo, [date–]
A mosaic of believers : diversity and innovation in a multiethnic church / Gerardo Marti.
p. cm.
Includes bibliographical references and index.
ISBN 0-253-34482-4 (hardcover : alk. paper)
1. Christianity and culture—United States.
2. Ethnicity—Religious aspects—Christianity. I. Title.
BR115.C8M2398 2004
280'4—dc22

2004013521

ISBN 978-0-253-34482-3 (cl.)
ISBN 978-0-253-20343-4 (pbk.)

2 3 4 5 14 13 12 11 10 09

To Laura,
with all my love.

[Y]ou must learn to use your life experience in your intellectual work: continually to examine and interpret it. In this sense, craftsmanship is the center of yourself and you are personally involved in every intellectual product upon which you may work.

C. Wright Mills, *The Sociological Imagination*

CONTENTS

PREFACE TO THE PAPERBACK EDITION

A Mosaic of Believers was written quickly, completed within a few months of transcribing interviews and field notes, and themed around the initial question of ethnic diversity. It was also published quickly, and the response to the book was almost immediate. Many scholars have commented on the book in conferences and in their own writings, and church leaders have been challenged by the changing dynamics of American religion described in it. I hope this new edition furthers even more expansive, insightful, and productive conversations at the intersection of religion, race, innovation, and social change.

Although I moved away from Los Angeles a few months before the release of the first edition, I have kept up with happenings at Mosaic through friends, conferences, and the ever-ubiquitous internet. The core processes described in this book continue—and are expanding. In this preface, I bring readers up to date on Mosaic, briefly describe critical reactions to the book, and highlight continuing themes in my research.

Mosaic and the Rise of Entrepreneurial Evangelicalism

With more than 3,000 people attending nine weekly services in seven separate locations at the beginning of 2009, Mosaic remains one of the largest multiethnic congregations in the United States. The average member age continues to be 27 years with an ethnic composition similar to what was reported in 2005: 35 percent white, 35 percent Asian, 20 percent Latino, 5 percent African American, and 5 percent other. The study of this unique congregation continues to provide an opportunity to see how this one church achieves an exceptional degree of diversity.

Mosaic also remains one of the most innovative congregations in America, and this aspect, which I describe herein, is gaining greater attention. I now see Mosaic as part of an expanding religious orientation I am labeling "entrepreneurial evangelicalism." Processes of religious innovation are fundamental to the congregation, and a significant portion of the narrative implicitly accentuates the importance of religious creativity. My second book, *Hollywood Faith: Holiness, Prosperity, and Ambition in a Los Angeles*

Church, further taps into entrepreneurial evangelicalism through a focus on Christians working in the entertainment industry as members of the creative class. Considering how much Mosaic and other contemporary evangelicals draw on the nuances of entrepreneurialism, I intend to look more closely at entrepreneurial evangelicalism as a distinctive religious orientation that creatively and intentionally engages "culture" (as these believers understand it), especially through the use of art, media, and technology and energized through loosely coupled organizational networks. The vitality of organizational networks encouraging religious innovation is significant, especially in the ministry of Mosaic.

As I predicted when I originally wrote the book, the number of "Mosaics" is growing significantly. The successes of the church and its influential lead pastor, Erwin Raphael McManus, are making Mosaic a worldwide phenomenon in local church belief and practice. Pastor Erwin has authored seven best-selling books over the last seven years, which are translated and distributed across the globe. Through the non-profit organization Awaken, described as "a team of dreamers and innovators who specialize in the field of developing and unleashing personal and organizational creativity" (see www.awaken.org), Pastor Erwin produces conferences (Ethos), short films (Awaken Films), music (Wide Awake Records), and other experientially based materials (e.g., yelō) that further extend the reach of the congregation. And under Pastor Erwin's leadership, the mother church in Los Angeles supports the ministry of other congregations through a network of like-minded churches.

The innovative, entrepreneurial aspects of this church make it a network hub attracting the attention and collegiality of church leaders around the globe. The increased demand for consultation and partnership led to founding the Mosaic Alliance in 2002, which serves some 2,000 churches. More than a hundred churches participate at a higher level commitment within the network. Some have taken the name Mosaic (e.g., Mosaic Manhattan, Mosaic Atlanta, Mosaic Perth, Mosaic Sheffield), and all share a common ideological framework (as described throughout this book). In the United States, closely allied congregations stretch from California to Connecticut (with Texas and North Carolina well represented). Fully one-quarter of Alliance churches and one-third of highly committed churches are international. These non-U.S. churches cluster in the Anglophone countries of Australia, New Zealand, and the United Kingdom largely because the resources coming from Mosaic are produced in English. In order to share material in other languages, Mosaic hosts annual conferences in places like Germany and Switzerland with extensive use of translators.

The spread of Mosaic's influence will surely continue as the number of "Mosaics" expands and more representatives from the congregation (both

U.S. and non-U.S. based) spread the "cultural DNA" of the church. In addition, Mosaic recently formed the Origins Project, a new initiative among entrepreneurial churches that is intended to "inspire one another to embrace innovation and creativity." Ventures like these accentuate the importance of voluntary transnational organizational networks that actively promote religious innovation. More research on such networks is desperately needed.

Critical Reaction to Core Ideas

In my formal study of Mosaic, I was overwhelmed with the congregation as a complex organization with multiple and contradictory layers of history, identity, and theology. Initial readers drawn to the study of race and ethnicity are surprised to find how this book addresses many other topics, including

- the active negotiation of personal identity in a multi-identity society
- curious re-framings of religious tradition in response to local pastoral challenges
- alternative age dynamics and their implications to congregations
- insight into emerging variations in American evangelicalism
- the conscientious management of charismatic leadership and experimental—even disposable—ministry structures
- challenges to recruiting volunteers and crafting mission-driven lay leadership roles
- an intimate look at the internal workings of an American megachurch
- the conscious cultivation of distinctive religious frameworks that serve the growing creative class

These themes continue to feed my research, and my growing thoughts on these topics will become available in future talks, books, and journal articles.

The aspects of this book that are drawing the most vocal reactions from scholars include the process of ethnic transcendence, the notion of havens as a lens for understanding congregational cultures, and the challenge of ethnographic research involving religious insiders.

The Process of Ethnic Transcendence
in Diverse Congregations

A Mosaic of Believers is the first complete ethnography of an integrated congregation. Since its publication in 2005, other ethnographies of single churches have been published (see, for example, Kathleen Garces-Foley's

Crossing the Ethnic Divide, Korie Edwards's *The Elusive Dream*, and my second book, *Hollywood Faith*), in addition to other book-length studies of diverse congregations (including Michael Emerson's *People of the Dream*, Russell Jeung's *Faithful Generations*, and *Against All Odds*, by Brad Christerson, Michael O. Emerson, and Korie L. Edwards). There is also a growing stream of journal articles and research notes now available (see cited works in Marti, 2009). We are only beginning to understand the processes of congregational diversity.

My own approach to the study of diversity contrasts with most other published scholars because of its emphasis on the context-dependence of ethnic identity (see chapters 1 and 7 of this book; more extensive discussion can be found in Marti, 2008a, 2008b, 2009). Here and in later writings, I describe how the process of religious racial integration can be accomplished within specific congregational structures. In short, the complexity of personal identity and the malleability of ethnic identity allow members of disparate racial and ethnic groups the potential to join together under a collective religious identity. I label this process "ethnic transcendence"—a label I still like because of its provocative nature. Yet, scholars of race have questioned my seeming optimism (or perhaps, in their assessment, my naiveté) of what they perceive as a dismissal of the ever-present dilemmas of racial oppression and exploitation.

Ethno-racial distinctions do matter, and the sociological processes embedded within these distinctions leave members of various groups unable to enter willy-nilly into any congregation. In her excellent book, Kathleen Garces-Foley (2007) distinguishes between strategies of ethnic transcendence and ethnic inclusion to emphasize how some integrated congregations choose to highlight racial differences while others, like Mosaic, do not. However, I do not believe such a distinction is necessary and view her analysis as underestimating the processes of ethnic transcendence at work in the congregation she studied (see Marti, 2009). Other scholars, such as Korie Edwards (2008), suggest interracial churches only happen when non-majority racial groups subordinate their religious practices to white-dominant standards. Edwards's insightful study leaves us wondering if truly diversity-affirming congregations are ever possible (see Jeremy Rehwaldt-Alexander's review of Edwards's book in *The Christian Century*, January 2009). While *A Mosaic of Believers* is inconclusive as to whether the process of ethnic transcendence is relevant for multiracial churches with a significant proportion of African American attendees, my second book, *Hollywood Faith*, focuses on a successfully diverse black-white congregation and essentially argues that racial differences can be successfully negotiated without privileging white religious practices.

I clarify and expand on the process of ethnic transcendence in an article that was published in the *Journal for the Scientific Study of Religion* in March 2009. Without reducing the macro-structural difficulties of integrating ethno-racial groups, I show how micro-interactional organizational contexts can sustain cross-ethnic relationships. Even seemingly intractable identities like "Asian" and "African American" are malleable in the lived experience of actual individuals in diverse settings. Much more research is needed to locate the extent and nature of such dynamics among members of diverse congregations without dismissing the overall difficulties, pressures, and contradictions that persist in our racialized nation. Moreover, we need to pay much more attention to cross-ethnic diversity beyond the incorporation of nonwhites into Anglo-centered congregations.

The implicit debate within the literature wrestles with the relationship between processes of ethnic *transcendence* and ethnic *reinforcement*. Can diverse members "set aside" their racial identities in a religious multiracial setting? Or is it important to retain racially specific identities as a primary base of interaction and not be expected to "obscure" or "subsume" racial specificity in order to participate in a multiracial community of faith? I trust scholars will continue debating the relative merits of various perspectives until we achieve a more satisfactory consensus.

The Challenge of Ethnographic Research Involving Religious Insiders

Another aspect of this book entails the background of the researcher who wrote it. Scholars have spoken to me privately noting their appreciation for the methodological appendix included in *A Mosaic of Believers* on the tensions inherent to ethnography in which the researcher is a "religious insider." Although this is not a raging debate within the field, my sense is that the delicate task of studying religious settings by insiders is frequently, but quietly, discussed among younger and developing scholars. To the extent that one's biography is inextricably connected with one's scholarship, many social scientists desire to apply sophisticated methodological techniques to analyzing the religious settings that have intrigued them the most—the ones they participate in—whether they remain members of that setting or not.

These scholars seek models for how to study settings that are inherently personal while respecting the demands of responsible scholarship. The task is rife with difficulties as insider projects are not for the faint of heart. Data collection and analysis aside, there are considerable challenges to having one's work accepted as valid by the social scientific community. Certainly *A Mosaic of Believers* faced challenges getting published as a monograph with a respected university press. One reviewer for another press felt the book was "not theoretical enough." Another reviewer for yet another publisher believed that "the book should be published, but not by this press," and suggested the book be pitched to seminary, rather than social scientific, audiences. These reviews greatly distressed me, as I always understood myself to be a theoretically sensitive sociologist contributing to the research literature.

My graduate training, the motivation for the project, and the conceptualization of the original study (including its questions, its methodology, and its analytical technique) follow standard practices among qualitative researchers. To emphasize my approach and careful working through of any potential difficulties, I crafted the methodological appendix *after* its acceptance by Indiana University Press in part to alleviate potential criticism (which I have not heard) and in part to encourage other researchers wishing to do similar work (which I have heard). In addition, I inserted the epigraph (taken from C. Wright Mills's *The Sociological Imagination*) as it was going to press to underscore how biography is generative to scholarship. Evaluation of methodology is critical to social science, and I invite others to continue assessing the merits of insider ethnographies not only as they pertain to questions of religion but also to questions of race, gender, politics, class, and other aspects of personal identity.

One more thing—during my second ethnography, which was published in *Hollywood Faith*, I found the difficulties of determining the line between insider and outsider to be much more complex, entangled, and non-obvious. At the beginning of this subsequent study, I was conflicted about the degree to which I had insider status to a congregation that was not my own. For example, if I claim to adhere to a particular religious orientation, am I an insider to all varieties of that orientation? Is an insider determined only by membership in a specific congregation? Or is an insider determined by participation in a denomination? Or perhaps a geographic region? Playing with the possibilities, it seems easier to determine what constitutes an outsider than an insider.

In the end, any binary definition of insider/outsider resists the nuance of tensions between these terms in the lived experience of a researcher. The usefulness of the insider/outsider dilemma is to highlight and promote a productive investigation of how one's status as a researcher affects one's investigation. Following contemporary ethnographers, we can never eliminate personal involvement in research, but we can and should use a critical understanding of our involvement in productive ways.

Havens as a Lens for Understanding Congregational Cultures

Scholars often ask me where I got the concept of havens. To be clear, it is my own idea, a concept that came to me as a way to organize the data. *A Mosaic of Believers* is organized around the notion of havens, which I define as subtle, overarching structures that emphasize how people find a refuge or a sanctuary for a significant aspect of their religious desires, personal identities, and value systems. Havens are not static structures that exist in the abstract; they are dynamic structures created through shared activities and motivated by certain beliefs.

Scholars have indicated both privately and publicly the usefulness of this concept as a starting point for understanding the movement of people within and between religious settings (e.g., see Jerome P. Baggett's *Sense of the Faithful,* p. 262n.). This is how the concept is meant to be used. The notion of havens is not a theory but rather a sensitizing concept, a heuristic device for stimulating questions and advancing insights about the self-selective mechanisms that simultaneously draw and repel certain groups to a congregation. While it serves as a suitable organizing framework for this book, others may find the concept of havens more disposable as they progress in their own analysis.

As for myself, I was often reminded during my interviews that congregations are voluntary organizations and consequently some people join while others leave in the normal and ongoing activities of any congregation. Individuals connect to a congregation by participating in opportunities for relational interactions that appeal to at least one aspect of their social selves. But havens are not universally experienced; thus, havens exhibit an interesting dualism that I found critical to my analysis. As self-selective mechanisms, havens attract certain people and repel others. While I did not pursue this idea in *A Mosaic of Believers,* I now believe that distinguishing between racially specific havens that appeal to specific ethno-racial groups and racially diffuse havens that successfully appeal to members of all groups might contribute toward a better understanding of the alternate probabilities for achieving sustainable diversity. I suspect there are congregations that combine both types of havens and hope to write more about this at a later time.

Continuing Research beyond Mosaic

Ideas initially introduced in chapter 4, "The Hollywood Connection. . . ," are greatly expanded in my book *Hollywood Faith*. In particular, I now see how entertainment industry workers accentuate the situation of a broader workforce referred to as the creative class, a relatively new and growing stratum of American labor consisting of as much as 30 percent of the workforce (about forty million people) increasingly clustered in metropolitan areas (Florida, 2002, 2004, 2008; Reich, 1991). As capitalistic structures continue to shift long-term economic responsibility from the corporation to the worker, more workers pursue individual success in ways that appear like the efforts to become a celebrity; that is, being a person who commands attention and demand for one's labor from strangers. It is not merely workers in show business or sales or politics that must sell their identities, it is becoming the norm for a greater number of Americans.

For good or ill, self-branding is a phenomenon of modern work life, and individuals increasingly become entrepreneurs regarding their own public self. The combination of self-promotion, popularity, and celebrity becomes an indispensable quality for successful economic achievement and for attaining a steady flow of income through a seamless succession of projects. Congregational leaders are being forced to refine their ministries to account for these changes. The question to explore is whether such individualism is contrary to religious devotion or whether the value of individualism can be negotiated within a religious framework that propels believers to accentuate their duty toward God and others. I label one such development as "ego-affirming evangelicalism" in an article to appear in the journal *Sociology of Religion*.

With respect to the conditions for stimulating ethno-racial diversity, the study of liturgy has become more important to my research. Building on themes in *A Mosaic of Believers* and *Hollywood Faith*, a new book project focuses solely on music and worship in multiracial churches. I began to suspect that attendees remained in congregations that reflect their musical tastes; church leaders believe this and consequently focus much attention on the construction and performance of music in hopes of attracting and keeping diverse congregants. I conducted new research among successfully diverse congregations and expected music to be one of the greatest determinants of racial composition. As it turns out, I was wrong, and this new research reveals how my naïve expectations mirror those I found pervasive among scholars and practitioners. I will show how we must fundamentally reorient our observations on music and worship to uncover essential social processes responsible for bridging the racial divide.

Finally, I am conducting research focusing on the formation of political identity in local churches. The idea for this project came when I compared the lack of discussion of politics in my studies of Mosaic and Oasis (two churches that represent innovative aspects of modern evangelicalism) to the emerging emphasis on political attitudes increasingly evident across the country. A growing number of evangelical congregations are moving away from a form of political neutrality (as the Seeker Church orientation so dominant within modern evangelicalism tries to stay above the divisive fray of political discourse) to openly embracing more liberal political agendas. I suspect congregational leaders and their church attendees are actively negotiating a new form of political identity, one that leaves behind much of the rhetoric of the Religious Right and embraces values and perspectives that have been traditionally associated with the socially progressive left. I also suspect this is a highly contentious process with unanticipated outcomes. I look forward to pursuing this—and other interesting contemporary religious developments—much further.

REFERENCES

Baggett, Jerome P. 2008. *Sense of the Faithful: How American Catholics Live Their Faith.* New York: Oxford University Press.

Christerson, Brad, Michael O. Emerson, and Korie L. Edwards. 2005. *Against All Odds: The Struggle of Racial Integration in Religious Organizations.* New York: New York University Press.

Edwards, Korie L. 2008. *The Elusive Dream: The Power of Race in Interracial Churches.* New York: Oxford University Press.

Emerson, Michael O. 2006. *People of the Dream: Multiracial Congregations in the United States.* Princeton, N.J.: Princeton University Press.

Florida, Richard. 2002. *The Rise of the Creative Class: And How It's Transforming Work, Leisure, Community and Everyday Life.* New York: Basic Books.

———. 2004. *Cities and the Creative Class.* New York: Routledge.

———. 2008. *Who's Your City? How the Creative Economy Is Making Where to Live the Most Important Decision of Your Life.* New York: Basic Books.

Garces-Foley, Kathleen. 2007. *Crossing the Ethnic Divide: The Multiethnic Church on a Mission.* New York: Oxford University Press.

Jeung, Russell. 2004. *Faithful Generations: Race and New Asian American Churches.* New Brunswick, N.J.: Rutgers University Press.

Marti, Gerardo. 2005. *A Mosaic of Believers: Diversity and Innovation in a Multiethnic Church.* Bloomington: Indiana University Press.

———. 2008a. "Fluid Ethnicity and Ethnic Transcendence." *Journal for the Scientific Study of Religion* 48: 11–16.

———. 2008b. *Hollywood Faith: Holiness, Prosperity, and Ambition in a Los Angeles Church.* New Brunswick, N.J.: Rutgers University Press.

———. 2009. "Affinity, Identity, and Transcendence: The Experience of Religious Racial Integration in Multiracial Churches." *Journal for the Scientific Study of Religion* 49 (Mar.): 53–68.

———. Forthcoming. "Ego-Affirming Evangelicalism: How a Hollywood Church

Appropriates Religion for Workers in the Creative Class." *Sociology of Religion: A Quarterly Review.*

———. Forthcoming. *Worship Across the Racial Divide: Notions of Race and the Practice of Religious Music in Multiracial Churches.* New York: Oxford University Press.

Rehwaldt-Alexander, Jeremy. 2009. Book Review: *The Elusive Dream: The Power of Race in Interracial Churches. Christian Century* (Jan. 13): 45–48.

Reich, Robert B. 1991. *The Work of Nations: Preparing Ourselves for 21st-century Capitalism.* New York: Knopf.

ACKNOWLEDGMENTS

Scholarship is a collective endeavor, and it is my privilege to thank many people for their gracious support and assistance. My special thanks go to Jon Miller of the University of Southern California for his investment over many years in my development as a scholar. He is a discerning listener with keen observations that stimulate my thinking with every conversation. Donald E. Miller, also from USC, earned my gratitude with his enthusiasm for this project and his continuing encouragement in my research. H. Edward Ransford is to be thanked for reading through an earlier draft of this manuscript and providing many helpful remarks regarding racial and ethnic dynamics. My thanks go to Jon Johnston at Pepperdine University for many years of goodwill, especially in the years of developing this project for eventual publication. Other scholars and friends read earlier drafts of this work and provided many useful suggestions, especially Michael Emerson of Rice University, an anonymous reviewer, and Carolyn Sillman.

To the people of Mosaic, thank you all so much for sharing your lives with me. Dozens patiently spoke with me before or after church services, during church events, and over meals at various social gatherings. I especially appreciate those who carved out time for in-depth interviews to answer questions, offer insights, and respond to my own observations. To those of you who were willing to sit and talk, our time together was both profitable and enjoyable.

I am also grateful for two days of interdisciplinary dialogue in the company of both junior and senior scholars during the Lived Religion workshop organized by Alan J. Wolfe and Patricia Chang at Boston College in 2002. Our conversations prompted several ideas and served to bring many thoughts to fruition. I deeply appreciate the spirit of collegiality and camaraderie nurtured there.

Finally, this work would not have been possible without the loving support of my wife, Laura, who always encourages the endeavors of an intensely curious husband, lets me hog the computer, and tolerates piles of books stacked around the house. To her and our children, Miranda, Zachary, Nathan, and Genevieve, thanks for letting this learner pursue his quest for insight, understanding, and inspiration.

A MOSAIC
OF BELIEVERS

INTRODUCTION

MANDY: I was looking for something more multiethnic.

ERIC: I think we are the future. The future will look more like Mosaic. The church cannot remain homogeneous and be relevant in the future, and I think we've already tapped into that.

It is a Sunday morning at San Gabriel High School, and the congregation is gathered for a "Quest service." Quest services are deliberately orchestrated to appeal to the unchurched, and members are mobilized to bring as many guests as they can. Every person involved in the production of the service knows that the main reason for participating today is to see people in the audience make commitments to become dedicated followers of Jesus Christ. Twenty minutes into the service, the worship band stops playing, and the stage is bare. The lights go down. A deep, dark jungle rhythm rises from the back of the auditorium as white lights become yellowish-brown, and the red velvet curtain at the front of the auditorium opens. Four men appear. They are naked except for cloths around their waists. They are covered from head to toe in mud. These four clay-covered figures dance together. Despite the mud clumped on them, their hair, eyes, and physique show these men to be different from one another: one has white skin and blond hair; another has light skin, black hair, and Asian eyes; a third has brown skin and short, black hair; and a fourth man with nappy hair is darkest, the brightness of his palms and the soles of his feet contrasting with the rest of his body. The message of the "dirt dance" is simple and rooted in theological imagery. In dirt, the four men all return to Adam, the One Man, emphasizing our common heritage and our common connection as people created by God. They dance in a circle, taking turns stepping into the center. Each man performs his own unique dance as the others move approvingly around him. The song ends, the curtain closes, and the crowd roars with enthusiasm.

For many in the auditorium that Sunday morning, this was their introduction to Mosaic. With weekly attendance approaching two thousand people at the end of 2003, Mosaic is one of the largest multiethnic congregations in the United States. The church has not only won adherents but has done so while overcoming ethnic barriers—a significant accomplishment, considering that 94 percent of churches in America continue to be separated by race and ethnicity. Churches are not unusual; multiethnic churches are. Partly because 2000 census data suggest that, by the year 2050, the United States will have no single majority race or ethnicity and partly because of notable gains in desegregation following the civil rights era, social scientists believe that our society in general will become integrated well before our churches. This study provides an opportunity to see how one congregation breaks the norm to achieve an exceptional degree of diversity.

Mosaic is also one of the most innovative congregations in America. Churches continue to be among the most robust organizations in society. By whatever means and name—proselytizing, evangelism, propaganda, recruitment, brainwashing, or acculturation—congregations, by and large, remain robust because they continue to attract new participants in every generation. Yet congregational forms have changed significantly through the centuries to accommodate broad shifts in social structures, cultural imperatives, political ideologies, and philosophical fashions. In the midst of continual social change, some churches innovate, opportunistically finding points of leverage in the surrounding social structure. While Warner (1994:54) states that congregations remain "the bedrock of the American religious system," Carroll and Roof (2002:

32) go on to assert that "congregational leaders and their members must—if they are to survive—adapt to new challenges as the population and cultural context change."

Innovation happens at Mosaic because the church strategically interacts with its social environment in pursuit of explicit goals. Mosaic appropriates regional characteristics of a changing Los Angeles. Through selective accommodation to its social environment, Mosaic creates multiple havens of inclusion and commonality which render ethnic differences inconsequential. These havens emerge from a creative engagement with the surrounding social environment that includes innovations in theological articulation, ways of mobilizing and acculturating members, empowerment of leaders, and incorporation of younger cohorts. Indeed, Mosaic is an organization crafted for Los Angeles. First, large numbers of immigrant children growing up in or moving to Los Angeles are in the process of escaping "ethnic entrapment," the feeling of being bound to honor and practice their parents' or grandparents' native culture. Second, Los Angeles is an urban region historically devoted to artistry in arenas such as film, drama, music, and the visual and graphic arts, and many people there work in these fields. Third, Los Angeles attracts people who accept social change, enjoy it, and desire to contribute their own changes. Fourth, these dynamics are experienced most acutely by single adults in their twenties and early thirties. Understanding these significant social patterns within Los Angeles contributes to understanding the congregation.

In short, Mosaic is attracting an ethnically diverse group of primarily young adult urbanites who are open to artistry, creativity, and change, and who ultimately act on a mission-driven theological framework. It interacts with the ethnic fluidity of the Los Angeles region, co-opts creative arts as a base of influence, strategically leverages culture by embracing and pursuing innovation and change, and reverses the typical age hierarchy of churches by giving young adults power and influence. Mosaic appeals to an emerging culture and younger age base, giving young adults an opportunity to respond to the church's mission and mobilization. Mosaic attracts an ethnically diverse population because it captures an emerging culture concentrated in young adults who have fluid personal identities, are open to artistry, and wish to both embrace and effect social change.

This is a study of a church that continues to diversify as it grows. Overall, the strength of Mosaic, as a congregation, lies in its continual ability to innovate in the face of ongoing challenges to win new adherents in the midst of Los Angeles's continually shifting culture. While I began this extended case study by asking how this one Los Angeles church attracts and keeps its ethnically diverse population, I found that ongoing innovation is a fundamental feature of this congregation. In the end it became a critical part of the answer to my question. While it was not the feature I initially set out to uncover, it highlights the continued importance of religious creativity even among the broader and more mainstream currents within contemporary Christianity. Certainly the structure of congregations (e.g., the rituals they practice, the reasons people join them, etc.) have changed over the centuries, but we have rarely been privileged to see so closely the practices within a particular church and to hear so clearly the voices of those within it. This study reveals how unique historical circumstances manifest themselves in one local church and contributes to understanding the relation between broad patterns of social change and the local church. Mosaic affirms that local churches are resilient social organizations willing to strategically identify, embrace, and adapt to aspects of the surrounding culture to further their mission.

Finally, Mosaic is a growing phenomenon in local church belief and practice. As part of the modern evangelical movement, the successes of the church and its influential lead pastor, Erwin Raphael McManus, are attracting increasing attention. The mother church in Los Angeles has started other "Mosaic" churches in Berkeley, Pasadena, Manhattan, and Seattle in the past five years and is attracting "Mosaic" imitators in other American cities—even a few in cities outside the United States. Some churches have only taken the name; others share the original's ideological framework. Pastor Erwin is now a bestselling author with one of the largest Christian publishing houses in the world. Mosaic hosts an annual conference for church leaders, and the establishment of the Mosaic Alliance in 2002 created a growing network of like-minded churches under Mosaic's leadership. The number of "Mosaics" is expanding and expected to grow further.

Mosaic Havens: Dual Movement of Escape and Refuge

My study began with the question "How does Mosaic attract and keep its diverse population?" In the end, I found my study was not just about multiethnicity, although this is a basic and undeniable aspect of the church. Mosaic is multiethnic, but multiethnicity does not define Mosaic. Mosaic is multiethnic because the mission of the church prompts creative, resourceful, artistic, and pioneering corporate activity. It is a congregation committed to innovative evangelistic effort that embraces

Los Angeles's diverse population. The organizing principle at Mosaic is "What must we do to reach Los Angeles for Christ?" Mosaic cultivates a warmly relational and catalytic community in the conviction that Jesus calls his followers to love all people and to disciple them city by city, region by region, until he returns at the end of history. Common biblical references emphasizing the mission of the church include Matthew 24: 14, 28:19; Luke 24:47; Acts 1:6–8; and Romans 10:9–15. In the process of carrying out this mission, multiple havens have been created, i.e., safe places for building relationships while moving forward with the mission. These havens are subtle, overarching structures emerging from a church whose goal is to create an organization that evangelizes the entire metropolitan region of Los Angeles. Personal identity is accessed and reconstructed by church leaders within these havens. And these havens are populated by ethnically diverse people.

I collected data through in-depth interviewing and participant observation. While the emphasis of this analysis is on those who remain at Mosaic, those who fail to stay are addressed as well. I tried to stay very close to the lived experience of the participants in this organization. I interviewed sixty people currently attending Mosaic, including those who made commitments to become dedicated followers of Jesus Christ at Mosaic and those who had made such commitments elsewhere, long-time members and recent attenders, men and women, young adults and senior citizens, single and married people, whites and nonwhites. (To preserve the anonymity of respondents and significant figures in the history of the congregation, the majority have been given pseudonyms.) I pursued an understanding of Mosaic's sixty-year history based on the memories of long-term participants as they correlated with each other and with the few print resources available. I consulted my own field notes, written over twelve months from 2001 to 2002. I also drew on seven years' experience as an attender, a member, and then part of the pastoral staff; for the purposes of this study, I shed the role of pastor in order to become a sociologist in my own congregation. Such work carries its own dangers, and I hope the following pages reveal also that such work is valid and can carry certain advantages (for an expanded discussion of insider/outsider methodological issues, please see appendix A).

Looking over all the information received during my research, I found that the reasons for the attraction and retention of members and attenders in this ethnically diverse congregation fell into a pattern best summarized as what people are coming for and what people are escaping from. Every respondent had had past experience with other churches. More specifically, nearly every respondent had had a *negative* experience with one or more churches. Even those who made decisions to identify themselves explicitly as Christian at Mosaic vividly remember bad experiences with prior churches. I noted early in my interviews that individuals came to Mosaic within a context of past church experiences. Most had some sense of what to expect or what they considered normative of churches in general when they came. Most said they were pleasantly surprised by what they discovered. Not everyone experiences a sense of refuge within these havens; inadvertently, by their nature, every haven tends to deter participation by certain people. Mosaic's attractiveness seems to derive partly from contrast with what was *not* attractive at other churches. However, what I am describing is not a feeling of discontent. People at Mosaic did not join the congregation merely because it is the antithesis of places they did not like. My respondents indicated that they would rather not attend church at all than simply come to a church because it was "less bad" than a past experience. Their explanations point to something much more subtle.

Organizational diversity like that found at Mosaic requires people to cultivate bases of affinity which are inherently attractive. Stephen Warner (1994:65) states, "If the proletarian, the capitalist, the woman theologian, and the superstitious man occupy the same pew today in the United States, it is because they are somehow drawn to be there together. As a voluntary organization, those who come must be attracted to coming. They do not have to be." People at Mosaic constitute communities not by social designation, but by their own voluntary choice. Gilkey (1994:104–105) discusses how pluralism and diversity mean that "communal membership becomes a preference, not a matter of social or family destiny; it is contingent on choice and not on inherited necessity. Correspondingly, the ground for such choices becomes inescapably those of self-fulfillment—what contributes to one's personal growth and well-being." People are looking for self-fulfillment. Havens at Mosaic are a means toward personal fulfillment because they provide places for people to belong.

Mosaic attracts and keeps people with dual motivations for moving to Mosaic: what they are escaping from and what they are finding shelter in. The concept "haven" summarizes this movement. It emphasizes that people find at Mosaic a refuge or a sanctuary for a significant aspect of their religious desires, personal identities, and value systems. Ethnic identity is selectively accentuated or obscured according to context. I find that people at Mosaic consistently put aside their ethnicities in favor of other identities. Havens provide shelter in the context of escape. The concept of haven is dynamic and accentuates the perspective of the individual. While havens provide refuge for some, they do not provide refuge for all. Each haven provokes reactions from those who do not experience that aspect of the congregation as positive, or who find it personally troublesome. These havens constitute a self-selective mechanism simultaneously drawing in certain groups and repelling others. There is an implicit "us" and "them" in the concept of haven. Mosaic, like any other organization, defines places of inclusion and exclusion. In that sense Mosaic is magnetic, drawing certain social clusters while deterring others. Thus visitors can, and do, opt out of opportunities to engage in the congregation. Each haven is publicly evident in the celebration services and embedded in the fabric of Mosaic's congregational activities.

Within these havens identity is eventually reconstructed away from particular ethnic affiliations toward a religious affiliation. All of my respondents indicated they were "dedicated followers of Jesus Christ." It is within havens that leaders leverage their own identities toward reconstructing a common identity which is rooted in the mission of the church.

I find five distinctive havens at Mosaic. These five havens are the relational spaces for communal activity at Mosaic and will serve as launching points for understanding this congregation. The havens explored are

- Theological Haven
- Artistic Haven
- Innovator Haven
- Age Haven
- Ethnic Haven

Since these havens simultaneously draw and deter congregants, Mosaic exhibits interesting tensions in the ongoing operations of the church. Utilizing respondent accounts, I will emphasize those who chose to stay at Mosaic. Implications about those who leave are constructed from respondents' recollections of conversations with others as well as the accounts of respondents who considered leaving or even actually left for a time and later returned.

Theological Haven

At Mosaic I encounter many people coming from very conservative, even fundamentalist, religious backgrounds. They are sincere Christians who are ashamed, embarrassed, or reluctant to identify with a church. All of them describe their previous churches as boring and irrelevant. Some described unpleasant experiences; several described bad experiences with Baptist churches in particular, in part because they eventually discover that Mosaic is associated with the Southern Baptist Convention. Experiences with past churches contrast with the experience of Mosaic. Emily, who previously attended a Chinese church, tells her friends, "I don't go to church; I go to Mosaic." People at Mosaic think of it as different from other churches they have experienced. Ralph stated, "This feels like a fundamentally different groove, different vibe, a very different approach fundamentally." Mosaic sometimes performs its activities in unconventional ways, yet affirms orthodox beliefs. The affirmation of conservative beliefs combined with a more open, relevant expression of contemporary culture in public worship services is a unique haven cultivated by Mosaic.

However, many who come from traditional church settings find Mosaic's approach to the celebration services to be "too wild" and even "unbiblical." Those expecting a traditional service and framework are not just disappointed but often distressed at Mosaic's services. A college-age white male left the nightclub Urban Mosaic service in the fall of 2001; greeters overheard him saying, "This is not a church, this is not a church." He never returned.

Chapter 3 describes the practical theology that guides and motivates church activities. Because of his influence as the primary shaper and articulator of Mosaic's ideology, I will explore the distinctive theological emphasis of the current lead pastor, Erwin McManus.

Artistic Haven

Mosaic provides a haven for creative artists who escape from isolationist, "world-fearing" churches and find refuge for their passion for film, art, dance, drama, and multimedia. When Samantha, a Chinese American interior designer, was asked what motivated her to stay at Mosaic over other churches, she said, "For me it was the emphasis on art and the creative energy that was there. . . . There were so many artists at Mosaic that were Christians, and I never knew they existed before. That was really cool." Mosaic encourages artists to practice their craft through the public celebration services and initiates projects that stimulate artists to be purposefully creative in community with each other. African Americans who did not relate to other havens often found this one.

Not everyone enters the artistic haven. The progressive nature of speech and action from both the platform and the pew has kept more than a few people from making Mosaic their church. One Hispanic woman, a dancer and member of the congregation, left because Mosaic was becoming an "entertainment church" that was not focused enough on "the Word." There is also apprehension among those who do not feel that they are creative enough, who feel marginalized because they are not part of an artistic subculture. One Caucasian woman talked about the artists, saying, "You see them and you go,'Wow, they're really artsy.' You just take things in a whole different way than the rest of us, the rest of me."

Chapter 4 describes how the church mobilizes artistry for ministry. A striking affinity exists between the organizational nature of Hollywood productions and the infrastructure of Mosaic. Moreover, the public display of artistry has become a consistent message that the church welcomes any gift, skill, or talent that contributes toward its goals.

Innovator Haven

Mosaic is also a refuge for people who in other churches have been called mavericks, rebels, or freaks. These are catalysts, change-friendly and change-initiating individuals interested in making a distinctive mark in the world. Trevor, a white Southerner, said, "We have a lot of crazy people in this church." When I asked him to describe what he meant, he told me, "Individuals who want to change the world, who want to make a difference; when I say crazy, they actually believe that they can change the world." According to the lead pastor, Erwin McManus, people at Mosaic "lean toward innovation, toward change, toward the invention, toward risk, toward adventure." Mosaic draws those who see themselves as movers, visionaries, and world changers.

Others see too much change in the church. When I asked Emily why people leave, her first response was, "Sometimes it's a little bit *too* fluid." Molly, relating comments from people who have left, said, "It's okay to change, but stay with tradition, change within tradition." Mosaic deters people who desire stability, predictability, and highly structured programming.

Chapter 5 describes how the church recruits innovators who take ownership of congregational goals. It also describes the importance of certain attitudes and perspectives which channel potentially disruptive leaders toward corporately productive efforts.

Age Haven

The age haven at Mosaic is for those in their twenties and early thirties. These are mostly singles without children who are escaping from churches dominated by "old people" and finding refuge where they can cultivate leadership, creativity, and meaningful responsibility. Young adults at Mosaic are looking for relationships with people their age; they want to make friends, to get involved, to contribute, and to have their voices heard. These young adults include both spiritual seekers and the "true believers" who bring them. What attracted Derek, originally from Texas, was that Mosaic "places a value on twenty- and thirty-year-olds and gives them a chance to have responsibility towards leadership in ministry." In his experience, "[o]ther churches just wouldn't." For several African Americans like Bridgette, age was more important than race in connecting with the church. She immediately noticed that people at Mosaic were "still young." Bridgette got involved with creative arts in her first month of attending, and co-led a small group the following year.

The age haven deters people who feel they are too old to be included. One senior adult told me, "I know some people left because it was too youth oriented." The irony is that the complaint that the church is too "youth oriented" has come from those in their twenties. Lindsey, twenty-nine years old, said, "I'm getting to feeling like I'm too old for Mosaic." She added, "I don't like being the old person in the group." The youth orientation that attracted young adults can be distressing as they get older and the congregation continues to attract people who are as young as they were when they first arrived.

Chapter 6 describes how the typical age hierarchy of churches was reversed in this congregation. Moreover, the chapter argues that Mosaic appeals to a younger generation because it leverages the trends of an emerging culture. In the coming century, Mosaic is positioned to appeal to all ages.

Ethnic Haven

Mosaic provides a haven for second- and third-generation ethnics escaping from mono-ethnic home churches. Churches have historically served as an ethnic haven for recent immigrants as part of the experience of assimilating and acculturating to a new culture (Burns, 1994; Papaioannou, 1994; Shaw, 1991). The sons and daughters of the immigrants who formed such churches are now finding their way into more broadly Americanized settings. In contrast to immigrant churches, Mosaic provides a different kind of ethnic haven. Within the broadly Americanized culture of Mosaic, they find refuge for "being" ethnic without having to "act" ethnic. This ethnic haven is also attractive to Caucasians who value diversity because it offers them a safe place to mingle with various peoples and cultures without an excessive burden of constant cultural adjustments.

Mosaic's ethnic haven is not suited for ethnically committed individuals and more recent immigrants. Families of immigrants do not come together to Mosaic; their acculturated children do. Mosaic also does not provide an ethnic haven for African Americans. For Blake, "There's nothing in Mosaic that even says 'black,' culturally speaking." African Americans who stay at Mosaic do so because they find shelter in other havens.

Chapter 7 describes how a new, shared identity is reconstructed within the congregation. Through the strategic assertion of charismatic authority and participation in particular activities and rituals, congregational leadership channels the fluidity of ethnic identity by socializing individuals toward a new personal identity as dedicated followers of Jesus Christ who are on mission together.

Max Weber and the Dynamic Nature of Ethnicity

The dynamics of ethnic identity at Mosaic cannot be understood from any static conception of ethnicity; to understand the ethnic identity of respondents, we must work with a more fluid understanding of ethnic identity developed originally by Max Weber. My examination is neither a comprehensive social history of this one congregation nor a "how-to" manual for revitalization or church growth. This book is a sociological interpretation. And the story of Mosaic is, like its dominating metaphor, multifaceted. For the purposes of this study, my observations and conclusions are arranged in a framework emphasizing the multiple havens found at Mosaic. The book is organized around the concept of haven, which summarizes the movement of people who escape from certain settings and seek refuge in others. This organizing framework is not meant to oversimplify the multivocal and multitextured realities in this multiethnic church. Rather, this framework builds on theoretical concerns regarding the fluid nature of ethnic identity, beginning with the writings of Weber. (Those who wish to proceed directly to the significance of multiethnic churches in general, and Mosaic in particular, may skip the rest of this introduction and go directly to chapter 1.)

Everyday assumptions about ethnicity include that one is born with an ethnic identity, that (like race) it is unchanging, and that everyone in an "ethnic group" has the same traits and customs. Many sociologists in the past have leaned toward a static definition by defining ethnicity as a social group distinguished by race, religion, language, or national origin (e.g., Gordon, 1964; Schermerhorn, 1970). "Primordialists" understand ethnicity to be the tie of ethnic attachment which binds individuals through birth and early socialization (Brenton and Pinard, 1960; Geertz, 1963; for critique see McKay, 1982). Such views of ethnicity are gross oversimplifications. While primordialists and other social theorists emphasize the "givenness" of ethnic identity, more recent theories of ethnicity (theories of instrumental ethnicity, situational ethnicity, social constructionism, and ethnic identity management) severely criticize and amend these notions, emphasizing the circumstantial and contextual nature of ethnic identity (Cornell, 1996; McKay, 1982; Roosens, 1989). I found that by avoiding static and deterministic conceptions of ethnicity and embracing these more recent notions of ethnic identity I was better able to account for the ethnic dynamics among people at Mosaic.

Fenton (1999:95), in discussing the unique challenges faced by immigrant children like those found at Mosaic, writes,

> The children of migrants, born in the new home country, become aware of their parents' expectations and have to square these with what may be differing expectations of their school friends and teachers. These differences are sometimes portrayed as the problems of young people "caught between" two cultures, but in fact young people become skilled at coping with different sets of expectations, a skill that is for most people an essential, even commonplace, means of dealing with a life which crosses many institutional areas in which the audiences differ.

In acknowledging the reality of such ethnic negotiations in the lived experience of immigrant children, especially in a setting like Los Angeles, research on ethnic identity must reconsider typical assumptions about ethnicity. Recent biological and genetic research fails to find any physiological basis for commonality among races or ethnicities (Smelser, Wilson, and Mitchell, 2001; Ehrlich, 2000). Racial identity has been shown to emerge contextually and be either accentuated or disclaimed (e.g., Patterson, 1975; Van den Berghe, 1967; Wagley, 1952). The scholarly consensus today is that race and ethnicity derive from sociocultural factors that are produced, sustained, and reproduced by social actors (Baumann, 1999; Prince Brown, 2001; Guillaumin, 1995; Jenkins, 1997;

Livingstone and Dobzhansky, 1962; Waters, 1990; D. Wheeler, 1995). For example, Baumann (1999:64) writes, "Ethnic identities can be stressed or unstressed, enjoyed or resented, imposed or even denied, all depending on situation and context." The precedent for understanding these complex constructions and negotiations of ethnic identity was established by Max Weber.

Though seldom acknowledged, Max Weber's writings are critical to understanding the dynamic nature of ethnic identity. Weber (1978:389) defined ethnicity as rooted in a "belief in group affinity, regardless of whether it has any objective foundation," and ethnic groups as "those human groups that entertain subjective belief in their common descent because of similarities of physical type or of customs or both, or because of memories of colonization and migration." It is *belief* that is important; actual objective kinship or bio-genetic relationships are not. For Weber, "Race [and, by implication, ethnicity] creates a 'group' only when it is subjectively perceived as a common trait" (385). Weber anticipated contemporary approaches to ethnicity by recognizing the subjectivity of ethnic affiliation and the societal forces that contribute to the emergence and salience of ethnic bonds. For Weber, the bases for ethnic group consolidation are varied and constantly shifting. In much the same way that Barth discussed ethnic group formation as based in boundary creation (1969), Weber claims that "any cultural trait, no matter how superficial, can serve as a starting point for the familiar tendency to monopolistic closure" (388). Fenton (1999:62) also states, "Ethnicity refers to the social mobilization of ethnic ties."

What conditions cause people to form ethnic groups? Weber suggests that they do so primarily out of mutual self-interest as a foundation for joint action. Yet he also writes that "a comprehensive societalization (focus on interests) integrates the ethnically divided communities into specific political and communal actions" (Gerth and Mills, 1946:189). In other words, when a concern emerges relevant for the entire society (such as war), ethnic distinctions are suspended as the entire society engages in communal action. Weber understood that people (and peoples) can and do alter their own and others' ethnic ascriptions in circumstances and environments that create common mutual interests. This insight is acknowledged by more recent ethnic theorists like Gleason, who states (1996:469) that "ethnicity is not an indelible stamp impressed on the psyche but a dimension of individual and group existence that can be consciously emphasized or de-emphasized as the situation requires." Cornell (1996:266) agrees: "As circumstance or context changes, so does the calculus of ethnic identity claims and assignments, and likewise ethnic identity itself. Ethnicity becomes, for the most part, a situationally-determined byproduct of more 'fundamental' forces." Gleason and Cornell both exemplify the instrumentalist or situationalist perspective emphasizing plasticity in ethnic identification and, therefore, in the composition of ethnic groups. Weber's and more recent theorists' views of ethnicity accentuate the fluidity and variable significance of ethnicity as an organizing principle. Ethnic groups divide due to opposing interests; ethnic groups can also unite in pursuit of common interests. How these interests are defined is most critical.

Sharing assumptions with Weber, social constructionists view ethnicity as comprising meanings that are created, accessed, and managed through human interaction. Social constructionists emphasize "ways in which ethnic boundaries, identities, and cultures are negotiated, defined, and produced through social interaction inside and outside ethnic communities" (Nagel, 1994:152; see also Alba, 1990; Royce, 1982; Waters, 1990). Ethnic groups are "agents in their own construction, shaping and reshaping their identities and the boundaries that enclose them out of the raw materials of history, culture, and pre-existing ethnic constructions" (Cornell, 1996:266). Group identity bases itself on a belief in such things as a common ancestry, a shared past, and common cultural behaviors such as kinship relations, religious belief and expression, and language use. These elements are not static but are shaped and reshaped over time.

Moreover, one's ethnicity consists of a complex set of repertoires accessed at different times according to different contexts. From the social constructionist standpoint social actors construct ethnic identities that suit varied purposes, since ethnic repertoires are learned and reconstructed for purposes at hand using available symbolic resources (see Alexander, 1992; Conzen et al., 1992; Leonard, 1992; Nagel, 1994, 1996; Royce, 1982; Sollors, 1989). Fenton (1999:95) succinctly states, "No one is a full-time ethnic." Ethnicity emerges as a "contingent, volitional, negotiated phenomenon in which both societal circumstances and the creative assertions of human groups play variable and interacting roles" (Cornell, 1996:266). It is in this sense that ethnicity may become for certain social actors in certain social contexts a primary aspect of individual identity, while at other times ethnicity is ignored.

Ethnic identity must be enacted and affirmed by others. If on the basis of visible characteristics (hair, facial features, skin color, etc.) a community does not affirm a person's "choice" of ethnic identity, community members will simply act according to their own internalized categories rather than a seemingly arbitrary announcement of individual choice. One cannot simply "choose" ethnic identity, since ethnicity is both ascribed by others and achieved in performance. As Fenton (1999: 12) writes, "Ethnic identities are not made and remade at will." The most prominent constraint on ethnic identity is physical appearance, which includes such things as skin color, body shape, facial features, and hair type. Individuals distinguish among others according to these qualities and accept such distinctions as real; therefore (per W. I. Thomas's theorem: "If men define situations as real, they are real in their consequences") these distinctions become real in their consequences. Many aspects of one's own appearance and mannerisms are not only immediately visible but often outside of one's ability to control (Lyman and Douglass, 1973; Royce, 1982).

These constraints of recognition (i.e., the way in which most people immediately assign ethnic categories to others) mean that ethnicity cannot be ignored as a fundamental aspect of social behavior. Outward features of ethnic affiliation often generate immediate, unintentional yet meaningful affective response. As Royce (1982:167) states,

> In order for interaction to occur at all in multi-ethnic settings, there must be shared understandings and common conventions. This necessity gives rise to ethnic stereotypes, which are generalizations about the different groups they describe and which indicate appropriate attitudes and actions toward those groups. We "see" situations and individuals in terms of our predetermined and often inflexible definitions of them.

Thus, social actors have a limited number of ethnic categories to choose from, and yet within these choices they choose whether to assert or obscure their ethnic identity. Royce affirms this by acknowledging that ethnic identity is "a negotiation within constraints" (184).

Building on Goffman's "impression management theory" (1959, 1963, 1967), ethnic identity management theorists focus on the day-to-day or moment-to-moment variability in the manifestation and salience of ethnic identity (see De Vos, 1975; Lyman and Douglass, 1973; Royce, 1982). Impression management is the selective display of symbols of identity to maximize status within an interaction. Social statuses other than ethnicity may be put forward instead to enhance social standing such that, as Okamura (1981:460) states, "Ethnicity may be of critical relevance in some situations, while in others it may be totally irrelevant." This perspective introduces a strategic element of human behavior; actors tactically manipulate their ethnic identity in conforming to expectations when necessary and avoiding disruptions or embarrassment when not (Nagata, 1974; Okamura, 1981; Eriksen, 1992, 1993). James (1950:294) notes that an individual "has as many different social selves as there are distinct groups of persons about whose opinion he cares. He generally shows a different side of himself to each of these different groups." Different audiences call for different performances. Baumann (1999:21) writes, "Just as people emphasize different aspects of their language, body language, behavior, and style in different situations, so too do they emphasize or abjure the attributes of their ethnicity."

Since the presentation of ethnic identity is selective, I agree with Fenton's argument (1999:12) that "We need to consider the manner in which ethnic identities...are constructed and the contexts within which ethnicity takes shape as a dimension of structure and action." Summarizing recent theories of ethnicity which are found to be consistent with Weber's own view, I assert the following (adapted from Royce, 1982:26):

- individuals negotiate, within constraints, a variety of identities,
- individuals maximize the options available to them using aspects of their ethnic identity if they perceive an advantage in so doing, and
- individuals contend with others engaged in the same process whose interests and perceptions may be quite different.

Ethnicity is a complex attribute of the self with different aspects that can be highlighted or obscured, constructed or reconfigured according to the demands and constraints of presentation. Since ethnic identity is guided by interests that involve social status and social mobility, its importance and priority vary depending on the context of social action (see Nagata, 1974). Whether and how ethnic identity emerges is determined by its salience, and ethnic identity falls somewhere within a "salience hierarchy" in differing situations (Stryker, 1981). The salience and malleability of one's ethnic self-presentation is situationally contingent. Ethnicity must be internalized through self-definition, it must be recognized as a valid group identity, and it must be actualized, that is, credibly enacted through a set of ethnic-specific practices. Moreover, the malleability of ethnic identity is such that it is often obscured in favor of other aspects of self to maximize personal status. As circumstances require, other social statuses are emphasized in favor of ethnicity.

Mosaic shows that membership in a religious community can suspend or supersede ethnic identity and become the basis for a new type of status honor. Perhaps instrumental and situational theorists are correct in asserting that ethnic groups emerge out of material interests, yet this implies that ethnic affiliations can recede when other interests (e.g., otherworldly, value-rational interests) are emphasized. Shaping people toward a new identity framed around new interests overrides the divisive aspects of ethnic identity. Charismatic authority which catalyzes diverse groups toward a common mission will supersede other group identities and highlight the identity that plays a role in completing that mission. A new identity can be created around the value-rational mission of the organization. (The relation between charismatic leadership and the reshaping of identity to achieve ethnic diversity is further explored in chapter 7.)

Ethnic transcendence, superseding ethnic identity in favor of other identities, is the strategy most consistently and most explicitly found at Mosaic. Spiritual leaders construct a new, inclusive "Christian" identity that redefines relationships between people of different ethnicities. For some who already see themselves as followers of Jesus, spiritual leaders gain their charismatic authority quickly. For most, the exercise of charismatic authority is dependent on a status boost that lends credibility to leaders. Therefore, in interaction with potential followers, leaders in multiethnic churches like Mosaic find some ground for status by which to transcend ethnic and other status identities altogether, moving toward a new shared identity on a new base of affinity and legitimacy. Status honor, whether claimed through shared ethnic membership or another means, undergirds the legitimacy necessary for the reorientation of identity based on a common corporate mission.

A common identity begins with a base of affinity. The five havens described in this book constitute the overarching spaces of interaction at Mosaic which allow for the reconstruction of personal identity, grounding interaction less on ethnic difference than on religious similarity. The construction of this new religious identity has its beginnings in the havens found at Mosaic. These havens represent distinctive, defining aspects of the congregation (a form of truth, a valuing of creativity, an openness to ongoing change, a priority on cultural relevance, and a common set of commitments and practices) by which individuals find a connection to the community. Those who stay at Mosaic resonate with one or more of these havens. A person need only find one haven in which to stay, but many people find shelter in multiple havens. The deeper people's involvement, the more likely they are to access multiple havens simultaneously.

Overview

This study explores the unique and interrelated havens of inclusion and commonality that have emerged from interactions between the regional characteristics of Los Angeles and this particular congregation in the pursuit of its evangelistic mission. Havens are not static structures that exist in the abstract; they are dynamic structures which are created through corporate activities and motivated by certain beliefs. Havens represent a constellation of corporate interests that, in effect, vitiate ethnic boundaries, making them less salient. These havens encompass diversity because people are willing to obscure their ethnic identifications in favor of other group ties.

The following chapters will show how these havens emerge out of a series of simultaneous ongoing constructions of the church involving corporate ideology, individual involvement, a dominant organizational imperative, age-based power structures, and personal identity. Together, these elements result in a reconstruction of the institution of the church. The sum total of these reconstructions is an innovating Christian community that provides multiple spaces of inclusion and gives a new praxis for an emerging generation of followers of Jesus Christ.

This first chapter describes several characteristics, including multiethnicity, which make Mosaic an important site for research. Chapter 2 provides an oral history of Mosaic and gives a glimpse into its current atmosphere. Chapter 3 describes the prominent role of Mosaic's lead pastor, Erwin McManus, in shaping the current ideological framework within the church. Although Mosaic is guided by an orthodox evangelical theology, the practical theology followed by any church is selective, emphasizing certain beliefs that frame the activities of the congregation. Chapter 4 describes the emphasis on artistry in the ongoing activity of the church, especially in its construction of weekend celebration services. Chapter 5 describes the distinctive role of catalysts within Mosaic. Catalysts are defined as change-initiating and change-friendly people given privileged positions of influence so that they can carry the adaptive, creative mission of the church forward. Chapter 6 describes how Mosaic co-opts elements evident in the emerging American culture in such a way that it resonates with young adults living in this urban cosmopolitan region. Chapter 7 focuses on the fluid ethnic identity of people at Mosaic and how that fluidity is reconstructed by leaders into a new shared identity as dedicated followers of Jesus Christ who are "on mission" as members of a catalytic, apostolic community. The chapter will describe the enacted rituals, common commitments, and shared activities that define and foster such an identity and acculturate individuals into it. Finally, the book concludes with discussions of the nature of religious movements today, the significance of these movements to younger generations in their religious experience, the effort of white pastors to cultivate diverse congregations, the relation of all these developments to African Americans, and the future of Mosaic.

1

MULTIETHNIC CHURCHES, MOSAIC, AND SOCIAL CHANGE

CRYSTAL: If you're used to a typical church, you are surprised when you come to Mosaic. It's cutting edge, and the people are nice, and the people are interesting. It's so "unchurchy"; it's not like the church where you grew up reading the bulletins and passing notes and sleeping in the balcony.

GERARDO: What other churches are like Mosaic?

DEREK: What other churches are like Mosaic? Is this a trick question?

In June 2001, I was busy around my office in Los Angeles answering phone calls, returning email, and looking through letters, when I came to an abrupt realization. Dozens of church leaders had called in the past several weeks asking how their churches could become more diverse. I knew that I and other staff members received ten or more requests for information each week from church planters, seminary students, sociologists, journalists, pastors of churches of all sizes, church consultants, and professional religious researchers. Half of my phone messages in any particular month came from those wanting to ask a question, distribute a survey, pursue an internship, or experience a Sunday celebration service. The most frequent question was "How did Mosaic become multiethnic?" Christian leaders, in particular, were consciously rejecting the mono-ethnicity of their own churches. They desired to diversify their congregations and embrace various ethnic groups in their communities. They asked how they could recreate what Mosaic had become. Mosaic was now a locus of research, a place others went for answers to questions related to the church they wanted to change or the church they wanted to start. And by virtue of my six years on the pastoral staff of this particular congregation, I was now an "expert" on how churches can become multiethnic.

I stepped into Mosaic after being a member of four other churches and a pastor at three of them, all of them middle- to upper-middle-class, suburban, and overwhelmingly white. My wife and I began attending Mosaic in 1996. While I was struck from the start by the variety of ethnic groups represented there, Mosaic's unusualness was driven home to me a few years ago when I attended a conference at Willow Creek Community Church in Illinois, well known for its impressive growth and a standard stop for any pastor seeking to "do church" in a contemporary, relevant way (see Sargeant, 2000). Our group from Mosaic was the most diverse, with Hispanics, Asians, and a couple of "token whites." The contrast of this visiting group against the virtual sea of thousands of white faces made me aware of how utterly normal diversity had become for me.

I see now how the significance of Mosaic's ethnic diversity grew on me as a sociologist. Yes, I was aware that Mosaic was somehow different from other churches. Sitting in my office that June day some years after my first Willow Creek visit, I realized that I was at the center of a unique phenomenon. I listed several characteristics that made Mosaic distinctive. Mosaic had become a large, multiethnic church, one of the largest and most diverse congregations in the United States (DeYoung et al., 2003). Moreover, its congregation was young and getting younger. Of the 1,200 attending in any given week at that time, the average age was twenty-nine. And while the organization had been established by a group of Southern Baptists in 1943, the most dynamic period of growth and diversification to date had occurred in the last four years, since 1997, with more ethnically diverse and more geographically dispersed people joining the church. Furthermore, Mosaic was attracting national and international attention. The church had been cited in book chapters, articles, and newspaper stories for such things as the structure of its small groups, the youthfulness of its congregation, its missional orientation, and its emphasis on creativity. Leaders of various denominations were requesting special meetings. Increasingly, the lead pastor and other staff members were solicited for speaking engagements and church consultations. Vans full of pastors, youth workers, and seminarians showed up unannounced to observe our Sunday celebration services. Our lay leaders became accustomed to being interviewed spontaneously during and after services and made themselves available throughout the week to guests wishing to learn more about the church. We always answered questions openly and honestly, with as much information as was available, yet our day-to-day ministry had never been examined systematically. The in-depth research I carried out for this study was the most extensive ever done, testing commonly held notions of "what makes Mosaic tick" and exploring overarching patterns that could explain how we got here and where we are going.

Significance of Multiethnic Churches

The importance of diverse churches like Mosaic is at least partially connected to several interrelated trends in American congregations, especially evangelical congregations. These trends demonstrate the importance of examining the multiethnicity of Mosaic.

ETHNIC DIVERSIFICATION IN AMERICA

The United States continues to become more diverse in every societal sphere, bringing a new challenge of integration to both civic and religious organizations. Demographers estimate that by the year 2050, America will have no single majority group (Smelser, Wilson, and Mitchell, 2001). Increased racial and ethnic diversity is most anticipated in port-of-entry metropolitan areas such as Los Angeles, New York, and San Francisco. Specifically, according to the 2000 census, people of Hispanic/Latino origin make up 44.6 percent of the total population of Los Angeles, which is much higher than the national proportion of 12.5 percent. The census also shows that more than half of the United States' Asian population is in Los Angeles, San Francisco, and New York. In Los Angeles the proportion of Asians grew significantly in the 1990s, such that L.A. is now 11.9 percent Asian. Given the increased level of diversity and assuming less isolation of ethnic groups, the opportunities for sustaining multiethnic congregations and transitioning mono-ethnic churches into multiethnic ones will grow in the United States during the twenty-first century.

SEGREGATION IN AMERICAN CHURCHES

Researchers have repeatedly demonstrated the overwhelming ethnic and racial homogeneity of American churches. Emerson and Smith (2000: ix) indicate, "Evangelicals desire to end racial division and inequality, and attempt to think and act accordingly. But, in the process, they likely do more to perpetuate the racial divide than they do to tear it down." Focusing on the black/white racial divide, Emerson and Smith describe the races in American churches as moving from "separate pews to separate churches" (48). Their argument shows that such a separation is almost inevitable, because of what they describe as "the overwhelming push toward internal homogeneity" (136). According to data from the National Congregations Study, in 90 percent of American congregations, 90 percent of the members share the same race or ethnicity (Chaves, 1999). And according to Yancey (1999:299), "The dearth of interracial churches within American society undoubtedly reflects the continuing and persistent racial gap." Indeed, church growth theorists have called ethnic homogeneity a positive element in the growth of churches; they advise church planters and church revivalists to use the "homogeneous unit principle" as part of their strategy (Wagner, 1976, 1979, 1984, 1996; McGavran, 1990; for critique see Fong, 1996; Nees, 1997; Shenk, 1983).

Mosaic violates the principle of homogeneity. In early 2000, the Congregational Project, funded by the Lilly Endowment, interviewed about twenty churches in America that it considered "multiracial," meaning that at least 20 percent of the congregation was of a different race or ethnicity than the rest (DeYoung et al., 2003; Emerson and Kim, 2003). Mosaic was one of these churches. Attendance records for 1997–2001 show that overall attendance is growing as it becomes more diverse. In the world of American churches, Mosaic is an anomaly, and one of the most fruitful scholarly endeavors is the examination of anomalies. One of the elders of Mosaic, Ramon, puts it this way:

> Churches tend to be protected preservations of groups. You go there, and it's all white, it's all Russian, it's all Chinese, it's all Mexican. It reflects more of what America *was*—very segregated—yet Mosaic represents what America is *today*. It's not segregated. You go to the university, and it's not segregated; you go to high school, and it's not segregated. Generally speaking, I mean, it depends on what community you go to, but here in L.A., most of L.A. is not segregated.

With the emergence of other multiethnic congregations, greater attention is being paid to how to foster and manage such congregations (for example, Foster, 1997; Foster and Brelsford, 1996). Because Mosaic violates the segregation of racial and ethnic groups, it may suggest ways church leaders can actually promote rather than hinder ethnic diversity.

RACIAL RECONCILIATION AND THE EMERGENCE OF INCLUSIVE CONGREGATIONS

Marshall and Rossman (1989:29) state that "questions and problems for research most often come from real-world observations, dilemmas, and questions." Churches whose neighborhoods or communities are experiencing racial or ethnic shifts face real-world dilemmas and must confront issues of ethnicity, community, authority, and common activity. Leaders are attempting to answer several questions, including how churches will survive, how to reach out to ethnic groups different from the majority within the congregation, and how to blend ethnicities together into a smoothly functioning organization that provides both inspiration and care. The majority of literature on multiethnic churches emphasizes community, or the bringing together of races and ethnicities into a common fellowship (Branson, 1998; Lupton, 1996; Ortiz, 1996; Spencer-Byers, 1996). Some works describe how races and ethnic groups have successfully come together into a single community (Rice, 2002; Smith and Johnson, 1999; Thurman, 1979, 1959; Fisk, 1975); others urge the creation of such a community (Foster and Brelsford, 1996; Harms, 1999; Kliewer, 1987; McKenzie, 1997; Patterson, 1997; Rhodes, 1998; Rhoads, 1996; Thurman, 1971, 1965). Most of these are written predominantly for white pastors wishing to encourage or expand the ethnic presence within their congregations, and they focus almost exclusively on the white/black divide and the possibility of togetherness.

Racial reconciliation has been a dominant topic of discussion among evangelicals since the 1990s, in part because of the continued segregation of American churches. The priority they have given it is evidenced by the explicit goals of parachurch organizations such as Promise Keepers and Intervarsity Christian Fellowship, the organizational restructuring of denominations like the interracial Pentecostal Churches of America, and statements by such prominent Christian leaders as Billy Graham. Yet racial reconciliation is a very specific project aimed at accomplishing very specific goals: that whites acknowledge that blacks have been oppressed, that they ask forgiveness of blacks, and that blacks grant it to them. Yancey (1998) describes the process of reconciliation as having four steps. First, individuals from different races must develop friendships with each other. Second, "all" Christians must recognize social structures of inequality. "All" here means "white," since

Yancey implies that other races are already aware of social inequality in their lived experience. Third, as the main benefactors and creators of racial inequality, whites must repent of personal, historical, and social sins. Fourth, African Americans must be willing to forgive. Racial reconciliation literature assumes that there are only two races (white and black) and that it is these two races that must be reconciled to each other, starting with friendship and ending with whites seeking forgiveness from blacks with whom they have relationships.

Racial reconciliation certainly raises awareness of racial and cultural issues; however, the program of racial reconciliation maintains distinctions between two races while ignoring prejudice and discrimination between others: white/Hispanic, white/Asian, Asian/Hispanic, Hispanic/black, etc. This is evident in both the scholarly literature (Rice, 2002; M. Emerson, 1998; Emerson and Smith, 2000) and popular works (Collum, 1996; DeYoung, 1995, 1997, 1999; Law, 1993, 1996; Meeks, 1992a, 1992b; Okholm, 1997; Shearer, 1995; Yancey, 1996). Also, the focus on friendship and forgiveness emphasizes community and interpersonal relationships but ignores how leadership and authority are enacted between individuals of different group memberships. While there are resources explicitly urging churches to become multiethnic, there are no resources for organizing interethnic activity or exercising spiritual authority in such congregations. Discussion of nonpeer relationships is absent. Racial reconciliation is a specific agenda that does not address, and often fails to recognize, complex issues of interethnic organizational behavior in our increasingly multiethnic society.

Despite the limitations of racial reconciliation literature, Yancey's (1999) recent testing of contact theory came to an important conclusion that affirms that Christian leaders are right to desire inclusive congregations. Whites who attend interracial churches engage in less negative stereotyping and maintain less social distance from African Americans than whites who do not. Inclusive congregations reduce prejudicial attitudes. Yancey states, "Religious institutions can help to promote harmonious relations, or they can reinforce racial segregation," because "they are influential in shaping the values and ideologies of those who join them." He adds, "Much of the current sociological literature on race overlooks the importance of such organizations. It seems imperative that those who desire to promote harmonious racial relations begin to examine how to use religious institutions in this regard" (299).

In addition to the exhortations and studies discussed above, several recent biblical studies and theological resources have addressed multiethnic churches. Perhaps the most interesting are those that emphasize the diversity of the first Christian communities (R. Brown, 1984, 1979; Bruce, 1985, 1979; E. Jones, 1970; Kee, 1995; LaGrand, 1995). Recent theological works incorporate postmodern conceptions of identity and power in discussing the marginality of ethnic groups (Lee, 1995) and the interaction of exclusion and embrace within Christian communities (Volf, 1996). Constructions of multiculturally based theologies help shape a multicultural ecclesiology to produce a vision of how the Christian church can become integrated in the future.

My study goes beyond the forming of friendships between racial groups to examine the active involvement of volunteers in the ongoing activities of Mosaic, how authority is exercised in the context of ethnic diversity, and the ideology shaping the organization as a whole. Mosaic does not explicitly concern itself with issues of racial reconciliation but does value diversity and substantive relationships between people of all ethnic orientations. This study articulates the beliefs, attitudes, and behaviors that stimulate and promote diversity within this congregation.

Lay Leadership Movement

Research indicates the importance of lay leadership in local churches. One of the best indicators of lay leadership is the proliferation of small groups in American congregations (Wuthnow, 1994, 1993). Forty percent of all Americans meet regularly in a small group, from AA to Bible studies (Wuthnow, 1994:314). And according to the Barna Research Group (2004), 20 percent of adults nationwide attend a specifically Christian small group that meets weekly for Bible study, prayer, or fellowship. Small groups are usually led by laypeople and are likely to remain an important strategy for church growth and assimilation.

Mosaic has several dozen small groups within its structure. There are two main types. Home-based small groups meet throughout Southern California during the week, while task-oriented groups called "service teams" accomplish various aspects of ministry within Mosaic. All of these groups have at least one designated leader exercising some form of spiritual authority. Recruitment and training of these leaders is a constant concern.

Interest in the mechanics of small group ministries and the mobilization of team-based ministries is growing; practical guides and professional conferences for church leaders have proliferated in the past decade. But little systematic research has examined the dynamics of lay leadership. The lack of systematic research does not stem the tide of a staggering number of conferences produced for Christian church leaders to help them "equip and mobilize" their lay leadership. Parachurch consultants and leaders of large Christian churches are publishing their programs and biblically informed philosophies for a clergy eager for advice on developing lay leadership (Cordeiro, 2001; Christensen, 2000; Mallory, 2001; Mallory et al., 2001; Mittelberg, 2000; Morgan and Schaller, 2001; Ogden, 1990; Steinbron, 1997; Warren, 1995, 1997). Church leaders understand that the primary resource for the operation of their congregations is not money but people, and their eagerness for advice has led to a lucrative market for resource material on recruitment, assimilation, and leadership training.

A glance through these program guides and training materials reveals a woeful neglect of issues of diversity. I have not found any resources that explore mobilization in the context of ethnic diversity. Perhaps church leadership in the context of diversity is ignored because the standard strategy for dealing with diversity is to subdivide groups into more homogeneous units. As Foster (1997:xiv) asserts, "congregations divide people into groups according to age, marital status, sex, and often professional and educational experience." Such divisions now include ministries targeting certain ethnic groups and led by an ethnically appropriate staff member. In contrast to other churches, Mosaic does not have ethnically segregated groups.

The more that churches succeed in creating diverse groups that are cohesive and purposeful, the more likely they are to become significant social forces in the coming century. And if diversity is to characterize groups at every organizational level within congregations, the work of such integration will lie mostly with lay leaders mobilized to lead such groups.

Significance of Mosaic

Mosaic is a congregation, a group of people who regularly meet together for the express purpose of enhancing and extending their religious convictions. All congregations, including Mosaic, are vital arenas for study as "embodied systems of mutual action (social organization) and shared meaning (culture)" (Warner, 1988:64). Broadly speaking, American churches remain important as a dynamic site for examining human sociality. As Brasher (1998:28–29) reflects,

> Placed on the human social body at its warmest, congregations are religious thermometers that take the temperature of American existence. They are social sites where groups maintain particular values

over time; thus, they are among the first places where changes in the composition of public or private moralities become obvious. Especially given the increasing pluralism and uncertain homogenization of the American public, we need more extensive congregational studies examining how communities are living out their religious beliefs if we are ever to extend our understanding of the human religious impulses taking shape in the spiritual amalgam of the United States.

Congregational studies began in the early twentieth century with the studies of H. Paul Douglass and Edmund de S. Brunner, and such studies are of interest to a growing number of social scientists today (see Chaves, 2004; Wind and Lewis, 1994: vol. 2). Because American congregations are voluntary organizations with no central administrative system, it is difficult to gather comprehensive and systematic information on them. For this reason, congregational studies have often pursued very fruitful investigations focused on understanding single churches in depth (e.g., Ammerman, 1987; Neitz, 1987; Brasher, 1998; Sargeant, 2000; Wilcox, 2003). Congregations chosen for study are notable for their location, their ethnic culture, their distinctive practices, or their local expression of broad social trends. Besides multiethnicity, several other characteristics of Mosaic make this church notable and, therefore, a significant site for social research.

RECENT SCHOLARLY, PASTORAL, AND MEDIA INTEREST

Mosaic has drawn the attention of scholars, pastors, and journalists in recent years. For example, Mosaic is one of several multiracial congregations nationwide whose members were interviewed in depth by scholars working on the Congregational Project, which found Mosaic to be one of the most diverse congregations in America (DeYoung et al., 2003; see also Emerson and Kim, 2003). A discussion of Mosaic as an innovative congregation is featured in Alan Wolfe's *The Transformation of American Religion* (2003). Richard Flory and Donald E. Miller published a chapter in *Gen X Religion* (Prieto, 2000) on Mosaic's Sunday evening service, emphasizing its diversity, innovation, and embrace of creative artists. Leonard Sweet, professor of postmodern Christianity and for five years dean of the Theological School at Drew University, repeatedly refers to Mosaic as a model church suited for today's American culture, calling it an "edge-church" that has "placed both feet in the postmodern waters" and "one of the largest multicultural churches in North America" (1999b:440, 441). Dan Kimball, an author and the pastor of an innovative church in Santa Cruz, California, is one of many evangelical writers who cite Mosaic as a model for postmodern ministry. Mark

Mittelberg, executive vice president of the Willow Creek Association, highlights Mosaic's effective use of interactive dialogue and creative arts such as fashion design, film, and music (2000:266, 283–284). The Southern Baptist denomination, to which Mosaic belongs, highlights Mosaic's activity not only in Los Angeles but also in other countries, giving attention to innovation at home and preparation for missionary work abroad (Conner, 2002; Dotson, 2002; Welch, 2002). And the leadership of the Lutheran Church, in their Missouri Synod of March 2000, named Mosaic their national model for how to "do church" in America. Mosaic now hosts annual conferences for church leaders, and its lead pastor, Erwin McManus, has written several bestselling books endorsed by popular Christian figures like Dallas Willard and Rick Warren. As for journalistic attention, the *Los Angeles Times* and other L.A. newspapers have often looked to Mosaic for stories on ethnicity, creativity, and church growth (Bradley, 1995; Luo, 1998, 1999; Lobdell, 2001a, 2001b; Ramirez, 2000). Even local television news media has taken an interest in Mosaic. Recognizing that Mosaic is already of interest to scholars, practicing pastors, and journalists, this qualitative study will answer some of the most persistent questions already being asked of Mosaic.

TRULY MULTIETHNIC

Research and popular literature describing multiracial, multicultural, and multiethnic churches uses similar labels to mean different things. In this study, I wish to be clear about the meaning of "multiethnic" in describing the composition of Mosaic. The small amount of literature on multiracial churches is often framed by white/black relationships; multiracial most often means biracial, a congregation with significant proportions of both whites and blacks (Emerson and Smith, 2000). In addition, I am cautious in my understanding of the concept of "race," for fear that use of the term "multiracial" could unintentionally reinforce socially constructed racial boundaries. For the purpose of this study, I avoid using "multiracial" as a category. I also want to make clear that Mosaic is not a multicongregational church. A multicongregational church describes itself as diverse because two or more ethnic congregations share worship facilities (Ortiz, 1996). Multicongregational churches are also often multilingual churches, since the congregations have separate languages and leadership. Mosaic is not biracial or multicongregational or multilingual. Mosaic is multiethnic.

A multiethnic church has at least two distinct ethnic groups sharing a common congregational life and governance (see Ortiz, 1996). For purposes of this study, ethnicity derives from a shared ancestral group, broadly defined by a common language, region of birth, lineage, religion, or customs. Ethnicity implies greater fluidity between such groups than does the concept of race. It may be argued that almost every congregation is multiethnic, since the category "white" includes subgroups, such as Germans, Swedes, Dutch, and others, who have intermarried (see Waters, 1990). However, most researches subsume these national heritages in "Caucasian" or "white." As a church that includes national heritages other than those called "white," Mosaic is a rarity. Data cited by Flory and Miller (2000) for the Sunday evening Urban Mosaic service in downtown Los Angeles indicate that 48 percent of the congregation is of European descent, 27 percent Latin, and 18 percent Asian. However, figures drawn from Mosaic's own database reveal far more diversity in the congregation as a whole (Mosaic People Database, 2003). In each of the past three years Mosaic has held two or three celebration services in as many locations, and ethnic diversity was evident at all of them. Mosaic recently attempted to determine the level of diversity of attenders at all the services. Data were collected at all celebration services in January and February 2000, with a simple fill-in-the-blank card requesting basic information such as name, address, and age. The bottom of the card listed "Ethnicity" and "Country of Origin," each with a blank line next to it; no other instructions were given. Just under six hundred respondents, approximately 75 percent of the average weekly adult attendance at the time, filled in something for "Ethnicity," and the aggregated results are presented in table 1. A further examination of paid staff members at the time revealed similar proportions. Of twenty paid staff, six (30%) were Asian, eight (40%) were Hispanic, and six (30%) were white. Even the elders of the congregation showed a similar pattern: two (25%) Asian, three (38%) Hispanic, three (38%) white. (At that time, all of the Caucasian elders were serving overseas in India, Turkey, and Indonesia.) At every level of organization, Mosaic reveals a surprising consistency of ethnic diversity among the three ethnic groups of white, Asian, and Hispanic.

Results of Mosaic's survey show a small percentage of African Americans at Mosaic. At 1.7 percent, the proportion of blacks attending is well below the proportion of blacks in Los Angeles County, which 2000 census data placed at 9.8 percent. The percentage is low despite the fact that for five years (1991–1996) Mosaic had a black worship leader. The discriminatory history of the Southern Baptist Convention may contribute to the paucity of blacks. The denomination was formed in 1845 when the Alabama State Baptist Convention was asked whether missionaries sent by the convention could bring their slaves on mission,

Table 1. Proportion of Ethnic/Racial Groups at Mosaic

Ethnic Diversity at Mosaic
(n = 599)

Caucasian	32.8% (largest group: white, non-Hispanic, 31.8%)
Hispanic	30.3% (largest group: Mexican American, 25.6%)
Asian	27.8% (largest group: Chinese, 14%)
Other	8.9% comprising:
Middle Eastern	4.8% (majority USA born)
African American	1.7% (all USA born)
Armenian	1.2% (majority USA born)
American Indian	1%
Creole	0.2% (all USA born)

with the convention covering the costs of doing so. The convention refused to commission slave owners (or slaves) as missionaries, which rural whites felt denied them the right to own slaves; they therefore split off and formed the Southern Baptist Convention (Copeland, 1995). Blacks, therefore, have not associated historically with the Southern Baptist Convention. Through the civil rights era, blacks reportedly were not welcome in many Southern Baptist churches ("Southern Baptists," 2000). The Southern Baptist Convention apologized in 1995 for its history of racism and became more conscientious in placing blacks in key positions within the denomination, apparently succeeding in creating prominent leadership roles for blacks (J. Jones, 1998). The number of black (and other minority) Southern Baptists appears to be growing, and the number of homogeneous black Southern Baptist churches is increasing as well.

While the discriminatory history of the Southern Baptist Convention might have an influence, the more likely reason for the low proportion of blacks in this specific congregation is the location of Mosaic's activities. Until 2003, Mosaic owned three-quarters of an acre in East Los Angeles, the portion of the city known as the "barrios of East L.A." Garfield High School, the site of Jaime Escalante's notable achievements in teaching mathematics to Hispanic minorities, is around the corner. The strong Hispanic presence combined with the history of gang activity in the area meant that East L.A. was not a comfortable place for blacks to visit, let alone live. The location was not as important to whites in the congregation since whites most often came with a missionary mind-set, several moving from the South or the Midwest to live within walking distance of the church building. Furthermore, in 1997 a change in the location of the Sunday morning celebration service attracted more Asians to the congregation. The service moved roughly a mile west, to East L.A. College. This junior college is located in Monterey Park near Atlantic Boulevard, a notably Asian-friendly city and street. Because the Asian population has grown and moved southward from Alhambra and Monterey Park toward the 60 freeway over the past two decades, and because a celebration site outside of the barrio was now available, the number of Asians in the congregations grew. A move to a more "black-friendly" area has not yet occurred in the history of the congregation.

A final factor regarding the relatively small proportion of blacks in the congregation might be that blacks favor homogeneous congregations almost as much as whites do. Data from a paper presented by Michael Emerson (2000) show that among white, black, Hispanic, and Asian respondents, whites were least likely to attend mixed congregations: 11 percent of them did so, followed by 18 percent of black respondents (Hispanics and Asians reported 28 percent and 44 percent respectively). Alternatively, it may also be the case that blacks are "forced" into ho-mogeneous churches because they are not accepted as easily as other races or ethnicities into predominantly white or multiracial churches. Even more, residential segregation further contributes to the lack of interracial blending (Massey and Denton, 1993; for critique, see Thern-strom and Thernstrom, 1997). The distinctive difficulty of African American assimilation into diverse churches is explored in more detail in the last chapter of this book.

LARGE WEEKLY ATTENDANCE

The distinctiveness of Mosaic's multiethnicity is compounded by its size. Less than 1 percent of all churches in the United States see attendance over seven hundred; this has led to a designation of such churches as "megachurches" (Schaller, 2000). The great majority of megachurches consist of white, well-educated boomers, and exceptions tend to be either all-black or all-Hispanic congregations (see Thumma, 1996). From June 2002 to June 2003, Mosaic's weekend celebration services had between 1250 and 1550 attenders; the average attendance on any given weekend is about 1400. At its current size, Mosaic is larger than over 99 percent of American churches. Larger attendance translates into more small groups, ministry teams, and lay leaders than at other churches, including multiethnic churches.

MANY COMMITTED LAY LEADERS

Also, a large number of unpaid lay leaders are engaged in the ongoing creation and execution of Mosaic's organizational activities, increasing the number of sources from which to gather data. Mosaic's broad base of leadership provides a large number of ethnically mixed group experiences for attenders. When I set out to examine attenders' reasons for coming to and staying at Mosaic, many potential respondents were available.

For example, small groups are led by members of Mosaic, and almost every group has multiple leaders, variously called "leaders," "co-leaders," and "apprentices." Every group has at least one lay leader who takes responsibility for the life of the group. The 2003 brochure lists 116 group leaders by name, including 50 women, of whom 33 lead groups together with their husbands. The parity in the number of women recognized as leaders is interesting in light of the fact that while women make up the majority of believers in mainstream Christianity, men dominate religious authority (J. James, 1989; Batson, Schoenrade, and Ventis, 1993; Braude, 1995). At Mosaic women share many of the significant roles of spiritual leadership with men (see appendix B for a discussion of women and leadership at Mosaic).

According to a June 2003 flyer, there are forty-three small groups across metropolitan Los Angeles. Groups extend as far west as Venice, as far east as Riverside, south to Cypress, and north to Sherman Oaks. Mosaic small groups have many similarities to "cell groups" (Galloway, 2000; Comiskey, 1999; Cho et al., 1987), which are home-based small groups intended to grow and multiply as group members are added by either assimilation or conversion. As another observer of Mosaic wrote, "Primarily, [small] groups are considered to be the base source of church social interaction, as well as a method of introducing non-church-attenders and potential converts into the church" (Prieto, 2000: 60). Groups are not categorized by age or life station, yet they often center on affinities of geography, marital status, and involvement with the creative arts, such as dance, painting, and film. "Creating this kind of community is a distinctive feature of Mosaic as it seeks to secure a place for persons to belong" (Prieto, 2000:61).

In contrast to other multiethnic churches, Mosaic does not have ethnically designated small group ministries (e.g., "Asian Groups" or "Mexican American Groups") and does not target its programs to specific ethnic groups (e.g., Hispanic ministries). Instead, small groups at Mosaic are ethnically mixed; for example, groups of eight or twelve members will routinely include at least one Caucasian, one Hispanic, or one Asian, in addition to African Americans, Middle Easterners, or others. Mosaic small group attenders are choosing to build relationships with people of different ethnicities, since within the structure of Mosaic the choice of group is left to the individual.

In addition to small groups, Mosaic has "service teams," task-oriented groups that accomplish some aspect of Mosaic's overall activity. For example, there are at least three worship bands, four tech and multimedia crews, a dance team, a visual arts team, two Café Mosaic teams, two ambiance teams, a writer's group, and several follow-up teams. These groups are varied in purpose, but all are smaller communities of four to ten people responsible to one or more designated leaders, who exercise spiritual authority in the group. These teams show as much ethnic diversity as the home-based small groups.

Part of the Evangelical Movement

Mosaic is part of a significant aspect of American Protestantism. Thirty-nine percent of Americans describe themselves as evangelical Christians (see Hunter, 1983; Quebedeaux, 1974, 1978). Although publicly acknowledged for creativity and innovation (Sweet, 1999a, 1999b; Luo, 1998, 1999; Prieto, 2000), Mosaic is a doctrinally conservative Protestant church sharing evangelical convictions. Mosaic is affiliated with the Southern Baptist Convention, which is by far the largest American Protestant denomination; Southern Baptists have more churches (over 37,000) in the United States than any other religious body, even more than the Roman Catholic Church. According to a Mosaic congregational audit conducted by the Gallup organization in 1999, an overwhelming 98 percent of attenders at Mosaic believe in the full authority of the Bible and 95 percent believe their religious faith is the most important influence in their lives (Prieto, 2000:65–68). Mosaic embraces the evangelical priority of sharing the "good news" of salvation in Jesus both locally and internationally. Gallup's congregational audit revealed that 98 percent of those surveyed were active in sharing their faith in Jesus

Christ with others. Internationally, Mosaic sends more missionaries overseas than any other Southern Baptist church. Missionary efforts target areas of the world considered "least evangelized" by the denomination.

Almost 90 percent of Americans calling themselves evangelicals are white (Emerson and Smith, 2000). With the notable exception of ethnic diversity, Mosaic is part of the broader evangelical movement, especially in its evangelistic activity locally and overseas, its emphasis on the authority of the Bible, and its overall conservative doctrine. This study examines its ability to attract and retain a diverse population within the general subculture of evangelicalism.

EMPHASIS ON ARTISTS AND ARTISTRY

Sociologists of religion are now focusing much more attention on artistry within the local church. Chaves (2004) demonstrates that more church attenders are involved in church-related artistic pursuits, including music, skits and plays, and dance, than in either social service or political action. Wuthnow (2003) goes further to assert that art is the means by which churches are being revitalized today. The critical mechanism for him is "selective absorption," which emphasizes that "religious organizations do not respond passively to social conditions but negotiate with their environment" (14). Wuthnow shows how exposure to the arts is widespread and possibly increasing, and suggests that those with a strong interest in spirituality are also interested in artistry and consider experience a valuable means to knowing God. He found that 30 percent of people in church-sponsored small groups say they discuss the arts or music as part of their weekly group activity (116–188). Churches develop programs to take advantage of local opportunities to involve and engage people in religious activities. He states that "churches are readily taking advantage of the present interest in the arts as a way to maintain the loyalty of members and attract new ones" (237).

Although there is no choir at Mosaic, the artistic focus is evident in artists painting during the celebration services, multiple bands, special music pieces, integrated dramas, multimedia presentations, glossy invitation cards, weekly re-creation of ambiance, new dance pieces, fashion shows, colorful bulletins, and more. For Wuthnow, "the innovations involving music and the arts reflect an awareness that churches must work harder than they did in the past to make the liturgy a meaningful worship experience" (177). Since 1997, Mosaic has expansively embraced the arts and is becoming a reference point for other churches seeking a model to emulate.

A "New Paradigm" Church

Mosaic exhibits almost every characteristic of reinvented, postdenominational, or "new paradigm" churches as described by Miller (1999, 1998, 1997). For example, Mosaic actively uses contemporary cultural forms in music, visual arts, graphic arts, and dance. Mosaic has a very fluid organizational character, accentuating the Protestant principle of the priesthood of all believers in emphasizing that being on mission is not the prerogative of professionalized clergy but is fundamental to all believers. Part of the significance of Mosaic is its membership in this broader class of organizations emerging in America.

As a "new paradigm church," Mosaic is not necessarily a "seeker church" as described by Sargeant (2000). It is indeed entrepreneurial and innovative, deemphasizing denominational identity while maintaining a broadly conservative doctrine. However, Mosaic is not consumeristic in its approach. Rather than constituting a straight-forward marketing mechanism intended to draw masses of attenders, the ingenuity manifest in the worship services is part of a distinctive theology focused on creativity. Sunday messages are not so much pragmatic as they are provocative. Leaders do not rely on methods they have learned at conferences or from books, preferring to spontaneously craft whatever is needed to address new problems or begin new initiatives. Mosaic is not a spiritual shopping mall with well-ordered programs and calendars but a changing kaleidoscope of projects, events, and activities. In terms of age, Sargeant defines seeker churches as providing religious significance to "spiritually seeking baby boomers" (14), while Mosaic's greatest growth is occurring among "Millennials," post–Gen X young adults in their twenties and early thirties. Seeker churches are suburban phenomena; Mosaic and its sister churches are urban. Sargeant clearly distinguishes seeker churches from new paradigm churches, saying that "seeker churches are generally less charismatic and more middle class" than new paradigm churches, yet "both share the same entrepreneurial innovation, contemporary cultural style, empowerment of the laity, and antiestablishment or antidenomination sentiment" (172).

Miller (1999:1251–1252) seems to be describing Mosaic in his list of characteristics of new paradigm churches, which includes such elements as a free-spirited worship environment; a focus on the application of Scripture to personal life rather than the encyclopedic exposition of theological doctrine; small groups that focus on worship, Bible study, and mutual care; strict moral standards with a tolerance for different personal styles; a "culturally hip" atmosphere; great freedom for lay leaders in developing ministry programs; the lead pastor's serving as "teacher, visionary, and trainer" while congregants accomplish the ministry; independence from denominational affiliation and identification as part of a broader movement; ongoing commissioning of leaders for new churches and ministries throughout the world; members' sense of themselves as empowered, inventive, and resourceful; little concern for fund-raising; radical decentralization; and having fun in worship celebrations. For Miller, churches like Mosaic are forerunners of postdenominational Christianity, ushering in a Second Reformation.

This study explores an exceptional case among new paradigm churches. The diversity of the church forces us to ask how the texture of innovation in this congregation allows it to embrace different ethnic groups. If Mosaic becomes even more influential as a model for congregational diversity, could it be that the Second Reformation will include the overcoming of church segregation?

A Glimpse into the Future

Mosaic is a bounded system, examination of which can "reveal the properties of the class to which the instance being studied belongs" (Guba and Lincoln, 1981:371). Studying Mosaic is seeing a "new paradigm church" in action. If Mosaic's style and structure of ministry continue to grow in influence, then it may help demonstrate how to lead and grow a church in the context of ethnic diversity. In a society that will become increasingly diverse in the coming millennium, such learning could serve to accelerate the growth of these churches as a whole, such that multiethnicity could become a significant part of this emerging movement. The next chapter will provide historical context to the congregation, tracing the development of the church from its founding until the present day. The chapter will also present the uniqueness and significance of Mosaic today.

2

DESCRIBING MOSAIC

DAVE: People who have left the church sometimes say maybe they'll come back. The first thing I tell them is a warning, a caution, that whatever you remember about the church when you were there, it's not anywhere near that. In fact, you might want to think of it as a whole new church.

BROOKE: I come from a very traditional Southern Baptist background. *Very* traditional. I walked into church, and this Latino guy was standing up there bouncing around on stage leading worship, and everybody is clapping and all this kind of stuff. And I was just looking around like they're freaks. I'm like, "What the heck? Is this a cult?"

The history of specific congregations emerged in the last decade as an explicit focus of research (Warner, 1988; Wind, 1990; Wind and Lewis, 1994: vol. 1). Such histories provide a necessary context for the beliefs, activity, and local culture of a particular congregation, and that is my aim in pursuing a history of Mosaic. Putting together such a history is challenging. I often heard from leaders that Mosaic is an "oral culture." Very little of Mosaic's sixty-year history is documented. Only a few pamphlets and bulletins survive, the oldest, dating from the mid-seventies, describing the church's building program. Without a doubt, the best and most detailed sources are the oral histories obtained from longtime members. Eight of my respondents had been at Mosaic over twenty years, so my account of the earliest history of the church draws heavily on them. They learned the history of Mosaic through direct questions, extended conversations, and chance encounters with previous leaders and members. Fortunately, Mosaic has had only two lead pastors in the past forty years; the continuity of its leadership lends coherence to Mosaic's story. This chapter will briefly review the history of Mosaic and describe the church from different angles. Having done so, it will describe significant shifts over the past decade that have contributed to the uniqueness of this congregation.

An Oral History

The history of the church reveals a pattern of growing ethnic diversification, a focus on missional theology and personal evangelism, a growing use of creative arts, a commitment to creating an organization responsive to change, and an ongoing effort to appeal to young adults. The history given here is not comprehensive nor does it give equal weight to every aspect of the church's corporate experience; it addresses those themes and events most relevant for people who are still in the congregation today. Most names have been altered.

Home away from Home

Mosaic began as a church for people like Carl. Originally from Tennessee, Carl is a white, middle-class Midwesterner who moved to Los Angeles in his early twenties and worked as an attendant at a gas station, where he met his wife, Clara. When in their late twenties, Carl and Clara drove some distance every Sunday to a Southern Baptist church in downtown L.A. where Carl's uncle was the interim pastor. After some time Carl's uncle told him, "There's a church down in East L.A. with mainly people from the Midwest. You'd be right at home there." His uncle was right. They visited it the next Sunday, and, according to Carl, "I felt right at home."

Their new church home, the First Southern Baptist Church of East

Los Angeles, had already existed for over twenty years. Thirty-five transplanted white Midwesterners and Southerners established the church in 1943 at Carpenters' Union Hall on Whittier Boulevard. At that time, such halls were rented for parties on weekends, so setting up for church on Sunday morning meant sweeping out Saturday night's beer bottles and peanut shells. In 1947 the congregation, then numbering about a hundred, purchased property with a small church building a few blocks away on a little street called Brady. Over the next five years, more property and buildings were purchased, and some structures were torn down to make way for a new sanctuary. The total size of the property owned by the church was three-quarters of an acre.

Worship service attendance in the next few years more than doubled, to 250. Then came decline. The shrinking congregation consisted of whites in their forties and fifties. As people left, few new people were added. According to a building program brochure, "Pressures in a changing community shattered the dream. It faded. The Sixties were hard times for our church. It was the death of a vision. Many left. Few people hung on through that decade. It seemed like the end."

When Carl and Clara arrived at the little church on Brady Avenue in 1967, church attendance was about a hundred. Most attenders were still white Southerners and Midwesterners. There were a few Hispanic families. Few in the congregation lived in the immediate neighborhood. Carl remembers one Hispanic family leaving the church "because they said they didn't like the people from the neighborhood. They said, 'These people are not for us,' like they were lower class." Brother John Ashcroft, pastor at that time, was in his late fifties or early sixties and wanted to retire. When he left, the church appointed Mike Norfleet, a man in his twenties with a thick Texas accent. Within two years, however, Brother Mike went to the mission field in China, and the church appointed a new search committee.

The Urban Apostle

According to the building program brochure, the church nearly died in the 1960s. "Then God brought a man," it declares. A longtime member recalls that the church narrowed the candidates down to three men: one African American, one Mexican, and one Caucasian. Each was given an opportunity to preach, and one, a young Caucasian student at Fuller Seminary, stood out as an outstanding communicator. In 1971, after a unanimous vote, Philip Bowers, or Brother Phil as he asked to be called, became the pastor of the church. He was in his early twenties, and remained its leader for over twenty years.

Brother Phil was on his way to the mission field before he felt a calling to East Los Angeles. His orientation was not that of a suburban church pastor looking to build a comfortable parish; rather, he was a fervent missionary-evangelist mobilizing people to reach the world. The church had dwindled to forty-five members, almost all white, almost all fifty or older. The church was very traditionally Southern Baptist in its doctrine, music, order of worship, and organized activities. Brother Phil wanted to draw more people by leading the church to become more relevant to its East Los Angeles setting. He began introducing various changes. Fueled by passion and disciplined initiative, he set out to create an organization that would be an evangelistic force locally and globally. He would ingrain into the congregation a single, clear mission statement: "To be a spiritual reference point east of downtown Los Angeles and a sending base to the ends of the earth."

At first, he drew new, younger members into the church. Carl told me, "He attracted a lot of university students and a lot of young seminary students, so the church began aging down." Brother Phil moved his family into a house one block from the church and befriended Hispanics in the surrounding neighborhood. He participated in civic agencies, interacted with minority activists, and created ministry programs to help the poorest in the area. Walt, one of many who lived for a time with Brother Phil, spoke about Brother Phil's engagement as a white man in the Chicano culture. "In some homes when he visited," Walt said, "he had to go in through the back door. And he did. He submitted himself to that as a way of entering people's minds." Through his relational approach, lively teaching style, and active involvement in the local community, the number of Hispanics in the church increased. The congregation was guided to welcome guests. According to church records, attendance at weekly worship services grew from forty-five to two hundred in the first three years of Brother Phil's leadership, to four hundred in the next three years, and peaked in 1981 at 585.

During that time, Brother Phil changed the name of the congregation to "The Church on Brady." Such colloquial church names are not unusual now, but Brother Phil is believed to have been the first to remove the denominational label from a Southern Baptist church. One reason for the change was that people had difficulty finding the church. Around the neighborhood, members would refer to it as "the big church on Brady." Another reason, and perhaps more significant, is that the new name was more acceptable to local Hispanics who had been raised Roman Catholic and whose family and friends considered entering an evangelical church to be a betrayal of faith. Some Hispanics would start attending but not tell others that it was a Baptist church. According to Walt, the new name "created a kind of A.K.A., a subversive, underground way of doing ministry." Such a "subversive" attitude suited the cultivation among members of an attitude of being on mission.

First Changes in Ethnic Composition

The ethnic composition of the church changed to such an extent that Ramon, arriving five years later in 1976, described the church as filled with English-speaking Hispanics:

> That made it very comfortable for me. There were very few Asians and an interesting group of white people coming. Being in East L.A., it drew a noticeable white group, a minority, but a group of white people nevertheless. It was relatively young, pretty much young families in their twenties to thirties; no one was much older than that. So, young beginning families with kids were mostly there at the time.

According to another longtime member of Mosaic, the white members did not come from the immediate community. At the founding of the church, neighborhoods just a mile north of the church building and in nearby cities to the east and west were mostly white. But immigration from Mexico made the area predominantly Hispanic. However, it was not the Hispanics living around the church building who attended the church. According to Ramon, Hispanics at the church "tended to come more from the greater East L.A. area. Maybe they had grown up nearby, but they no longer lived necessarily nearby." According to him and others,

> many of our parents were immigrants. . . . It was really more the Mexican Americans, the English-speaking ones, who were coming to the church, not the Spanish people. Often they didn't even speak Spanish.

Ramon called them "Americanized Latinos." These Hispanics were mostly working-class, second-generation or later Mexican Americans; often they had moved away from East L.A. to be closer to work or to live in a nicer neighborhood. Brother Phil brought a Mexican American on staff to be the director of evangelism for the congregation.

Older whites became a minority, and the number of younger whites grew. In the late '70s and into the '80s, Brother Phil networked with Southern Baptist groups on college campuses. He appealed to the missionary-minded students by announcing that Los Angeles was a place that could affect the world. "The nations come to Los Angeles," he would say, and by offering a compelling vision of how God was orchestrating a global movement to reach the nations starting from Los Angeles, he actively recruited students and seminarians to join his ministry in East L.A. Dozens of students responded to the message and relocated from places like Texas and Oklahoma. They moved into the neighborhood and became interns. Many lived closer to the church property than established members, and many of them remained in Los Angeles permanently.

Church members generally saw the involvement of these young Midwesterners as positive, although there was some tension. It seems that these young white people came eager and ready to work. "The thing that struck me," said Luis, a longtime Hispanic member, "is they were so ready to assume leadership and do whatever God wanted them to do." Whether they were expecting to be in Los Angeles a few weeks or months, they brought zeal to whatever they were asked to do. Many took on a good deal of responsibility. They rose to leadership quickly. Luis said there was "some resentment from a predominantly Hispanic church who were wishy-washy or reluctant to take leadership positions in the church." One longtime church leader said, "The church was definitely led by those who grew up in a Southern culture, knew Christ, grew up in church, were very well discipled, and, really honestly, a lot of the Mexican people who were here felt like, 'How am I supposed to compete?' " Another longtime member explained, "If anything, the most verbal complaints were from the Latinos," but then quickly added, "but they would be overcome by the genuine love the people expressed in service. How can you argue if someone's genuinely there to serve you?" One member conjectured that Hispanics did not share these young, highly churched whites' aggressive drive to fulfill the goals of the church. Luis suggested that their attitude was one of *mañana*, i.e., that they felt no rush to do anything quickly. "[The Hispanics] just let other people step in and then [didn't] say much. I don't think they particularly cared much." Part of the tension came from the sheer difference in the time the two groups had available for church-related commitments. Hispanics were working full-time and raising families while these white, young, single college students gave their discretionary time almost exclusively to the church.

As for other ethnicities, since the coming of Brother Phil there had always been a few Asian and African American attenders. He and his wife modeled and encouraged hospitality to people of diverse backgrounds. The most prominent African American under Brother Phil's leadership was a worship leader I will call Ethan, who began participating in the worship ministry sometime in the mid-1980s. Having married a Mexican American woman from the congregation, he became an intimate member of the community. Ethan was an effective worship leader with a warm personal presence, yet he did not have much actual authority. According to a member involved with the worship team, "He would be the one singing up top, but he was definitely not the one who was in charge." Another staff member, named Susan, was in charge of church music. She had been hired by Brother Phil early in his pastorate. "She picked the songs, she directed the choir, she ran the rehearsals, and so Ethan would be one of the people up on the microphone." Nevertheless, his public presence gave a diverse feel to the worship services and led many to see the church as ethnically and racially diverse. As for Asians, a Japanese American man became a prominent Bible teacher in the congregation and, late in Brother Phil's ministry, a Chinese American couple became leaders in the college ministry.

Lay Leadership and Mobilization

Susan is universally considered to have been a versatile, hard-working, and missions-minded strategist, and was determinedly committed to understanding what made local church ministry effective. She networked well and was often consulted by other church leaders. Brother Phil and Susan became the central leaders of the church. "You talk to one, you're talking to both," said one member. A longtime church leader said, "Nothing of any major consequence was done without their approval." Brother Phil and Susan experimented with church structure in hopes of deepening the belief systems of attenders, developing strong volunteer leaders, and further enlarging the congregation through personal evangelism.

Under their leadership, changes were implemented quickly. They nurtured a responsive organization willing to implement their tactical initiatives in pursuit of long-range strategic endeavors. For example, the two most innovative programs of the church for many years were the Sunday school teaching program and the weekly small groups. The Sunday school curriculum was an intentional mechanism for Bible training and spiritual growth for all age levels. Weekly small groups provided group discipleship and a communal base for evangelistic activity. Both programs had stringent standards of operation. Weekly training provided leaders of classes and groups extensive and demanding guidance in working with people. Many of them expressed appreciation for what they had learned and were surprised other churches did not offer the same type of training. However, some leaders felt that the training was controlling and restrictive. One member who owned a business at the time described it as "meetings, a lot of meetings. Very high structure, very demanding in terms of time . . . a lot was expected of you." In the role of a Sunday school leader, he said, "I felt like I couldn't be creative. It constrained me, and the shoe didn't fit." A small group leader told me,

> Things were very restrictive then. We all had to do the same Bible study every week. One week I decided that I wasn't going to do it; I was going to do something else. When we all got together and were asked how the study went that week, I said that I hadn't done the study—that I had decided to do something else. After the meeting, I was taken aside and told, "If you want to continue to be a group leader, then you need to do the study we assigned to you."

Another leader agreed, "They had an intensely high level of commitment for training people, but it ended up standardized. Training was to 'put in to' people, not to develop them." He added, "While you could teach, you weren't allowed to innovate. And there's a difference." Another member summarized the culture of the church then as "highly structured, heavily programmed, leadership encouraged but not entrusted, a certain sense of being very convicted as far as spiritual values, and, while feeling loved, not feeling significant as far as roles within the church."

As the church shifted from an almost exclusively white congregation to one that was primarily Hispanic, and as a great number of volunteers became involved in the ministry, almost every paid staff member was white. The diversification of paid staff leadership lagged behind diversification of the congregation. People placed in the highest levels of leadership were often recruited from outside of the congregation, most paid staff had seminary training, and a high regard for educational achievement became part of the church's culture. An informal set of educational requirements may have hindered Hispanics from being hired as paid staff. A Hispanic member who had worked closely with Brother Phil and Susan said,

> One of the Latin members of the church eventually left because he felt they wouldn't appoint him or commission him as a pastor. In his

own perspective, they felt like if he didn't go to seminary and have a seminary degree, then he wasn't qualified to be a pastor. And he left and planted a church.

Tony, a Mexican American, recalled being asked by Brother Phil to join the staff. "The first thing I said was, 'I don't have a seminary education, not even a college degree.' " Tony thought that his lack of formal education was an obstacle. But he was brought on staff nonetheless. "He took me because I owned my own business." Tony showed evidence of being able to manage himself and others well.

While there were few Hispanics on paid staff, congregational lay leadership did become more diverse over the years, including two Hispanic elders, male and female Hispanics commissioned for overseas ministry, and a handful of Asians leading ministry programs.

The Church on Brady

In their first decade of working together, Brother Phil and Susan successfully implemented their strategies. The Church on Brady grew and carried on evangelistic outreach. Despite a woefully small property, in the 1970s the church grew from forty-five members to almost six hundred, and included children as well as adults. This remarkable growth drew attention from missiologists Donald McGavran and Winfield Arn, who prominently featured the church in a training film entitled *And They Said It Couldn't Be Done!* (McGavran and Arn, 1977:12–13). The sense of mission, Brother Phil's teaching style, the commitment to leadership training, and the warmth of the congregants in welcoming newcomers contributed to sustained growth throughout the decade. The church at that time reflected Holifield's (1994:47) conclusion that "people joined congregations to seek a sense of both belonging and meaning, and that congregations which made this a challenging and demanding quest in the 1970's seemed to flourish."

Located on three-quarters of an acre with forty parking places, the church property was much too small to accommodate existing ministry activity and further growth. The Church on Brady considered moving to a larger location, but all options were ultimately rejected in favor of expanding facilities around the current church building. A new, larger building was built over the existing sanctuary with much volunteer effort. Upon its completion, the old building was torn down and literally hauled out through the new front doors. Members describe a deep sense of community and purpose in completing such a large task. After the expansion, the church attracted younger students, a few more Asians, and still more whites. But the project was exhausting, and for many the new building implied a new level of committed service. "People left," one member said, "who had been or were committed to the building because they knew more was required of them." Attendance, which had peaked at 585 and had included both children and adults before the completion of the new building, now dropped down to the 300s.

While new people continued to come to services through connections with members of the congregation, the greatest draw in the 1980s became large stage performances. Dave Auda came to the church during his college years with broad experience in theater arts. He began writing plays and composing songs, creating sets, establishing production schedules, recruiting people to work on his productions, and directing the actors. Christmas and Easter plays were at first standard productions that were borrowed or purchased as packages, which then included one or two original songs written by a member of the congregation (usually Dave). Several successes permitted him, in cooperation with another member, named Jay Parker, to go beyond producing holiday plays to create dinner theater experiences that drew even more into the church. These were massive productions with elaborate set designs, dozens of actors and stagehands, and an orchestra, and they offered members an opportunity to work together in pursuit of the church's evangelistic mission. In one weekend over 1,500 people would attend such performances. Eventually, the church stopped using prepackaged productions and church members began writing original works. This was the beginning of the co-optation of the creative arts that expanded throughout the next two decades.

The church also created outreach programs to serve community needs. For the poor, a food pantry was established and, at Christmas, the congregation delivered groceries to needy families. For those legally required to do community service, the church provided opportunities to do so. The church also created its own twelve-step "Clean and Sober" program for those with alcohol and drug problems. And, in the early 1990s, the church obtained a government grant establishing a nonprofit organization to help the unemployed. By networking with local businesses and training individuals in new skills, the church placed ten to fifteen people in jobs every month. Many homeless people were served through these ministries.

In the late 1970s, the church began sending teams on short-term, overseas trips to locations from Belize to China. Over the years, the church succeeded in sending out more overseas missionaries than any other Southern Baptist church. The majority of these missionaries were "home-grown" through local ministry opportunities. This global missionary involvement fostered appreciation of other cultures and an emphasis on evangelism to all ethnic groups. Ramon told me,

> Through missionary trips, you had to address the fact that you're going to other countries with different customs and values and practices from our own and that we have to respect them and admire them and understand them. That helps you also to see that I have one way of doing it and they have another, and that's okay as long as the overriding issues of morality and life principles of the Bible were applied.

Sensitivity to cultural dynamics overseas and concern for people regardless of cultural background permeated the church and paved the way for further diversification.

Passing the Mantle

The Church on Brady was introduced to Erwin McManus, an ordained pastor and church planter born in El Salvador, when he came to speak at its annual missions conference in 1990. Susan had met Erwin through a mutual friend, and she and Brother Phil found him engaging. They met often over the next several months to discuss one all-absorbing topic: how to evangelize the world starting from Los Angeles. Erwin told me they wanted to start a church-planting project and believed he should lead it. "They were desperately looking for an ethnic minority because they thought that a church-planting movement in L.A. wouldn't work with a Caucasian leader." Their dialogues continued into the next year until Brother Phil and Susan reached a radical conclusion. Erwin recalls,

> They asked me point-blank at a restaurant: Would I consider becoming pastor of the church? And I said no, I had no interest. What they explained was that Phil had been there for twenty years, he was looking to transition into another role, taking over the seminary kind of thing that he was doing. They wanted me to do a five-year transition process under him where he would be my mentor as senior pastor. I had no interest in doing that. And so I said no. No, thank you.

Though failing to convince him to take the pastorate, they did succeed in winning him over to the original idea of taking on the church-planting initiative. Erwin moved to Los Angeles in 1992 to head up a project for establishing a hundred new churches. It was an unpaid post; Erwin earned money through consultations and speaking engagements around the nation. He accepted leadership of LASER because he became convinced that Los Angeles was a critical city in God's overarching work in history.

Erwin became a member of the church in order to continue his relationship with Brother Phil and Susan. He called them "catalytic and intelligent," and said, "I was attracted to the passion, the global vision, and the high level of thinking that was available." Brother Phil and Susan asked him to take several leadership roles. "They had a value for small groups, so I started a small group." He also played sports for the purpose of evangelism, taught Wednesday night classes, and headed up the singles ministry. Erwin began to do things in whatever way made sense to him, not knowing that he was often breaking many unspoken rules. He told me about one occasion:

> I started a small group on a Tuesday night, and I got confronted by leaders. They said, "How come you're allowed to lead life group on Tuesday nights? We all do them on Sunday nights. No one's allowed to do a small group except for Sunday night."

Erwin's assessment of the church was that "innovation was extremely low on a congregational level." At the time, "one of the highest values in this church was standardization. So whenever I destandardized, I would get in trouble. But not from them. What was interesting was they would never stop me." All this time, Brother Phil and Susan continued to prod Erwin to take leadership of the church.

By 1993, Erwin said, "I felt God commanded me to become pastor. I accepted the call." It was no surprise to anyone. The congregation had come to expect Erwin to be the next lead pastor, and embraced him in that role. They took a vote on his appointment, and it was unanimous. Ramon said, "I don't remember any issues or concerns from anyone. It was a slam dunk." Clara told me, "When Pastor Erwin first came to the church and preached on Sunday, I said, 'That's the first person that I have seen that I think can take Brother Phil's place.'" According to her, "It hasn't been a burden for me at all for him to become our pastor. It seems like that's the way it needed to be."

On a strategic level, Erwin was disappointed with LASER's progress in church planting. Though he remained committed to church planting (Mosaic still commissions church planters nationally and internationally under his leadership), his ministry shifted at that time from church planting to church building. He believed that investing in the growth of the church would be a more effective strategy for evangelizing metropolitan Los Angeles. He concentrated on the resources and influence of a growing church, and on what this church could accomplish if properly positioned.

Two Leaders, Two Cultures

The congregation accepted Erwin McManus as its new pastor in part because in many ways he was similar to Brother Phil. Both are outstanding speakers. Both are great storytellers. Both are interesting and insightful conversationalists. Both are committed to accurate, conservative exegesis of the Bible. Both place a high value on making their messages relevant to local culture. Both bring to the issues they address a global perspective drawn from their direct experience in other countries. Both have a strong missionary bent. Both are effective personal evangelists. Both exercise a charismatic style of leadership similar to that found among black preachers (Mamiya, 1994:233). Both inspire loyalty from their congregation. And both attract younger people.

Confident in the attractiveness of Pastor Erwin's messages to those outside the church, members increasingly invited "unchurched" friends and family to attend church functions. Indeed, Erwin's influence as a communicator is an important cause of the church's sustained growth. Kevin, a twenty-three-year-old Caucasian, talked about Erwin's "amazing sermons," saying,

> The first time I heard Erwin speak, I remember having the feeling like I can't leave the room unchanged. Like this is *crazy*. I've heard *tons* of sermons before, but he's speaking on a passage that I had read a thousand times before and [I had] missed treasures in it that I had never seen. I was like, "What? Where did *that* come from?"

African Americans spoke very highly of Pastor Erwin. For example, Jerome said, "It's weird, but it seemed like he was talking to me." Dela, twenty-four, described why she stayed at Mosaic:

> It was definitely Pastor Erwin, I know that. Without a doubt. Everything he said. You know how some people think you're supposed to go to church, and the pastor has a message just for you? . . . he said things that were right on. I just had to go back.

And Dylan, twenty-eight, said, "It wasn't like preaching, it was like talking, explaining things, and things made sense, and there it was. I was hooked."

Early on, Erwin changed the mission statement of the church. Eric, one of the pastors at Mosaic, said,

> He removed the word "east." Now it became a spiritual reference point *throughout* Los Angeles and a sending base to the ends of the earth. By changing that one word, decisions began to be made in terms of the whole city.

The scope of ministry activity changed to encompass all of metropolitan Los Angeles. The church under Phil believed "it's going to happen on Brady Street," while the church under Erwin came to believe the future of the church was in a bigger and more central location.

Conflicts emerged, especially regarding personal evangelism. Warner (1994:69) cites research by David Olson showing "that when a congregation is settled, its members tend to have all the friends they have room for, and they have less incentive to seek out new recruits." The Church on Brady had become settled. Erwin sought to reenergize the evangelistic intentionality of the congregation. He told me, "I had people in my office saying that the church was growing too fast. People were definitely anti-evangelism. There wasn't neutrality; there were definitely people against it." The conflicts were sometimes severe. According to Erwin, "Theologically, they were extremely reformed, a lot of hyper-Calvinists. I would say that was the doctrinal center of the church." Evangelism tended to be viewed as God, through the Holy Spirit, drawing people who were already to be saved by His divine providence. Erwin described the difficulty:

> Those people stay, and they win people to themselves, and they create small groups of people, and they begin to teach that what you're doing is wrong. I had small coalitions forming everywhere, even among new converts, people we would lead to Christ, and they would convince them that theirs was the right way. So we were not a church coalesced around a common value system into common vision.

Because of Erwin's emphasis on personal evangelism, he was accused of diminishing the priority of overseas missions. "I would kill the missions of the church—that was the accusation." In time, Erwin's influence would change the congregation's view of evangelism, so that it was seen less as God's exclusive activity and more as saved humanity's intentional and strategic effort to reach out to a world already being wooed by God.

Closely related to the controversy over evangelism was controversy over making the celebration services attractive and accessible to the unchurched. Mosaic's celebration services became more dramatic and interactive. Erwin recalls, "When I started using film clips, people said I was bringing the world into church." He was criticized for using a Bible translation intended for children. "Since I wasn't preaching from the New American Standard, I wasn't preaching the Bible." Changes in ambiance in the sanctuary were critiqued. "When I tried to introduce a value for aesthetics, that seemed very carnal and fleshly."

Despite criticism, church attendance dramatically peaked three times, increasing to eight hundred and then dropping back down to five hundred in the first three years of Erwin's leadership. The church seemed unprepared for new people, new guests, new leaders, and new growth. During this time, Pastor Erwin began attracting a younger and more diverse crowd. And a few more Asians joined the congregation.

Becoming Mosaic

A breakthrough in growth came in 1997. Attendance at a new Sunday evening service for young adult singles grew from twenty to over three hundred in six months. That service was called Mosaic. The name became a rich cultural metaphor for what the church was becoming. The church was a mosaic of "broken" people, differently colored and from different ethnic backgrounds, coming together into a single community of faith. Within the year, the elders asked the congregation to change both the colloquial and legal names of the church. On a Wednesday night with over four hundred people in attendance, the name change was overwhelmingly approved. In this one congregationally affirmed change, the arena of church activity was redefined. The change in the name combined with the change in the church's mission statement (from "*east of downtown* Los Angeles" to "*throughout* Los Angeles") to broaden the scope of thinking in the corporate culture of Mosaic.

When Erwin initially took the title of senior pastor, Phil took the title of teaching pastor and remained on staff with an office on site. The arrangement created more tensions than originally envisioned. After five years of transition, Phil Bowers left the staff of the church. Several said they felt it was a very good thing for the church. One longtime member stated,

> It freed Pastor Erwin to do what God had placed in his heart to do. Otherwise, I don't think he would've been able to do it because of the kind of authority Brother Phil carried. It was really hard to take our eyes off of Brother Phil and put it on Pastor Erwin and look at him as the pastor.

Phil's leaving generated many questions for those who had come to the church under his leadership. Why did he leave? Did he really have to go? Longtime church members were leaving while many new attenders were coming. Those uncomfortable with changes in the church took the opportunity to leave. Yet the number of new people coming in was greater than those leaving, so records show a steady gain in average attendance. Attendance rose again to around eight hundred, and a search began for a larger facility because, once again, the facility on Brady was too small for the scope of ministry activity.

Significant diversification occurred when a number of Asians were added to the mix of whites and Hispanics coming to Mosaic. This happened when the Sunday morning services were moved west of the original site to the auditorium of East Los Angeles College in 1997. The new site was less than a mile from the old one, but that mile was significant for the area. Those still tied to the church building took the move as another opportunity to leave. East Los Angeles College is located on Atlantic Boulevard at the southern edge of Monterey Park, a densely populated Asian area. It was also more conveniently located, with access from major freeways. Those who had been afraid to travel into an East L.A. neighborhood were now willing to visit the church for the first time.

East L.A. College was also the site of a breakthrough in the design of the celebration services. Genesis, a year-long series of sermons, drew on images of the elemental forces of nature (wind, water, wood, fire, and earth) as metaphors to emphasize various aspects of the nature of God, the nature of humanity, and the place of humanity in relationship to God. Short films, dramas, and works of music, dance, and painting were incorporated such that celebration services become multisensory experiences integrating the pastor's messages with all forms of the creative arts. Services were filled with live painting and sculpting, dance and dramatic performances, with dozens of participants. The creative integration of message, music, and the arts became the distinctive public signature of Mosaic.

Another important shift came in 1998 when the Sunday evening service moved to a downtown Los Angeles nightclub. The college ministry rented the site for a special outreach event, and it was a hit. Shortly afterward, the college leader and Pastor Erwin met with the owners of the site. The end result was that Mosaic was invited to use the facilities regularly. So began a friendly relationship that continues to the present. The service, called Urban Mosaic, gives the church a presence downtown, in the symbolic center of Los Angeles. It also allows weekly experimentation with facility design, ultra-modern ambiance, serial dramas, unusual messages, and untried ministry teams. Attendance at Urban Mosaic began with sixty and was over four hundred four years later.

Success at the nightclub location persuaded the congregation to continue using rented facilities in different parts of Los Angeles. For example, for eight months in 2000–2001, the church rented an artist's space north of downtown. Called the Loft, this site allowed further experimentation with ambiance in the celebration services. Attendance at the Loft grew from fifty young adults to over two hundred. And the Sunday morning service, called Metro Mosaic, was held at a high school auditorium in the northeastern part of Los Angeles, in the city of San Gabriel, from 2001 to 2004. The morning service is the only service with programming for preschoolers through high school students; its attendance was over a thousand in 2004. A Westside service in Beverly Hills was launched in the summer of 2003 with about three hundred people. The use of multiple temporary sites is part of the current structure of Mosaic, and in this Mosaic is similar to other fast-growing churches such as Saddleback Community Church and Calvary Chapel, Costa Mesa, both of which have used large temporary structures (rented facilities and oversized tents) until they were able to purchase suitable permanent facilities.

Finally, involvement in cross-cultural ministry has accelerated in the past four years. Short-term teams travel to places like China, India, Thailand, England, and Morocco. Career missionaries are sent as well; Mosaic has sent an average of one adult per month for full-time overseas work in the last four years. Most went to China, India, and the Middle East. Closer to home, Mosaic has taken over two thousand people to serve the poor in Mexico through a partnership with the civic leaders of the city of Ensenada. Cultural sensitivity and global awareness continue to be a theme among members of Mosaic.

What is next in Mosaic's future? The most urgent objective is to acquire property. Acquisition of property around downtown Los Angeles has been the goal of the church for many years. As stated by Greg, an elder of the church,

To be effective in L.A., you need to be multiethnic. For the kinds of things we do, for the kinds of people we're trying to reach, that is a nonnegotiable.

So, in the interest of maintaining and further increasing the congregation's diversity, a critical criterion for any new property will be its accessibility from all parts of Los Angeles. "We're focusing on downtown because it seems to be a common, centralized location." It may take years for the church's financial resources and available property to match up in a suitable package. Until that time, the use of rented property allows flexibility and innovation in response to shifting demands in this growing congregation.

Unique Aspects of This Congregation

Mosaic is a church with a long history of ethnic diversity, evangelistic focus, strong pastoral leadership, accentuation of the creative arts, innovation in programming, and emphasis on world missions. Still, several significant changes have occurred in the church's history over the last decade. This period corresponds approximately to the time the current lead pastor, Erwin McManus, has been involved with the congregation. Specifically, eight unique elements distinguish the Mosaic of the last ten years from its own previous history, from other Southern Baptist churches, and, more broadly, from other evangelical churches. (To paraphrase Stephen Warner, a world of difference lies between Mosaic and the Southern Baptist Convention. As he states, "that the first is a local assembly of persons and the second a national network of assemblies is the beginning of the matter" [1994:59].)

First, Mosaic is multiethnic with three dominant ethnicities (white, Hispanic, and Asian), none of which is in the majority (DeYoung et al., 2003). This is notable since biracial churches are rare, multiethnic churches even more so, and large multiethnic ones (with seven hundred or more attenders) even rarer. Even in cities and regions like Los Angeles where such diversity is possible, it is rarely realized.

Second, the congregation of Mosaic is young. Data drawn from weekly guest registration cards (Mosaic People Database, 2003) show that the average age of visitors between February 2002 and February 2003 was twenty-six. According to these registration cards, about 90 percent of the visitors are single (never married) with an average age of twenty-four years. The other 10 percent are almost all married couples with an average age of thirty-eight years. The average age of Mosaic's members is thirty-five years. About half are single (never married), and the other half married. These attenders are significantly younger than the attenders in any mainline denomination in the United States, especially in megachurches of seven hundred or more.

Third, attenders are coming from a wide geographic area. It was once believed that the church would never draw people from Whittier, a city several miles east of the church site in East Los Angeles, or from cities north of the 60 freeway. Today, the zip codes of attenders' and visitors reflect all parts of metropolitan Los Angeles, with the notable exception of South Central Los Angeles (Mosaic People Database, 2003); few people come from south of the 10 freeway between the 405 and the 710 freeways. With that exception, people come from as far west as Venice, as far east as Riverside, as far north as Van Nuys, and as far south as Irvine in Orange County. One respondent, Derek, said, "Generally people don't come to Mosaic because it's convenient. They come because they have a commitment, and they have relationships here."

Fourth, Mosaic actively welcomes creative artists. Film, video, visual arts, media arts, sculpture, dance, and drama are among the artistic elements encouraged and incorporated into various activities. The *Los Angeles Times* estimated that Mosaic has the highest concentration of people in the entertainment industry of any church in Los Angeles (Luo, 1999).

Fifth, Mosaic has multiple temporary locations rather than one large, central, and permanent location. In a move necessitated by the growth of the congregation and the inadequacy of its own facilities, the church sold its property in 2001 and chose instead to rent multiple sites for celebration services around Los Angeles. It is currently projected that even if a large site were to be purchased, multiple locations would still be used around metropolitan Los Angeles.

Sixth, Mosaic is a large church with a significant number of weekly members, attenders, and guests. The church has experienced steady growth in weekly attendance, from 500 to over 1900, over the last five years. The number of volunteers involved in various small groups and teams has grown as well.

Seventh, the people of Mosaic demonstrate a remarkable zeal for the common goals of the church. Members and attenders alike are actively mobilized to further these goals. Respondents frequently and spontaneously expressed enthusiasm for the church; this zeal is also manifest in the steady flow of overseas missionary workers sent out by the church.

Finally, the belief system of Mosaic favors innovation. Mosaic's theological emphasis has shifted from a more fundamentalist, polemical, Bible study approach emphasizing obedience to an inspiring, praxis-oriented, missional approach that emphasizes creativity and catalytic movement. While Pastor Erwin's approach sustains a high regard for the authority of the Bible, it embraces relevance and originality in its interplay of creativity with the historic mission of evangelistic outreach.

Mosaic changes quickly. As I wrote this book and readied it for publication, weekly attendance grew from 1200 to over 1900, the congregation sold all of its property, shifted its organizational structure, moved offices, gained new staff people, lost others, raised its internal budget by over 20 percent, created new, broad-ranging ministry initiatives, constructed an alliance of "like-minded" churches, and increased, reduced, and increased again the number of celebration service sites. And these are only some of the significant changes. While this book tries to capture the more enduring aspects of this sixty-year-old congregation, it is admittedly a snapshot of a church in motion. Longtime members tell me Mosaic is unrecognizable from what it was ten years ago; perhaps continued change will move it to be unrecognizable once again ten years hence. What is most important is that through adaptation and innovation Mosaic in Los Angeles succeeds in attracting individuals who not only attend but also commit to its ideology and embrace the mission of continually attracting more participants. And, significantly, as it grows it continues to diversify. Starting with the following pages, the analysis will focus on how this congregation successfully transcends ethnicity.

3

HISTORY, AGENCY, AND EVANGELICALISM: A RECONSTRUCTION OF IDEOLOGY

MIKE: Other churches may think, "The times are dark, things are going to get worse, let's not bother impacting culture in this way." They have a different theological perspective.

ERWIN: The church must be grounded in a proper theology of change, not simply to address the radically changing world in which we live, but to advance the cause of Christ in a world that cannot produce the real change that has to take place.

In the last two years, several churches have taken the name "Mosaic" as their own without consulting the leaders of the original congregation. Leaders of these churches may say they "agree" with Mosaic and are "just like" Mosaic; in actuality, they are not. By adding some contemporary music, including a few skits, or even having church in a night-club, church leaders say, they are becoming like Mosaic. Essentially they take on a form of Mosaic without the content. Sometimes the only thing they take is the logo. It is necessary to understand that activities within

Mosaic are guided by an overall ideological framework that emphasizes certain aspects of the nature of God, what human beings are intended to be, their individual role in redemptive history, and their role in relation to other people who are working together for the purposes of the God they have committed to follow.

At the same time a growing number of churches are connected to Mosaic by not just a name but a deep similarity in ideological orientation. As of 2003, there are allied congregations in Pasadena, Berkeley, and Manhattan, and two in Seattle. At least two dozen other churches, including churches in New Zealand, Australia, Taiwan, Kenya, and Central Europe, have also entered into a loose alliance with Mosaic. At the core of this shared theological framework is a belief that the local church is a tool created by God and entrusted to apostolic leaders who are to continue an expansive movement begun by Jesus. The growing number of registrants at Mosaic's annual Origins conference for church leaders and the increased popularity of Erwin McManus's bestselling books suggest that an increasing number of churches will seek partnerships with this Los Angeles congregation for more than permission to call themselves "Mosaic." There will be more "Mosaic" churches that will share a common ideological framework.

Browning (1994: 206) defines "descriptive theology" as that which "is interested primarily in describing the potential dialogue between the narrative tradition of the researcher and the narrative tradition of the person or group being described." It is in the spirit of descriptive theology that I wish to discuss the theological perspectives held by Mosaic as expressed in its primary spokesperson, Pastor Erwin McManus. His speaking and writing best represent what Browning calls the "operative theology" of the church (205). Grasping the ways in which Mosaic makes theological distinctions is important since they describe the impetus and motivation of congregational activities. They are the source of the theological articulation actively invoked by church leaders through the public celebration services, membership classes, small group Bible studies, and leadership meetings. The theology of the church also provides frameworks that are reemphasized through drama, dance, music, video, and décor. Spiritual leaders use every opportunity, both planned and spontaneous, to promote the theology of the church. It is vital to apprehend both the explicit and implicit meanings of this theology.

This chapter focuses on the distinctive theological haven created at Mosaic, which provides a base for overcoming racial and ethnic differences. By "theological haven" I mean that Mosaic provides a haven for those who have fled boring conservative Christian churches with venge-ful gods and find a place where orthodox Christian beliefs are articulated in a culturally relevant manner. The nuances of Mosaic's theology mat-ter. Those at Mosaic are not like Ammerman's (1987) fundamentalist "Bible believers" who choose and maintain a life in opposition to the world. Instead, Mosaic provides a shelter for people escaping traditional churches that have isolated themselves from the surrounding culture. People at Mosaic are more broadly evangelical, affirming conservative beliefs through a more open, relevant interaction with contemporary culture, especially through the public worship services. The theology promotes an active, cause-oriented engagement through activities in the local church. While not all of those who come to Mosaic agree with conservative Christian worldviews, all of them have had vivid experi-ences of them. And these people come from many different ethnic back-grounds.

In addition to formal interviews, informal conversations, and my field notes, the descriptive theology given below draws on Erwin McManus's bestselling book, *An Unstoppable Force: Daring to Become the Church God Had in Mind* (2001), written in response to people asking about the ideological framework of Mosaic. Among Mosaic's paid staff members, this is known as "The Book," and it is becoming essential reading for lay leaders who want to understand the ideology of the church. Pastors and church planters expressing a desire to lead "Mosaic" churches both nationally and internationally whole-heartedly agree with the theological and philosophical views expressed in this text. It sum-marizes many of Erwin's sermons at Mosaic as well as messages he has shared in hundreds of churches and conferences over the past decade.

Exploring Mosaic's Theological Haven

People at Mosaic describe their previous churches as boring, irrelevant, closed communities that remain isolated from the world around them. Their collective assessment supports Peter Berger's (1961) classic state-ment that American congregations are places whose chief function is to keep religion irrelevant to the dominant challenges of contemporary life. Berger questioned the church's ability to affect any community and abandoned the notion of the local church as a place of mission. Winter (1961) also criticized suburban congregations that isolated themselves to become exclusive, homogeneous communities. Peshkin (1986), using concepts derived from Goffman (1961), labeled one fundamentalist Protestant church a "total institution" because of such apparatus as high walls, locked doors, and imposing structures that created an exclusive private sphere in a public world. Many Mosaic attenders who have come from conservative, fundamentalist religious backgrounds agree. Even the "unbelievers" who come to Mosaic have been influenced in their views of God, pastors, and Christians by experiences with traditional churches.

SHELTERS PEOPLE ESCAPING TRADITIONAL CHURCH BACKGROUNDS

In describing past church experiences, respondents describe unpleasant incidents. Several specifically describe bad experiences with Baptist churches, perhaps because more Protestants are Baptist than any other denomination, or perhaps because of the irony that Mosaic is affiliated with the Southern Baptist Convention. Jamie described how when she was a kid her parents dropped her off at a local Baptist church while they went to breakfast. "I have an impression of Baptists as being legalistic, wives submit, get ten feet behind, you know, just the legalistic realm." Jamie struggles with becoming a member. "If I would have known Mosaic was a Baptist church on the Website, I would not have gone." She told me, "The Baptist thing is a big deal to me. Well, oh, I'm not quite ready for that word." But, she said, "I found out it was Baptist too late. I already got hooked in." She concluded, "The whole Baptist thing is still . . . *eeuw*." (Jamie eventually became a member a few months after our interview.) Ralph had also had bad experiences with Baptist churches, saying, "God has a sense of humor in the fact that this is a Baptist-based church. But I didn't know it. It wasn't [clear to me] for a long time. If I'd known that coming in, who knows?"

People consider Mosaic to be different from other churches. Emily, who previously attended a Chinese church, tells her friends, "I don't go to church; I go to Mosaic." The contrast she draws is significant, distancing Mosaic from a popular understanding of church. As Kevin said, "This church is not a Christian church in the typical stereotypical description of it." Ralph describes his initial expectations after being invited to come:

> My expectation was that I was going to go down to a stuffy, boring service, the kind of service that you had to go to as a kid and just sit there for an hour listening to a guy talk about something you just couldn't relate to. And believe me, I showed up with bags full of judgment and prejudice and just hostility.

When he arrived at the service, Ralph was pleasantly surprised.

They took me down to Urban, which was quite a shock, you know, walking into a nightclub that looks like the home of the Oakland Raiders on the inside. Of course with the band and the multimedia and what have you, it was pretty amazing to me.

For Ralph, "This feels like a fundamentally different groove, a different vibe, a very different approach fundamentally." Attenders at Urban Mosaic really enjoy the fact that it is in a nightclub. Lindsey has had a lifetime of church experiences, but Mosaic is the first church she has joined as a member. "One reason why I go is because it's easy for me to bring people to church, to say, 'It's a cool place.' " The nightclub is a setting that allows the church to remain conservative in belief but nontraditional in expression. It also gives people opportunities to challenge their friends' stereotypic notions of church.

Both African Americans and white Southerners among my respondents shared the experience of growing up in churches they found obligatory, dull, irrelevant, and, certainly, not a source of pride. Dela had spent a lot of time in church when she was younger:

> When I was fifteen, I was baptized and everything. I did go to the church, but after a while I was like, why am I going here? I would be looking at my watch or the clock, stuff like that, and I just never really liked going to church that much.

Blake, another African American, described going to church as "torture," saying,

> [Y]ou did it out of obligation, and everybody else there seemed to be there out of obligation. No one there was going to church because they wanted to go to church. It was really more of a culture than a faith for a lot of people.

Blake then added, "It always seems so difficult to find a congregation where you can become part of the community without becoming part of the rot, you know?" Trevor, a white Southerner, was embarrassed by the church and reluctant to identify with any particular one. He wanted to apply the gospel using film and creative media but believed that he was alone in these aspirations. At Mosaic, he found a community that shared them:

> I'm surrounded by people who, like me, really believe we can change the world with the gospel of Jesus Christ and see lives transformed.

It's what I've always believed, but I've never thought it could happen in church because the churches I experienced were irrelevant.

His dreams of influencing the world for God through drama and film seemed to be coming true in the context of a local church. After being involved with the production of sketches and dramas for Mosaic, he was invited to come on staff. He told me that during a ministry meeting

> I started to cry. I discovered that my whole life I had been ashamed of church. I was ashamed of the church. I wasn't ashamed of Jesus Christ; I wasn't ashamed of Christianity; I wasn't ashamed of what Jesus did for me. But I was ashamed of the church. [...] This was the first church that I was proud to talk about and bring someone to. [...] I loved Jesus, but now I loved Jesus' bride.

Small group experiences at Mosaic were often compared with experiences at previous churches. Kevin said, "My idea was Bible study. You get eight, ten, maybe twelve guys; sit down in a room; you open up the Bible; you study it; you talk about it; you leave. The group never expands." He was discouraged. "I remember feeling frustrated that we would meet every week and I didn't feel like we were going anywhere or learning anything." Kevin found that at Mosaic a small group "actually expands and multiplies and invites people that aren't Christians. ... Never thought of that before." And the content of the study was different:

> It isn't sitting down and taking out Romans and going through Pauline theology and the doctrine of blah, blah, blah. It was not about transforming minds, but hearts. And to me that's what was missing. We would talk about how to change the world in our men's action group, but we never did anything about it. We never invited people into it. It was very stale and boring. At Mosaic, I heard that the Word of God is a verb, not a noun, and that it's supposed to go somewhere and not just be head knowledge.

This orientation toward action was significant and different. For Emily, it was the challenge of making friends with people in her group and cultivating relationships with strangers that came as a personal revelation. "It's all about relationships," she said.

People who stay at Mosaic are not looking for five-point sermons or messages that merely regurgitate information. Zack said, "Why do we need to wait for Sunday to get the Cliffs Notes version from somebody who's studied it for us?" and added, "If I'm interested in that, I'll do that on my own time." Rather than hear abridged summaries of Bible passages, people indicate they are looking to actively participate, share an experience, and hear a message that contributes something novel. The theological haven is attractive to those looking for theological conservatism that is packaged in a fresh way.

The Lord's Supper is one of the most prominent occasions for expressing conservative beliefs in a nontraditional way. Lindsey said, "I love the Lord's Supper, and I love how creative it is. I love it." The Lord's Supper is an innovative union of an orthodox understanding of the event with multisensory interactivity. In the last three years the Lord's Supper has been celebrated using metaphoric elements from different cultures around the globe. The liturgical aspects of the Lord's Supper feel more church-like, yet attenders cherish them because the Mosaic experience is executed differently from the church experience they escaped. Various forms of music, participation by the attenders, visual art forms focused on the theme of the evening, ethnically specific types of bread, and experimentation in seating arrangements (sometimes no seats at all) have contributed to a very sensual, surprising experience of the Lord's Supper. When a woman was being commissioned as an overseas missionary to India, *nan*, an Indian bread, was used to partake of what participants understand to be the body of Christ. On the occasion of a young couple's being sent to North Africa, woven prayer mats were placed all over the floor of the sanctuary for people to sit on. A dozen drums of all types were beaten in a deep, resounding rhythm that began, punctuated, and concluded the service. The evening felt like an ancient tribal ritual. Despite the time spent weaving elements of the evening together into a contemporary, participatory, and multisensory experience for all who come, the actual "feel" of the evening is numinous, worshipful, and sacred. Lindsey remembers the last Lord's Supper she attended. "It was amazing; it was awesome. Very creative. And it was very solid too because it was the truth that we were celebrating together." Asked why it made such an impression on her, she said, "I am a very visual, very imaginative person, and I like to experience with my senses too. And yet I like to know the truth; I like to have the foundation." As the most liturgically oriented experience at Mosaic, the Lord's Supper holds nostalgic meaning for those who grew up in church. The ritual is familiar to almost everyone from childhood. Brett, an ex–Roman Catholic from the East Coast, told me that experiencing the Lord's Supper was what convinced him to join the church. "It felt like communion, but it was so free and expressive." Through the Lord's Supper, Mosaic preserves something that is important to these believers, something to which they feel deeply emotionally connected.

DETERS CULTURALLY CONSERVATIVE CHRISTIANS EXPECTING TRADITIONAL SERVICES

Mosaic may be a theological haven to some people, but not to all. Mosaic services contain traditional elements found in almost any evangelical church, such as the singing of congregational music, public prayer, public reading of Scripture, a message from the pastor, an invitation to respond to the message, and a closing song. Yet many who come from traditional church settings are not just disappointed but often distressed at Mosaic's services. They find Mosaic's approach "too wild," even "unbiblical," and find that getting over the nontraditional aspects of the church is a challenge. Brooke, a white Southerner, vividly remembered her first Sunday:

> I come from a very traditional Southern Baptist background. *Very* traditional. I walked into church and this Latino guy was standing up there bouncing around on stage leading worship, and everybody is clapping and all this kind of stuff. And I was just looking around like they're freaks. I'm like, "What the heck? Is this a cult? What is this?" And then Pastor Erwin began to speak and I was just like [making a face] "huh??" And the more I met people, the more conversations that I had, I realized Mosaic was different from any church I had ever experienced anywhere.

An African American woman I spoke with in 1999 came to Urban Mosaic and was "offended" at the service because bottles of liquor were visible behind the bar at the nightclub. She felt the church should remove them before starting the celebration service. She never returned. Other people leave because, in their view, Mosaic doesn't "focus on the Word of God." Emily says this is particularly true of Asian visitors. "When I'm trying to connect them the first time or second time at Mosaic, they are looking for a Bible study." According to her, they may visit a small group but are soon disappointed because it does not fit their expectations of a Bible study. In March 2002, I met a young Korean woman who had been attending Mosaic for several months but was still undecided about whether to become a member. When I asked her what held her back, she answered, "I know the church is very evangelistic, but where do people learn the Bible?" Her concept of discipleship was textual analysis of the Bible, and she felt that not enough of such study was programmed into the ministries of the church. In discussing why people leave Mosaic, Molly said, "a lot of the families that left went to traditional churches." All of these comments indicate people who fail to find a traditional church experience found in many evangelical, Bible-emphasizing churches.

Catalytic Preaching and the Shaping of a Congregation

The weekly sermons given by Mosaic's lead pastor cannot be ignored, because they shape the congregation as a whole, especially through their ideological elements, and have contributed toward the ethnic diversification of the church under Erwin's leadership. Preaching is one of the primary catalysts for the diversification of the congregation. Franklin (1994: 264) describes the importance of preaching in the local church, saying, "Within the context of worship that stimulates the senses, preaching is the central sacred act and may be the chief mobilizing catalyst for mission activity." Becker's (1998) qualitative analysis of two "multiracial" congregations in Illinois considers pastoral preaching critical to cultivating diversity. Pastors in both congregations "mined their religious traditions for metaphors of community" (451) in order to address the most pressing problem in both congregations, namely their decline in membership due to the shifting ethnic and racial compositions of their neighborhoods. This kind of symbolic work has been noted by other researchers; in particular, Becker cites Hart (1996), Feher (1997), Griswold (1992), Swidler (1986), and Hobsbawm (1983) in asserting that religious traditions are not monolithic, but "cultural archives that are mined as needed, where individual elements can be selected or ignored, built upon, reinterpreted, or forgotten in specific institutional and historical contexts" (467). Pastors used metaphors to develop concepts in sermons, using the power of the pulpit to broadcast important ideas. Sermons allowed quick access to ideas which were quickly adopted by other congregational leadership. Such ideas were adopted only because they seemed to be logical extensions of congregational tradition. "Both pastors succeeded in making their new mission focus seem not only legitimate but natural" (467). This is the distinctive cultural work of pastors in transitioning their congregations: they present ideas that can be perceived as extensions of familiar ideas into new arenas rather than pure innovation. Barbara Wheeler (1990: 228) expresses the importance of such consciously crafted relevance in writing that congregational leaders "harvest the local knowledge" of a congregation. Metaphors that were invoked through preaching and linked to the congregation were accepted by them as guidance in matters of inclusion. Such conscious symbolic work is evident in Pastor Erwin's theological articulation. His metaphors reinforce concepts of a community in mission. These are presented as natural extensions of the historical Christian faith.

In addition, Pastor Erwin puts a high priority on making connections in every message to both the historical Christian faith and the surrounding culture. Relevance is an important and consciously stated goal. Paige, a recent member of Mosaic, calls this "paying attention," a quality she praises in Pastor Erwin. When I asked her to describe this quality, she said, "Constantly paying attention to what's going on in our world, and I don't mean the headlines in the newspaper, but what's real, everything that's going on." Pastor Erwin fits Stephen Warner's (1994: 85) description of Pastor Eric Underwood, who, he says, "reframed [people's life] stories in biblical terms and helped even the near secularists in this congregation understand the relevance of Christianity for their lives, even as he prodded them to acts of humility, decency, and generosity."

For Pastor Erwin, preaching is an act of leadership, not education. He sees preaching as prophetic and catalytic. Preaching is a catalyst for moving people to respond to God's activity. He believes his primary responsibility is to prod people toward mission. The ideology articulated by Erwin McManus is activated not in mental assent to propositional truths but in a personal, behavioral response to a message. In this concern for a personal response to preaching, Mosaic is historically connected to "revivalism," which has been called "one of the primary engines of American religion" (Wind and Lewis, 1994: vol. 1, 4). Revivalism at its heart constitutes a call for individuals to engage with a Christian God who demands a personal response. Wells (1994: 312) wrote, "Evangelical religion stands in a long tradition of protest movements against superficial Christian profession." At Mosaic, the crucial difference between superficial profession and authentic faith is manifested in evangelistic activity rather than mere pietistic devotion. Erwin consistently prods people to respond to the gospel message and take that message to others.

A Theology of Mission

To understand the theological framework of the church one must first grasp that the root theological impulse at Mosaic is missiology. Missiology is concerned with understanding God's mission in the world and humanity's mission in partnership with him. Several people at Mosaic, like Mike, said the church has "a missiological perspective on the Bible." In our conversations, Pastor Erwin said it very simply: "Mission shapes theology." Erwin would concur with the assertion by the systematic theologian Clark H. Pinnock (1990: 5) that "theology performs a missiological function. Although the Church has often seemed to forget it, missions is the mother of Christian theology." A missionary theology is not necessary if theology is only for theologians, as elite insiders. Pinnock states, "A secret society that cares only about itself and doesn't have to worry much about communicating its beliefs to others does not have to be concerned about being understood by outsiders" (6). Systematic theologians pursue a more perfect base of knowledge through conversations among themselves. The academization of Christianity equates theological education with moral perfection. The possession of "correct" knowledge is thought to signify a greater degree of moral righteousness. Erwin (2001: 72) highlights the danger in this perspective:

> A theological construct for interpretation finds success in the attainment of knowledge. The more you know, the more mature a Christian you are thought to be. And yet knowledge of the Bible does not guarantee application of the Bible. To know is not necessarily to do.

Pinnock asserts that a "missionary theology" would "insist on being faithful to the gospel" and yet "want to be open and adventurous and not at all rigid in its efforts to win a hearing for its message" (7). Pinnock's "bipolar method" of theology would "couple fidelity to the Word of God with the flexible and adaptable approach missionary communication always requires" (6). Noted theologian Gustavo Gutiérrez (1996: 177) similarly writes, "The theological enterprise is at the service of evangelization. Consequently, it must be very concerned for the communication and comprehension of the Christian message" (see also Gutiérrez, 1973).

Erwin's motivation for articulating a missiological theology grew out of questions posed by longtime Christians critical of the value he placed on relevance. While Mosaic has always been theologically conservative, in the past its response to local culture was also conservative. The theological climate of the congregation at the time of Erwin's arrival unintentionally deemphasized evangelistic effort and fostered cultural isolation. Since Erwin has always considered the Bible authoritative for life and practice, his challenge was to articulate a theology which was true to evangelical orthodoxy, was relevant to surrounding culture, and would inspire Christians to missional activity. Like Pinnock, he is a Christian who "wants to move beyond modernism and fundamentalism to a form of postmodern orthodoxy" (Pinnock 1990: v). His messages had to propel people toward creative evangelistic effort. This forced him to reconsider his theological framework. Erwin McManus carefully constructs his understanding of orthodox Christian faith because he, like other pastors and theologians today, sees a need for a restatement of the faith if it is to be meaningful to those not already committed to it. The praxis of mission contrasts with the usual articulation of theological concepts. For Erwin, maturity is found in missionary praxis. His theology paints a picture of a creative, catalytic God who calls out creative, catalytic leaders to nurture creative, catalytic teams in pursuit of global evangelization. His theology seeks to affirm the unique, creative contributions of individuals while also catalyzing leaders who will cultivate intentional communities that purposefully engage culture for the sake of mission. They will do whatever is necessary to serve people outside of the church and be relevant to the dominant culture.

Four dominant theological categories will serve to organize the missiological theology found at Mosaic. These four theological categories are derived from conventional theological approaches within Christianity: theology proper (the nature of God), anthropology (the nature of humanity), ecclesiology (the nature of the church), and eschatology (the nature of unfolding history). My understanding of conventional theology is based on a survey of standard works in systematic theology, especially those of Augustus H. Strong, Charles Hodge, William G. T. Shedd, Louis Berkhof, Lewis Sperry Chafer, Millard J. Erickson, and Henry C. Thiessen. These works emerged from a nineteenth-century attempt "to organize Christian beliefs and practices within a modern epistemic framework in response to the assault on theological knowledge by the Enlightenment" (Charry, 1996: 118). Although there is some diversity among these works, all of them are classical texts in systematic biblical theology, and evangelicals generally see them as fairly representing doctrinal understandings of the Christian faith. My discussion here is intended only to mark out broad areas of emphasis and contrasts in order to clarify where Mosaic's theological frameworks fit within the whole of evangelical thought.

THEOLOGY PROPER: THE CHARACTER OF GOD

"Theology proper" is the aspect of theology exploring attributes specific to the divine entity. Conventional theologians commonly describe God as immutable, which means that he never changes in any place or at any time (see Hodge, 1892: 390–392; Strong, 1907: 257–259; Berkhof, 1941: 58–59). This leads to a static conception of God. For Erwin, accepting the unchanging nature of God does not imply that God avoids change. "We must never forget," he states, "that we serve the changeless God of change. God is not satisfied with the status quo" (McManus 2001: 82). Erwin's theology incorporates and welcomes change in the world. "Why would anyone be surprised that the core of the New Testament church is radical change? . . . Everywhere God moves, there is change. Everywhere God moves, he creates the future" (85, 90). Change does not have to be feared; it can be embraced, especially if it accomplishes the purposes of God.

In arguing for the existence of God, conventional theologians focus on the role of God as creator of all empirical reality (see Hodge, 1892: 207–232). Erwin typically applies the concept of God as *creator* to conclude that God is *creative*. Emily, a Chinese American woman, discussed this, saying, "I never thought of God as being creative. He's the Creator, but Mosaic is just helping me to see who God is." The creative God is quickly used to encourage all followers of Jesus to be creative. Artistry reflects the nature of God.

Perhaps the best-known attributes of God are omnipresence (being present everywhere at all times), omniscience (knowing everything everywhere), and omnipotence (able to do anything without limitations). This all-powerful, all-seeing, all-knowing entity seems entirely self-sufficient, and for many this is an image of God as tyrannical and even abusive. As Crystal expressed it, "Growing up in other churches, God was kind of harsh, putting down the rules. He was much more legalistic and not lovable." With modern sensitivity to fascism, totalitarianism, and all forms of dictatorship, such a view of God is not readily acceptable today. Theologian Michael Welker (1996: 74) asks,

> Has theology taken seriously its task of bringing to people's attention God's vitality and love for human beings, God's creative and delivering power? Or has it rather directed their thoughts to some rigid authority in the beyond that has merely formal "relations" to the world and to human beings?

Why would such a god want a relationship with people? According to Welker, "This theism, characterized by the idea of a God who in absolute dominance and control brings forth and maintains both himself and everything else, is crumbling" (75). While not denying such attributes as the omnipresence, omniscience, and omnipotence of God, Erwin is in step with contemporary theological developments in typically emphasizing the communal nature of God (see Moltmann, 1974; Jüngel, 1983; Pinnock, 2001). "God is relational. God expresses himself through the Godhead as three persons: Father, Son, and Spirit. In himself God experiences perfect community. God is not absent of relationship; God is the essence of relationship" (McManus, 2001:171). Erwin emphasizes God's communal nature in order to explain God's desire to be in community with humanity and our need to follow God's example and pursue healthy relationships with each other. Experiencing community allows us to experience a primary characteristic of God. "It should not surprise us that we cannot properly experience God outside of community" (171).

The most prominent attribute in conventional theologians' descriptions of God is holiness, which, strictly defined from the original languages of the Scriptures, is "separation" (Strong, 1907:268; Thiessen, 1979:84; Berkhof, 1941:73; Erickson, 1985:284). This conception of God emphasizes distance. God is separated from creation and from humanity by his purity and moral perfection. God's holiness is related to his righteousness and justice. These are legal concepts that emphasize punitive correction administered by God. Erwin affirms God's holiness, but tempers it by discussing God as a servant:

> It sounds sacrilegious to say that God is a servant, but that's only because our value systems are so corrupt and distorted. We feel comfortable attributing to God those things we aspire to be. To describe God as all-powerful makes him only what we want more of. To describe God as all-knowing once again reinforces something that we value. To describe God as all-present is not only comforting, but it even affirms our personal value for control. We want God to be all-powerful, all-knowing, and all-controlling. It is not difficult to convince us that these should be attributes of God. But to say that God is a servant seems out of touch with our view of how God works. (McManus, 2001:156)

Erwin affirms conventional theism's presentation of God, but brings his power, presence, and knowledge into a form that allows him to be conceived of as relational and even generous.

God's servanthood is an extension of his humility. God desires to bring the overwhelming force of his essence into a form that aids and empowers humanity, not oppresses and exploits. Erwin insists that God's nature as servant contrasts with how human beings would utilize such force. He asks, "If we were all-powerful, all-knowing, and all-present, how many of us would choose to let servanthood be the ultimate expression of all that potential?" In this way, Erwin simultaneously counters the notion of God as dictator and reinforces a characteristic that his followers are to possess. Just as God is a servant, so his followers are to be servants to the world as well. Erwin writes, "We may never be more like God than when we're serving from a purely selfless motivation" (156). Followers are to channel their own talents and creativity, whatever powers of intellect, skill, and imagination they possess, into activities that help others. The injunction to "love your neighbor as yourself" is put into practice in serving others. Therefore, just as artistry expresses the nature of God, so does servanthood.

For Erwin, sacrificial servanthood is necessary to the cultivation of a multiethnic congregation. He writes,

> If your goal is a diverse church, then you need to ask God to give you love for people who are different from you. People go to church where they have friends or make friends. You can't expect people who are different from you to come to church simply because you want to paint a picture of diversity. This only happens when love actually brings people together. (54–55)

Servanthood reflects the nature of God and encourages people to go beyond tolerance or acceptance toward genuine, caring relationships between people who are different from one another.

ANTHROPOLOGY: THE CORRUPTED AND IDEAL NATURE OF HUMAN BEINGS

Theological discussions of anthropology revolve around the original, unspoiled nature of humanity at the creation of Adam and Eve, and the corrupted nature of humanity inherited from "the fall." Discussions are dominated by harmatology, the study of sin or transgression against a Holy God, since human beings are stuck in the mire of depravity. And any discussion of humanity's moving beyond depravity is relegated to soteriology, the doctrine of salvation. For systematic theologians, the spiritual quest of humanity becomes and remains the movement out of depravity to recover a state of innocence.

Erwin emphasizes that despite sin humanity still reflects the image of God. He writes, "For too long our only conversations related to the image and likeness of God have been about how we have defiled it" (181). Human beings are united less by sin than by their reflection of the image of the Creator. All systematic theologians agree that humanity reflects the image of God, although they do not emphasize this (cf. Erickson, 1985:512–514). For them the image of God is overwhelmed and obscured by sin. Erwin emphasizes that this image can still be seen and affirmed even in people who are not dedicated followers of Jesus. For him, "God is about reclaiming the divine potential he has planted within each individual" (180).

Erwin also stresses that spiritual life is a life of constant change. He writes,

> The whole theological concept of sanctification is rooted in the reality that God changes people. Repentance is change, conversion is change, regeneration is change, transformation is change, and sanctification is change. All of the deeply theological constructs that we have embraced and understand to be true cannot exist outside of a theology of change. . . . If you don't like change, you'd better not become a Christian. Once you belong to Jesus, change is inevitable. Our whole Christian experience is an experience of change. (81)

Such an emphasis on process, transition, development, and transformation is in contrast to the static categories of "depravity," "sanctification," "justification," and "redemption," which are typically presented in a binary manner: in or out, saved or lost, sinful or sanctified. The life of a dedicated follower of Jesus is full of change, and the best changes are the ones that followers initiate in pursuit of God's mission. The theme of personal change in pursuit of divine potential is so important to Erwin that it is the subject of his second and third books, *Seizing Your Divine Moment* (2002) and *Uprising: A Revolution of the Soul* (2003).

Conventional theologians define sanctification as a return to the original innocence of Adam and Eve, to "sinlessness." According to Erwin, "It's as if all God is trying to do is stop us from sinning" (2001: 180). Erwin does not express the goal of the Christian life in terms of either the vices we are to eliminate or the virtues we are to attain. The goal of the Christian life is not eliminating sin but making a creative contribution to the world. He asserts, "Our theology of character transformation needs to extend beyond the reestablishment of virtues to the reclamation of the potential in every person." The goal of spiritual development is found in our creative contribution.

> We preach against sin, but have we ever developed the anger of God when it relates to lost human potential? Have we ever looked at human lives and felt our hearts break not because of the sins committed, but because of the potential left unattended? (181)

The notion of man as a sinner gives way to a conception of humans with God-given desires and potential that is brought out truly and sincerely as they become dedicated followers of Jesus Christ.

Finally, the image of God is manifested in the uniqueness of every person. Erwin told me he sees this manifestation as vital to what makes the church multiethnic. In his view, people are drawn to Mosaic because there they "are seen as unique creations of God, and . . . who they are in Christ will be discovered, respected, and nurtured." Valuing human uniqueness is Erwin's theological alternative to focusing on group differences. Talking about the uniqueness of individuals is an alternative strategy for discussing diversity. To force people into one mold is to demean them. Instead of collapsing individuals into ethnic or racial groups, Erwin individualizes diversity and challenges congregants to acknowledge and respect *whatever* differences they may encounter. He writes that upon receiving new members,

> we invite them to change who we are, that we may become who God desires us to be. Our commitment is not to clone them to who we already are, but that each person who joins our community is a promise from God that he is not finished with us yet. If we respect the gifts, talents, and uniqueness of each individual, then we must be willing to change. If a person's contribution is to be honored and respected, then he will make a difference. (173)

If churches only know how to "clone" people, they will never become multiethnic. Creative potential is to be discovered and actualized.

ECCLESIOLOGY: THE MISSION AND MOVEMENT OF THE LOCAL CHURCH

Ecclesiology concerns itself with the nature of the church. The "ecclesia" are the "called-out ones," brought out from the world to be in a special relationship to God and to each other (Thiessen, 1979:311). Some theologians see the church, therefore, as the "community of the elect," consisting only of those who have been predestined to be part of it (cf. Berkhof, 1941:567). Conventional theologians concern themselves with power structures within each congregation as well as how separate congregations should understand their relationship to each other. Conventional theologians also predominantly discuss the nature of the church in terms of the "means of grace," which refers to rituals such as preaching, administering the sacraments, and exercising church discipline. The primacy of these topics is due to systematic theology's roots in the theological concerns of the Reformation, which were reactions to the medieval institution of the Roman Church. Moreover, systematic theology's discussion of the church is internally oriented because it assumes the church exists in a context of Christendom, a society organized around the church in which people are saturated with a Christian message. As a result, systematic theologians are more concerned with how the church relates to itself than with how it is to engage society.

For Erwin, Los Angeles is not Christendom, and therefore the call to be a follower of Jesus there is not the same as it would be in a culture steeped in Christian tradition. Pastor Erwin explains this using biblical images, comparing Jerusalem (Acts 2) with Athens (Acts 17). In Acts 2, Peter spoke in Jerusalem, at Pentecost, to a Jewish multitude that already believed in the God of Israel and accepted the authority of Scripture. In contrast, in Acts 17 Paul spoke in Athens to Hellenistic Greeks who worshipped idols. Although Paul utilized pagan poetry, familiar proverbs, and observations from nature, they called him a "babbler" and didn't understand his message. Erwin argues that Christians today cannot pretend that Pentecost is about to happen when we are actually living in Athens. Paul spoke to people who were worshiping an idol "to the unknown God" (Acts 17:23). Erwin insists that people in Los Angeles are looking for God and already worshipping Him even though, like the Athenians, they may not know who he is. Erwin does not assume a Christian worldview in his hearers, but he does assume that every person has an innate desire to connect with God. Many times he has said, "If you believe people are looking for God, you will see people who are looking for God." Through such exhortations, Erwin mobilizes committed Christians to communicate a gospel message in a relevant manner.

Why the Church Exists

Mosaic's first and primary core value is mission: Mission is why the church exists. Eric, one of Mosaic's pastors, asks, "Is the church here for Christians? Or is it here for the world?" He answers, "We are here for the world." For those at Mosaic, the church is not for Christians. The church is to participate with God in redeeming people. Eric and many other members articulate their belief that "Jesus established the church to continue his mission."

Messages and the practical mobilization of people move them toward intentional involvement in evangelism. Some churches hire separate staff for evangelism and outreach: "evangelism pastors" and "missions pastors" who minister through separate boards and committees. Eric remembers, "I grew up thinking the pastor did that; I gave him money to do that." Several systematic theologians reinforce this impression in talking about the offices of the church (cf. Berkhof, 1941; Strong, 1907; Thiessen, 1979). Being an evangelist or a missionary, which is considered by many evangelical Christians to be the highest level of spiritual maturity, is, for Erwin, the most basic characteristic of any dedicated follower of Jesus Christ. Rather than relying on a professionalized, credentialed, and ordained clergy to perform the mission of the church, Mosaic understands all dedicated followers of Jesus to be engaged in mission (or at least believes that they should be). It is not leaders who do the work of the church; every member does the work of the church in carrying out world evangelization. Erwin is critical of "church shoppers" who see the church as a place for convenience and personal benefit (29–30). Instead, he writes,

> Becoming a member of Mosaic is a declaration that you are moving from being a consumer to being an investor, that you are joining not simply the community of Christ, but the cause of Christ. The motivation behind becoming a member is not what can be received, but what can be given.... What once was our standard for leadership is now our standard for simple membership. We have established a radical minimum standard. (215–216)

He writes, "The church of Jesus Christ is on mission. Every disciple is a missionary" (166).

Clearly the focus of Mosaic's mission is evangelism. This focus is not limited to personal relationships, and, increasingly, Mosaic's involvement with the entertainment industry (artists, actors, dancers, designers, musicians, etc.) leads it to consider a form of nonpolitical involvement in culture that has the potential to affect masses of people. Thus, while most researchers define engagement by churches in the public sphere as essentially political involvement (cf. Berger, 1961; Berger and Neuhaus, 1977; Marty, 1994), Mosaic is choosing to engage the public through the arts with the hope that individuals will respond and that systems or institutions will change as the underlying cultural ethos of society changes. (For more on Mosaic's connections to the entertainment industry, see chapter 4.)

Mission is the primary reason that Erwin places such priority on cultural relevance. He writes that "[i]n everything that is about style and preference, the church must be willing to change for the sake of those who are lost" (2001:87). The church should initiate whatever changes are necessary to get into relationships and inspire all people to make their own unique contributions to the ongoing mission of the church. And the driving force that will build networks of missional, creative communities is apostolic leadership.

Apostolic Leadership

Systematic theologians use roles such as pastor, elder, and deacon to describe spiritual leaders. Their conceptions of these roles are dominated by their vision of medieval priesthood and involve preaching and teaching, administering sacraments, and exercising church discipline. At Mosaic, regardless of titles or formal positions, Erwin calls for leaders who create missional communities that turn church outsiders into insiders. Mosaic's leaders are more like Hollywood producers, recruiting and cultivating talent for purposeful projects. Like a motion picture, the group's "product" is meant to be "consumed" by a much larger audience outside of the group. Erwin has described such leaders with terms like "spiritual entrepreneurs," "catalysts," and "cultural architects." The core theme is apostolic leadership.

Instead of focusing on the "office" of spiritual leadership, which brings distinctive rights and responsibilities with regard to sacred rituals (cf. Strong, 1907:914–916; Berkhof, 1941:585–588; Thiessen, 1979:320–322), Erwin stresses that apostolic leaders are not to be ritualistic experts. Instead, apostolic leaders are to strive to meet the personal needs of others. It is interesting to note that many words used to define church leadership, such as "minister," "deacon," and "pastor," are etymologically related to serving or care. Servanthood is a source of legitimation at Mosaic; when leaders serve others, they build trust and credibility.

The challenge for apostolic leaders is not to demand change from others but to model that change and bring others along with them. Erwin writes, "Spiritual leadership in the change process is not so much about being the primary advocate of change, but being the primary example of change" (198). Initiating change to serve people opens new initiatives, invites active experimentation, and promotes a willingness to deal with uncertainty. "We must leave the past, engage the present, and create the future" (93). Leadership is expressed in the ability to deal with one's own sense of ambiguity and manage the uncertainty of others. Moreover, apostolic leaders initiate change with an understanding of the cultural context in which they live and lead. Erwin writes,

> From the beginning, God has raised up men and women who have had the power of seeing. They understood the times in which they lived. They understood the context to which they were called. They had the ability to understand change and create change. (85)

They are like the "men of Issachar" who are said to have "understood the times" in order to make appropriate decisions (McManus, 2001:84–85; see also 1 Chronicles 12:32). Apostolic leaders cope with ambiguity because they combine a clear sense of mission with an understanding of the culture in which they live.

Apostolic leaders have a special sense of time. These leaders move quickly and live in a fast-paced environment. Erwin writes, "The leader learns to thrive in a world of what others consider to be blinding speed" (74). The leader's different pace accounts for the marginalization of catalytic leadership in other churches. Erwin again writes, "The leader who values a slow rate of change often perceives those who try to move faster as rebellious, insubordinate, undisciplined, and adversarial" (75). While the leaders' speed obscures some people from their view, it allows others to emerge in their field of vision. Speed allows leaders to create affinity on the basis of a distinctive pace of life. For Erwin, "Speed is an important leadership dynamic because it helps the leader identify emerging leaders, as well as helping others identify him or her as a leader" (75). And for those in the congregation who have a slower pace, apostolic leaders lead by ratcheting up the urgency of participating in purposeful projects. For Erwin, "Leaders create problems not only by changing the expectations, but by creating a greater sense of urgency" (193).

The central purpose of servanthood, cultural perceptiveness, willingness to change, and speed is to cultivate catalytic, missional communities. According to Erwin, "Successful leaders can rally individuals around shared beliefs and a common vision. While community is important, the marker of apostolic leaders is to build community that is moving forward on mission" (13). Apostolic leaders do not accomplish things by themselves but rather build communities of mission that accomplish great things together. Apostolic leaders cultivate intentional, visionary communities that give themselves sacrificially and move quickly, creating whatever is necessary to fulfill the mission. An apostolic leader "would rather have ten people on common mission than a hundred who are simply curious. He understands that, in the long run, the ten will impact far more people than the hundred would" (76).

Apostolic leaders shape the church's ethos, its underlying values and culture. "There is perhaps no better description of a leader than one who creates and shapes culture" (133). This notion is summarized in the concept of a "cultural architect." A cultural architect is an artisan who "carefully paints a picture of an ideal world—the leader's concept of what the emerging culture should look like" (137). Apostolic leaders give vision through stories and symbols. "They provoke the imagination through compelling vision. They inspire hearts to believe that, together, a new world can be created" (137). Such artistry includes using "the power of aesthetics" in creating a physical environment that shapes and reinforces values and objectives kinesthetically for the congregation (129). Stories, symbols, and metaphors are tools used by apostolic leaders to build warmly relational communities of servanthood and inspire the unique, creative contribution of each person toward the mission of evangelization.

Finally, Erwin insists that the marker of good spiritual leadership is the cultivation of creative talent. He writes,

> The marvel of leading a New Testament community is that the genuine measure of leadership is not simply in the calling out of the extraordinarily gifted and talented. Instead, it is in the creation of an environment where each individual discovers and develops her unique gifts and talents. (13)

He also states, "An apostolic ethos identifies, nurtures, and develops these capacities as stewardship before God" (181). The result is a release of creativity within the church:

> The church can become the place where the great artists of our time paint their first strokes and the great musicians sing their first notes. The church can become the place where the great thinkers and the great scholars and the great writers emerge. The church can become the environment where the future's poets and film directors, dancers, and doctors grow up in community and learn that their talents are a gift from God. (183)

Apostolic leaders constantly look to involve people in creative endeavors within the congregation, endeavors that contribute to the overall goals and objectives of the organization.

Eschatology: The Nature of Human History and Human Agency

Eschatology is the study of "last things" and can be divided between personal eschatology (e.g., What will happen after I die?) and general eschatology (e.g., How will the world end?) (Berkhof, 1941). Since eschatology has been a source of great debate, systematic theologians do not assume orthodoxy on these matters. They either summarize alternative positions or ignore the discussion altogether. For this reason, I will rely on supplemental texts for understanding the dominant evangelical position on such matters. Focusing on general eschatology, evangelical theologians generally assert that Jesus Christ will return to earth again but debate the meaning and sequence of events leading up to this return. Interest in general eschatology is high and the debate over specifics vigorous (cf. Reiter et al., 1984; Erickson, 1977). The aspect of eschatology that most influences the beliefs and activities of Mosaic is the relationship between the church and the tumultuous last days of history, known as "the tribulation."

PRETRIBULATIONALISM, PREMILLENNIALISM, AND CULTURAL ISOLATIONISM

The majority position among evangelicals is both pretribulationalist and premillennialist and is illustrated by the belief of Chuck Smith, pastor of Calvary Chapel, Costa Mesa, "that Jesus will return at any moment and thus render all of human history irrelevant" (Balmer and Todd, 1994:663). The modern origin of this belief was a nineteenth-century attempt to apply to Scripture a scientific method called dispensationalism, a theological perspective which divided world history into distinctive eras of God's activity in relation to humanity.

The Scofield Study Bible, first published in 1909, popularized dispensationalism and the pretribulationalist eschatology through extensive study notes appended to the Scriptural text. The edition was widely read and considered a "badge of North American evangelicalism" (Reiter et al., 1984:24; see also Marsden, 1980:43–71). In pretribulationalism, the sequence of events leading to the physical return of Jesus is initiated by a single, dramatic action: the "rapture of the church" (Pentecost, 1958; Walvoord, 1957, 1971, 1976). Rapture is the physical translation of Christians from flesh into spirit and their immediate ushering into the presence of Jesus in heaven. Study notes in the Scofield Bible describe the church as living in a distinctive era, a "parenthesis" of world history, which began at Pentecost and will end when the church is removed at the rapture. Because the church is the vessel for the Holy Spirit on the earth, it restrains evil in the world. Once the church is removed in the rapture, the Spirit's restraining power over evil will be taken away and the world will enter into "the tribulation." The practical effect of rapture for Christians is that it will allow them to escape the disasters of the tribulation period. Evil will run rampant in the world, which will trigger an outpouring of God's wrath on earth. God's wrath will be manifested through natural disasters, cosmic signs, and dominance of the world by a single government ruled by the Antichrist. Seven years of the tribulation will finally end in the physical return of Jesus Christ, who will set up an earthly kingdom. This new kingdom, characterized by peace and prosperity, will exist for a thousand years, and this period is called the millennium (Campbell and Townsend, 1992). The position is called "premillennial" because it holds that that Jesus will return before the millennium.

Since human history is on a downward moral spin, Jesus' return will abrogate it in any case, and Christians will be leaving the world with all its cares and pains, the "pretrib, premill" perspective tends to move Christians toward cultural isolationism. Mike, a Chinese American who discussed eschatology at length, said, "The rapture means that you're gone; you escape whatever comes." Pretribulationalists continually expect the imminent return of Jesus. "They've been saying 'five to ten years' for the past thirty to forty years," said Mike. Anticipation of their escape leads pretribulationalists to withdraw from the world. Mike labeled this "the bunker mentality."

In his social history of evangelicalism, Marsden (1980) demonstrates that the "pretrib, premill" framework discourages cultural engagement. Dispensationalists believe their actions are overwhelmed by cosmic forces. They simply have no confidence that the church can make any significant impact on civilization, since humanity has almost no influence on the historical process. Marsden writes,

> Clearly, this view of history is antihumanist and antidevelopmental. Natural developments in which humans are the key agents play little if any role. Rather, humans participate in a larger cosmic struggle, the details of which have been planned and often revealed in advance. (63)

Change in this framework is the prerogative of God alone "through dramatic divine intervention" (63). Marsden traces this belief to the marginalization of fundamentalists in the early twentieth century:

> [T]he most immediate heritage of fundamentalists comes from their twentieth-century experiences of being a beleaguered and ridiculed minority. Sin and secularism had run rampant over some key parts of American culture. Like twentieth-century sociologists, most fundamentalists believed in laws that declared that the process of secu-

[81]

larization was irreversible. In the fundamentalists' case these laws were drawn from dispensational premillennialism, which posited the steady decline of the modern era in preparation for a final world calamity resolved only by the personal return of Christ with avenging armies. Fundamentalists in this worldview were outsiders. (Marsden, 1991:111)

Ultimately fundamentalists rejected all nonchurch culture and a host of activities, including the arts, dance, and theater. Revivalism turned inward. Marsden documents the belief that "the church in particular is declining in the present era from its original purity, while the whole civilization is also becoming increasingly corrupt" (1980:63). Since the church was believed to be headed toward apostasy, leaders centered their efforts on cultivating congregations characterized by great devotional fervor while neglecting a surrounding culture believed to be irretrievably lost. Congregations were discouraged from actively engaging culture. In short, Marsden (1980:66) demonstrates that dispensationalism "had little or no room for social or political progress." Timothy Weber concludes that this view of history "generally broke the spirit of social concern which had played such a prominent role in earlier evangelicalism." Its popularity is evident in the huge sales of books such as Hal Lindsey's *The Late Great Planet Earth* (1970), the aggressive pretribulationalism of the Calvary Church movement, and the wide distribution of Christian films depicting believers disappearing while regret-ridden people make desperate professions of faith in the midst of tribulation horrors. With this eschatological framework, evangelicals "turned their backs on the movements to change social institutions" (Weber, 1979:183).

Posttribulationalism, Amillennialism, and Cultural Engagement

Although general eschatology is seldom discussed at Mosaic and never heard explicitly from the pulpit, it is my view that, of Mosaic's ideological bases, its eschatology has been among the most effective in spurring belief and activity. And this eschatology is not pretribulationalist, but posttribulationalist, holding that the rapture of believers will occur after or at the conclusion of the tribulation period. The posttribulationalist eschatological perspective was brought to Mosaic by Brother Phil when he became senior pastor over thirty years ago. Bible study classes on it were taught every year. Moreover, agreement with the position was required for membership.

Historically, the posttribulationalist position has been well articulated, but almost always in an effort to refute the dominant paradigm of pretribulationalism (Gundry, 1973; Ladd, 1956; Payne, 1962; Reese, 1975). Brother Phil also held his position in conscious opposition to prevailing evangelical currents. According to Stan, "He would say that everyone in America is teaching this sensationalism, the rapture, all that kind of stuff." Coming to his first pastorate in Los Angeles, he felt it was morally wrong to let people believe the church would avoid the tribulation. Stan recalled that Brother Phil believed "people weren't going to be raptured out and essentially saved from persecution or suffering, and he felt like that was very important for people to understand. Otherwise, they would be under false hope." So, in contrast to other evangelical churches in the area, Brother Phil taught and reinforced posttribulationalism, a minority view within eschatology.

I learned how important this doctrine was to Brother Phil when I was hired on staff at Mosaic. Knowing that I had come from a dispensational church background, Brother Phil wanted to speak with me personally about the issue. I went over to his house and had an interview with the doctrinal gatekeeper of the church. He was a very gracious host and pleasant conversationalist, yet he was clearly intent on assessing whether I would threaten the posttribulational position established at the church. Since we had each spent much time studying the issue, it was not difficult for us to discuss the intricacies of the doctrine and explore the various ambiguities inherent in both positions. We spoke for two hours. By the end, he was satisfied that I was not committed strongly to pretribulationalism and was open to further dialogue on the issue. I was hired shortly thereafter.

There is little doubt that Mosaic's view of the future affects its enactment of the present, particularly in its perception of its role in the unfolding of history. The posttribulational stance affects the substance and direction of ministry at Mosaic, since rejection of dispensational premillennialism laid the groundwork for a different view of time and of the agency of human beings within culture. The posttribulation framework paved the way toward seeing the future as able to be shaped by human initiative, especially in the missional impulse of spreading the gospel to the ends of the earth. It assumes that followers of Jesus Christ will work in poor spiritual conditions. The period of church history is not a parenthesis in world history, operating only while the Holy Spirit is still working in the earth, but continues to serve Jesus even in the difficult times of suffering and persecution. Mosaic's posttribulational orientation leads it to see itself as working within a culture more often misdirected than openly hostile. Its perspective on history is less "either-

or," encouraging a more sympathetic working with the ongoing activity of God, who is wooing the hearts of people across the globe. Rather than subscribing to the dominant image of a "sanctified" body of perfected saints who confront "wicked" sinners in league with Satan, Mosaic attempts to elicit compassion for the ongoing brokenness of the body of Christ, which reflects the brokenness of the world. Today, Pastor Erwin tries to persuade people to enter into an entrepreneurial partnership with God in romancing people into a relationship with him and recovering their intended humanity.

Brother Phil would openly speculate about the merits of amillennialism, the belief that no future physical reign of Jesus on Earth will occur, but that Jesus actively reigns today. While Pastor Erwin has never claimed to hold this position, the theology of Mosaic is much closer to amillennialism than premillennialism. This leaning toward eschatological amillennialism also contributes toward an action orientation. For example, in 2001 Erwin frequently cited Matthew 11:12, "From the days of John the Baptist until now, the kingdom of heaven has been forcefully advancing, and forceful men lay hold of it." Rather than, like premillennialism, stressing Jesus' *coming* kingdom, amillennialism emphasizes Jesus' *present* kingdom, asserting that the kingdom of God is active now and advancing forward through history through the agency of human beings.

One of the practical consequences of this position is that people at Mosaic communicate hope rather than pessimism for the future. In particular, I was surprised to hear Mike say,

> My Christianity is becoming more long-term. I see the arts as a means to impact culture. It's a long-term perspective. Other churches may think, "The times are dark, things are going to get worse, let's not bother impacting culture in this way." They have a different theological perspective.

The "other churches" he talked about include the dispensational church he had left. Mike and others at Mosaic think in the long term. Mike even said he enjoyed thinking this way, and saw it as the motivation behind Mosaic's involvement in the creative arts:

> I'm understanding Erwin's teaching and understanding Mosaic about how you can shape culture through the arts. It's good to be there. But it's a long-term process. You don't shape culture overnight. You shape culture throughout the decades, even the next hundred years. But you've got to take that step, whereas other churches are, say, dispen-

sational, they probably see these days as coming to an end. So they don't see that long-term perspective.

What is especially significant is that Mike still considers himself "pretrib, premill" in his theology. "I'm the kind of guy that really tends to believe that we have only five to ten years left. I'm more that kind of guy. But at the same time I appreciate this long-term perspective." He told me,

> I know Mosaic's position on the rapture, but I still like the long-term kind of thought, because you know what? I just want to live like that. I want to live life. There's a tendency for when it's difficult to say, "I just want to bail," "I want to collapse under," and "God, take me now." Whereas Mosaic's perspective is to engage the world. Yeah, it's going to be hard, like when Pastor says that when two kingdoms come together sparks are going to fly. I like that. That's the kind of bravado I hear from Pastor Erwin, and that's what I want to be like. I want to be made of that kind of stuff. I want to be in battle.

Mike believes that we must engage this culture regardless of difficulties. "We need to have that kind of perspective that we're going to go into this hard, that it could be harsh." At Mosaic, he is motivated to try to affect culture:

> Let's say things get really bad; God can still do stuff. We'll still impact culture. We'll still have a say if we choose to. Why not? Why not shoot for it? I like that. I like that. I think that Erwin's been a strong leader, he's a strong communicator, and that rubs off—the boldness to engage culture.

Mike emphasized that purposeful human agency can affect history to actualize the mission of the church. For him and others, the posttribulational stance of Mosaic encourages the church to take a long-term perspective on the missional engagement of culture.

The Apostolic Community and the Movement of History

What does Mosaic believe? The question cannot be adequately summarized in the doctrinal statements it shares with every other Southern Baptist church in America. Erwin's messages aim at cultivating a catalytic community that participates in the mission of Jesus, drawing out dedicated followers from Los Angeles who will, through their initiative and creative contribution, participate in God's plan to woo the world to himself. Sermons are more than simply a means of disseminating doctrine to attenders. Rather, Pastor Erwin's messages consist of a convenient summary of the beliefs and values that nurture, justify, and channel organizational activities.

The messages given at Mosaic are delivered while other churches neglect such purposes. The need to reach a population that is broad and rapidly growing motivates continual innovation, a commitment to relevancy, and quick responsiveness to culture. But churches are simply not moving fast enough. According to Erwin, "The reason so many of us are becoming more aware of the need for the church to regain its essence as a movement is that we can feel history, and our relevance to it, slipping away from us" (2001:80). Erwin asserts that it is difficult for many Christians to accept a church that changes, consciously and purposefully, in order to engage the culture. "The church became a refuge from the world rather than a force in the world" (30). Because the church is in hiding, it is unable to deal with the rapid pace of social change. Christians are more caught up with accommodating each other than with accommodating to the culture they desire to shape. Erwin writes, "[T]he church becomes the last bastion of protection against change; the reminder of what the world looked like before it changed; the preserver of tradition and ritual, rather than the catalyst and advancer of the kingdom of God" (31). Protectors of "tradition" hold back needed changes within the church and "stifle the imagination, bring an end to creativity, and make innovation impossible" (90).

For Erwin, the role of the church is to change history. With exuberance, he writes, "We can go beyond fearing and resisting change. . . . We are not only called to be changed and to embrace change but to be the catalysts of change" (90). The church becomes a collaboration characterized by creativity, innovation, dreams, and experimentation in fulfilling the mission. The theme is one of co-entrepreneurship with God in what he is accomplishing in the world. In his writing and in his conversations, Erwin characterizes churches as either institutions or movements: "The distinction lies in the fact that institutions preserve culture, while movements create culture" (34). Mosaic is a movement.

Finally, in his missiological imperative, Erwin insists that churches must be characterized by ethnic diversity to have a legitimate voice in the coming culture. He writes, "If a spiritual expression wants to be considered as legitimate in the emerging culture, it must be able to cross the barrier of racism and isolation" (54). He uses biblical images of Babel and Pentecost, both of which are expressions of multiethnicity in the scriptures. "The church has an opportunity to reverse this integration of Babel and—as at Pentecost—to become an expression of the nations coming together and hearing the gospel in their own languages" (54). Change and diversification will come if the church takes up the imperative of mission.

The seed of the other havens found at Mosaic—artistic, innovator, age, and ethnic—can be found in the church's theological framework, because each finds legitimacy within the total belief system of the church. The next chapter will describe Mosaic's artistic haven, which is part of how the church mobilizes people into congregational activity. Such mobilization initiates, cultivates, and sustains their self-identification as dedicated followers of Jesus Christ by connecting their own skills and interests with the overall mission of the church in pursuit of a mandate believed to be given by Jesus himself.

4

THE HOLLYWOOD CONNECTION AND THE MANAGEMENT OF ARTISTIC TALENT: A RECONSTRUCTION OF INVOLVEMENT

CRYSTAL: The vibe of the church is that this isn't a church run by staff, this is a church run by everyone.

EMILY: I think it was just clear that I wanted to be a part of this. I wanted to be a part of what was happening at Mosaic.

When visitors come to San Gabriel High School they expect to see just that: a high school. From the outside, the buildings and grounds are unremarkable. But before the start of the second Sunday morning service, the lot is already full of cars. Having parked, attenders must walk between and around buildings to get to the main auditorium. A few tents on the front lawn of the school mark the entrance, and the familiar smell of buttered popcorn wafts through the doors of the auditorium. Greeters smile as they hurriedly pass out bulletins to the growing rush of people who enter the transformed lobby. Brick and concrete give way to fabric, furniture, plants, and paint. Bags of fresh popcorn are handed out in front of a floor-to-ceiling mural made of strips of celluloid and empty film reels. Once in the auditorium, the crowd waits amidst ambient music, looking at a broad stage on which an easel holds a movie poster surrounded by flashing lights. The lights are dazzling, and a stool is placed on each side of the stage. Huge screens display a title rendered in a sophisticated graphic design: "Framing Reality: From Reel to Real." The lights go down, and the focus remains on the screens and the movie poster. The screens go blank, and the opening scene of *As Good As It Gets*, starring Jack Nicholson, Greg Kinnear, and Helen Hunt, is shown. When the lights go back up, Erwin McManus and his brother, Alex, another pastor, are sitting on either side of the movie poster. They begin a back-and-forth dialogue on the significance of the film, giving insights into what it says about who we are as human beings and about who we all want to become. Another brief clip is shown, followed by more commentary; this continues for about twenty minutes. Then they pause, the lights dim, and the band emerges for a congregational song. As the lights come back up, Pastor Erwin opens his Bible and weaves a message from a small book in the New Testament, 3 John, reading the whole epistle and discussing further the kind of person we all want to become, how the film demonstrates this kind of person, and how these themes are complemented and developed in the Scriptures. Then a prayer, an offering, announcements, and the service ends.

Mosaic's proximity to Hollywood and the popularity of movie-going in Los Angeles makes focusing a sermon series on film a good strategy for conveying culturally relevant messages. Such a series also incorporates the interests and activities of a great number of people already attending Mosaic. Both the *Los Angeles Times* and knowledgeable people at Mosaic estimate that one-third of the attenders at Mosaic services are involved in the entertainment industry (Luo, 1999). Yet the artistic haven created at Mosaic exists for more people than just those working in film. It is concerned with artistic expression of all types. Sketches and dramas have become more common in many contemporary church services in the United States (see Chaves, 2004), but Mosaic has gone beyond "adding a skit" to embracing the arts in an expansive and integrative manner (especially since the Genesis series of 1998, discussed in chapter 2). Both committed Christians and non-Christians have found Mosaic an attractive refuge for artistic expression in the visual and graphic arts, dance, drama, and music. The name "Mosaic" therefore reflects not only the ethnic diversity of the congregation but also the value placed on creativity, since a mosaic is an art form.

According to Stephen Warner (1994:64), the master function of congregations in America is fellowship, yet "fellowship" is an inexact term. The fellowship found in churches varies widely. At Mosaic, fellowship is not just being together; it involves working together on common projects in a common cause. Mosaic's various activities (motivated by the goal "to serve others with others") involve "a bewildering array of activities undertaken by members of the congregation . . . where sharing the activity is part of its meaning" (65). Winter (1961) notes that involvement in congregational activities develops loyalty to the church. Creative involvement is a significant aspect of ecclesiastical practice within evangelicalism as a whole. Wind and Lewis (1994: vol. 1, 2) write that congregationalism is "an organizational pattern that places considerable power in the hands of the local body of lay members." More importantly, providing a space for people to express their individuality significantly adds to their feeling of ownership of and participation in the ministry of a congregation. Lyon (2000:33) observes,

> If religious groups capitalize (deliberately or otherwise) on, say, expressive individualism, but are able to connect—or reconnect—this with aspects of ancient traditions, and to curb potential excesses of individualism with reference to communal loyalties . . . then the growth of major movements such as Evangelicalism . . . becomes somewhat less surprising.

Such mobilization consumes much of the energy of Mosaic's leadership. This chapter demonstrates affinities between Mosaic and the Hollywood entertainment industry in the ways creative people are mobilized to take on purposeful projects within the congregation.

Mosaic has embraced the arts, encouraging artists to develop their craft in the context of the public celebration services and initiating projects that stimulate artists to be in community with each other. Because Mosaic draws artistically oriented people from various ethnicities, the creative arts at Mosaic provide a productive place for ethnic and racial blending. By examining the construction of the artistic haven and how it shapes the church as a whole, I continue to refine the understanding of how ethnically diverse people are engaged, in different havens, in becoming dedicated followers of Jesus through concrete activities that support the mission of the church.

Exploring Mosaic's Artistic Haven

According to Samantha, church leaders "create a forum for dancers, for writers, for actors, for painters." In this Mosaic is different from other churches. Chaves (2004) indicates that artistic activity is prevalent in churches and more common than either social services or political activity. However, the lived experience of people at Mosaic reveals that a great many Protestant churches are still hesitant to utilize the arts. For example, Martha said "if I wanted to be an actress, I can't be an actress because I might play a part where I might have to curse." She enjoys the arts at Mosaic and made it clear that this enjoyment was distinctive because "in the whole Christian world it's so taboo." Wuthnow (2003: 222) indicates that church members continue to hear pastoral sermons preaching against the arts; indeed, according to his study 49 percent of people who had ever heard a sermon on "the dangers of contemporary art and music" expressed negative attitudes toward the arts. Stockman (2001:35), an observer of the evangelical music industry, observes, "The Christian Church has put a spiritual hierarchy on jobs. Ministers and missionaries are on top, then perhaps doctors and nurses come next, and so on to the bottom, where artists appear." The way in which one sociologist describes the African American church experience applies as well to Christian artists at Mosaic: "Behind the church doors was a friendly and warm environment where black people could be temporarily at peace with themselves while displaying their talents and aspirations before an empathetic audience" (Morris 1984:6). Mosaic provides a haven for creative artists who escape from isolationist, "world-fearing" churches and find refuge for their passion for film, art, dance, drama, and multimedia.

SHELTERS CREATIVE ARTISTS ESCAPING ISOLATIONIST CHURCHES

Initially, Caucasian involvement in the entertainment industry may be the most notable at Mosaic. Pastor Erwin notes, "There seems to be a disproportionate number of Caucasians from the Midwest, like Illinois or Ohio, who are trying to make it in the entertainment industry." Stephen, a full-time staff person in the creative arts ministry, said, "Our talent base is ultimately Anglo. They tend to be the most talented, the most ambitious, the most educated, and the most experienced in the industry." But Stephen also named many nonwhites who work on movie sets, write for television or film, play music, act, design, model, or otherwise work in the industry. I found several among my respondents and consistently found a high degree of ethnic diversity on the platform (e.g., performing music, dance, or drama), on video (e.g., doing interviews, appearing in visual montages or short films), and on creative arts project teams (e.g., as writers, directors, designers, producers, or technical support).

Moreover, creative artists of all ethnicities were enthusiastic about the church. Samantha, a Chinese American interior designer, explained her commitment to Mosaic, saying, "It was the emphasis on art," and "There were so many artists at Mosaic that were Christians, and I never knew that before." Charles, a Mexican American painter, came to Mosaic with a vision. "What I've been hoping for . . . when God's vision for me came to life was to use art for his mission." Mandy, a thirty-year-old Chinese American active in the film industry, talked about what she saw when she first came to Mosaic:

> I saw there were a lot of different people working in the industry that were part of Mosaic. I saw that there was a lead pastor, Pastor Erwin, that basically was saying creativity is the natural form of spirituality. He was encouraging the artists. And he was encouraging people who want to be part of the industry or be part of the arts to do that. I felt like a team was there. There was a group of people that would support me in being part of the industry.

African Americans who failed to find other havens at Mosaic often found the artistic haven. Dela said she stays because there are "good opportunities for people interested in the arts." Bridgette was one of the first artists to publicly display her work. Today, art galleries are a regular aspect of all celebration services. Blake, another African American, almost immediately worked with computer equipment, sound, and lights, and ultimately directed celebration services. Dylan, also African American, connected with musicians immediately and was performing original music at celebration services within a few months.

A significant development in the cultivation of the artistic haven was the founding of a "creative arts" small group in 1998. Charles told me, "Everyone who was involved in the arts, didn't matter what format, was in that group." It grew and multiplied into several artistic groups, including a visual arts group, a graphic arts group, and a dancers' group. Charles's request for space to store art supplies and for a studio in which to paint and create other artistic projects was ultimately answered with an apartment owned by the church for artists to use as they please. For Charles, "The 'Art House' became the center point for drawing people" and affirmed the value of artists at Mosaic.

Artists were also drawn to a perceived commonality in artistic life experience, especially Christian artists. Abby, a Korean American in the entertainment industry, gave her snapshot view of Mosaic artists:

They are trying to be on the edge and trying to be individual. A lot of these people have had drug problems or really partied hard. They got into stuff. So their slate is not as clean even though they have a Christian background. They really struggle today with maybe drinking or drugs or even homosexuality—really taboo kinds of things. They go [to Mosaic] because they feel that other people accept them there.

These Christian artists are marginalized in other churches not only by their artistic expression but by their experiences with behavior that is not acceptable among American evangelicals.

Finally, this haven also exists for creative artists not already Christian. Ralph remembered his first encounter with people from Mosaic. He was in his apartment. "I heard people downstairs singin' and playin' guitar. And I thought, 'Cool, musicians live downstairs,' because I play the congas. So I went downstairs." Ralph was not Christian, but he was drawn to the group as an artist. "I had spent a lot of time doing art and music." One of the most important reasons that Ralph kept attending Mosaic without having committed to being a Christian was that he felt an affinity with "the whole emphasis on the arts as an expression of the Spirit. That was very pleasantly surprising." Soon, he began working on the weekly celebration services. "I saw opportunities there, outlets for these expressions that I could never seem to make happen on my own." Through a process of working behind the scenes, making new friends, and exploring the Christian faith, Ralph came to formally join the community of Mosaic by dedicating himself as a follower of Jesus. He was baptized a year after he first started working with the tech team.

DETERS CHRISTIANS WHO ARE TROUBLED BY ARTS IN THE CHURCH AND PEOPLE WHO DO NOT FEEL "CREATIVE ENOUGH"

While Mosaic provides a haven for many creative artists, it deters those who see the arts as irrelevant to congregational life. One pastor told me some longtime members have complained, saying, "The artists painting during the service are distracting." Others have said the dramatic sketches are "corny," and they "don't connect with the messages." Summing up his conversations with Christians critical of the services over the past three years, Stephen, a leader in the creative arts ministry, said, "For them, congregational music should be real slow. The more meditative the better. Then there should be a straightforward message from the Bible. Everything else is fluff." These Christians see no need to include creative elements that relate to the unchurched. According to Stephen, they consistently make one recommendation: "We should have a giant worship service and sing for two hours; that's the way to win the world." Dramas, special music, and artists are superfluous.

The use of creative arts on the platform has kept more than a few people from making Mosaic their home church. Stephen told me about a Hispanic woman who had often danced on stage but left because she believed Mosaic was becoming "an entertainment church" and not focused enough on "the Word." A Chinese American member said he had brought people "who were more fundamental" and who "reacted to the 'Hollywood' of the service." His guests told him the creative elements distracted from the message, and they never returned. I noted similar reactions especially from white, churched Midwestern visitors. Another person told me about the visit of his Southern family. According to him, they really didn't know what to think about the creative elements introduced into the service. They much preferred to be in a church like the one they had "back home."

The artistry in Pastor Erwin's preaching has also been criticized. Since Erwin's messages are often image-based and integrate with other creative elements, some Christians leave, looking for a message that feels more like an intensive Bible study. They want preaching that is more explicitly doctrinal (focusing on what should be believed) and exegetical (emphasizing close textual analysis of Scripture verses).

Surprisingly, some of the more adverse reactions to the arts come from Christian artists themselves. Every artist involved at Mosaic interacts with David, the creative arts director, at some point. In discussing artistry at Mosaic, David told me, "Artists who are successful in the entertainment industry and have a church background have the hardest time." He believes Christian artists are not accustomed to combining their talent with their faith. He recalls a Caucasian writer working on a series of sketches for the church. "She told me she was going through turbulence; she was questioning decisions she had made in the industry." David said she was "experiencing conviction for the first time." Judging from his experiences, at least some Christian artists prefer to keep artistry in their job and leave church untainted by their work concerns, as well as by the nonspiritual connotations of artistry they experience outside of the church.

The artistic haven also seems to deter those who do not consider themselves creative, feeling a marginality based on not being "hip enough" for the culture. The father of one family that left explained that he was not "a creative type." Some people I interviewed explicitly discussed their lack of creativity. A Caucasian woman who had been coming for about a year spontaneously said, "I'm not creative like a huge proportion of the congregation." I asked, "Is your impression that most of the congregation is more creative than you?" She answered,

> Yeah, seems like it. These people are, like, just fun. I went to Urban a couple of times and it was like, oh my God. They're all so young, and they're all so creative, and they're all probably around the same age as me. . . . They have the freedom to dye their hair all these cool colors. What a fun job they must have. So I feel a little older sometimes. *I'm only 26,* but sometimes I feel a little stuffy in comparison. [emphasis added]

She later said, "There's a definite crowd at Mosaic who are the creative ones, you know. You see them and you go, 'Wow, they're really artsy.' You just take things in a whole different way than the rest of us, the rest of me." I asked if any of those people were her friends, and she replied, "Some of them. We don't seem to have as many in our small group. It's more like, 'Oh, look at those people. They're more creative than us.' " Overall, she enjoyed artists, but at a distance. "I really enjoy seeing that aspect of God's creativeness. It's really enriching." She continued:

> I'm being pushed here. I have room to grow in this seriously because I am nowhere near that. It's so fun to be a part of being around people who have such giftedness in such different ways that I don't have. It's neat to witness.

By talking about "those people" and calling herself a "witness" to their creativity, she places herself on the outside. Thus, while the artistic haven is not for her personally, she enjoys being around it.

Parallels between Mosaic and the Entertainment Industry

While Balmer and Todd (1994) describe Calvary Chapel's appeal to hippies and the counterculture, Mosaic has shown that it appeals to those in the arts and entertainment industry. Many churches fear the influence of Hollywood. Mike, a conservative second-generation Asian in his late twenties, articulated this fear most clearly. Calling Hollywood a modern-day "Sodom and Gomorrah," he said, "Why would you want to go to Hollywood? I don't want to go to Hollywood; no, I don't want to go to Hollywood. I don't like Hollywood. I hate Hollywood. Hollywood is too sinful, too evil." He admires people at Mosaic who are involved in the entertainment industry, but he has no desire to get involved. In contrast, an estimated 30 percent of Urban attenders are actively involved in the entertainment industry, and if students, adults making career changes, and those between jobs who anticipate getting another gig soon are included, the proportion increases to at least 50 percent. Others in the industry come to the larger Metro morning service. So, combining the adult attendance of all services at Mosaic, 25 to 35 percent of the congregation has a "Hollywood connection." I have met, through Mosaic, a dazzling array of people in the film and television industry: writers, actors, producers, directors, assistant directors, art directors, production assistants, publicists, videographers, video editors, animators, composers, vocalists, musicians, sculptors, costume designers, graphics designers, special effects designers, miniaturists, dancers, set designers, location scouts, corporate office administrators, storyboard artists, photographers, agents, media distribution specialists, studio office personnel, and more. I have also known people to get involved in the entertainment industry as a result of being at Mosaic. Even I have earned money starring in a short video and selling three short sketches to a script distribution service. Both opportunities were opened to me by members of Mosaic.

While not everyone at Mosaic is in the industry, Mosaic embraces Hollywood and is very much influenced by the ambitions, sensibilities, activities, and workings of the industry. Given that Mosaic regularly puts forward a mission which affects the whole world, it is not surprising that the church would actively seek an alliance with the Hollywood film industry, arguably the most globally influential sector of Los Angeles. As one artist put it, "By reaching Hollywood, you reach the world." Pastor Erwin certainly agrees. He writes,

> Without question, Hollywood's influence far surpasses that of any political leader or nation. The possibility of spreading the gospel through film, videos, television, live feed, and the World Wide Web—not to mention the continuous influence of print media and radio—gives us the real potential of saturating the planet with the message of Christ. (McManus, 2001:50)

The entertainment industry can be summarized as having six essential components: (1) The industry is project-driven (oriented toward clear goals, which are pursued by variable teams for variable times); (2) It connects with popular culture (stressing cultural sensitivity, prioritizing aesthetics, emphasizing the fashion of the moment, both hitting the heart and pushing toward the new); (3) It is characterized by a rapid work pace (requiring high flexibility and high intensity among those working on each project); (4) It prioritizes the ready demonstration of talent (requiring instantly recognizable competence); (5) It most often works through relational networks (relying on referrals, mentoring, and personal connections); and finally (6) It demands vigorous self-promotion. In what follows, I compare the entertainment industry to the mobilization of artists at Mosaic. I also describe how Mosaic challenges self-promotion by promoting transcendent, altruistic goals.

Both Are Project-Driven

In its project orientation, Mosaic has an affinity to the rhythms of work in the entertainment industry. In the entertainment industry, work moves from project to project. Project orientation in the entertainment industry is a response to the emerging economy, in which institutions are becoming flat networks of "entrepreneurial groups" with "temporary projects" (Reich, 2000:84; see also Peters, 1999). Florida summarizes the thinking of several economic analysts to say that "much of the economy is coming to operate on the same principles as the Hollywood movie industry" (2002:28; see also Pink 2001:24–29; Storper, 1989; Christopherson and Storper, 1989). He sees project orientation as fundamental, saying,

> Typically, a producer today will sell a group of investors on a script idea, then pull together an ad hoc team of actors, technicians and others to make the film. Once the project is done the team dissolves, and its members re-form in new combinations around other ideas. (29)

I find much of the ministry activity at Mosaic to be project-driven. People sign up to work on a new project for a period of time. Mosaic's leaders recruit and cultivate talent much like Hollywood producers, in order to carry out projects. Projects are staff-supervised, team-oriented, and often lay-led, and have clearly specified goals. Like Hollywood projects (e.g., motion pictures), Mosaic projects are meant for a much larger "audience" outside the group, i.e., the "unchurched" or other people who could become mobilized followers of Jesus Christ.

This organizational pattern represents a historical shift at Mosaic. Longtime leaders told me that before Pastor Erwin arrived, "You were in a position for life and the only way you leave that position is to replace yourself." This made it difficult to mobilize people in the congregation because, according to one church leader, "People stopped making commitments because they didn't want to be committed for life." At that time, years ago, the church was dominated by blue-collar, nine-to-five workers who had regular schedules and weekends off. Now, people's work cycles are varied and unpredictable, so that it is difficult for them to commit to long-term, regular work on Mosaic's events. Patrick, a speaker, writer, and video producer, can be traveling for one or two weeks at a time. Mandy, as a film and television producer, can be gone for months at a time. Such irregular schedules can be a challenge if opportunities for ministry are limited to regular weekly activities. Now people are free to be involved in projects as much as they can and add more as they are able. Projects are designed to allow both short-term and long-term involvement, to accommodate the schedules of people like Patrick and Mandy. People on teams contribute what they can, when they can. And the large number of projects starting at any time means that people moving in and out of Los Angeles can choose one that fits their availability.

These projects are critical sites for multiethnic involvement and interaction. Mosaic redefines involvement in the local church by embracing first artistry and then the gifts, talents, and skills of all congregants, so that everyone involved is encouraged and given the opportunity to contribute to the overall mission of the church. Mosaic's project orientation allows it to mobilize people to use their unique interests and passions and take up Mosaic's mission of reaching Los Angeles and the world. Crystal affirmed this core vision:

> What can you do? How do you fit into Mosaic? What are your skills and talents? Why aren't you out there doing them? Don't just talk to me about it, do them. . . . You do the evangelizing, you talk to people, and you bring people to Christ. . . . You do it. You do it.

Joseph, a fifty-one-year-old Hispanic business owner, said, "Mosaic is a place where the opportunities are just endless. . . . I want to help other people to get there and just unleash them."

The most powerful example of mobilization through artistic projects I have seen in this past year was the "dirt dance" described in the first pages of this book. Four men of different ethnic backgrounds danced together covered in mud. As an artistic project, it both assumed and accentuated multiethnicity. The project was short-term and constructed for a specific, transcendent purpose. It involved a professional dancer (Caucasian), who choreographed the movements and recruited another man (African American), who danced publicly for the first time. The dance was a corporately performed message requiring creativity, recruitment, and effective execution. It supported and augmented the theme for that morning's service, which was "Earth," and complemented every other element of the service in portraying humanity's relation to God. The "dirt dance" drew on theological imagery of the first human, Adam, and brought four men together, emphasizing a common heritage as people created by God. Each man's performance of his own smaller dance manifested interplay between commonality and individuality and demonstrated a self-conscious coordination of body and mind in a syncopated rhythm for a single message told for a shared purpose. And the dance as a whole created a bond of friendship between the men that had not existed before.

The project orientation of Mosaic is most prominently seen in the ongoing construction of the Sunday celebration services. Mosaic produces its weekly celebration services in keeping with "evangelicalism's aversion to high liturgical forms" (Balmer and Todd, 1994:680). Rather than simply seeing a pastor speaking from a pulpit or a worship leader alone at the microphone, every Sunday includes dozens of artists on or around the platform. Painters work at the front of the platform during the sermon, young performers present original music, and short films are shown that encompass original poetry, cutting-edge editing, and sophisticated computer animation. In addition, attenders can often watch painters, sculptors, potters, and live models working both outside and inside the auditorium. Mosaic engages the congregation through the use of dance, drama, integrated lights and sounds, and messages that are interwoven throughout the services to create a fuller experience. These artistic spaces opened at Mosaic are characterized by ethnic inclusiveness, and are familiar to those involved in the entertainment industry. The weekly celebration services represent a bundle of projects both on and off the platform. While celebration services are broken up into multiple-week series, each series is a large project that requires a set of writers, dancers, tech people, and actors to produce it. To illustrate, a Sunday order of service in April 2002 was

"Jesus in Film" Welcome Video
Sound Clip of a Heart Beating
Four Congregational Worship Songs with Seven Musicians
Sound Clip of a Heart Beating
"Fratelli's New Family," Dramatic Sketch with Three Actors
Sound Clip of a Heart Beating
Pastor Erwin's Message, Part One

"Sounds of Golgotha" Audio Presentation
Pastor Erwin's Message, Part Two
"Love in a Moment," Special Dance, including Auditorium Aisles, with
    Five Dancers
Sound Clip of a Heart Beating
Pastor Erwin's Message, Part Three
Invitation
Offering Buckets Distributed by Ten Ushers
Announcements
Closing Worship Song

The components above represent the work of over two hundred individuals. The unifying element in all of them is the theme of the message given by Pastor Erwin for the week. The filming, editing, and producing of the "Jesus in Film" video involved at least five people working over several weeks. Audio sound clips involved another four. Not only were the worship songs performed by the band, most of them were written by someone at Mosaic. The tech crew for sound, lighting, and video accounted for another dozen volunteers. The sketch was written by one person and directed by another. The dance was performed and choreographed by members of a dance ministry at Mosaic. The team of ushers is one of several off-platform teams that greet, give bulletins, serve coffee and a continental breakfast, set up tables and chairs, decorate, put up signs, and manage parking every Sunday. Announcements represent events being hosted by groups in the church with team sizes ranging from five to forty-five people. During the service, an artist was painting to the right of the platform. Also, thirty-five to forty-five adults were involved in preschool, children's, and student ministries in adjacent buildings. And finally, still other teams after the service took everything down and hauled it away. These were the same teams that had set up that morning, three hours before everyone else arrived. Since services are held in a rented facility, nothing is stored on-site; rather, moving trucks are loaded and unloaded with all the elements required for producing every celebration service. In the evening, everything is repeated at the nightclub, except for the children's and student ministries. The celebration services demand careful coordination and often change from week to week, representing a constant shifting of teams, projects, and relationships.

Such activity is part of a broad historical movement in which churches have structured their services to allow more active response by congregants. Holifield (1994:46) noted that "even before the building boom of the 1940's, congregations began to move away symbolically from a conception of worship as a performance for passive observers." In the Second Great Awakening, Charles Finney spurred church services to become far more active and create a vital connection between platform and audience; the process continued with the revivals of Dwight L. Moody. Platform activity and the desire to engage and focus the attention of the audience even prompted changes in church architecture (for a fascinating discussion, see Kilde, 2002). And Warner (1994:64) describes worship as "sensual" in that "one's faculties and senses are mobilized" and church leaders tend toward sensualizing various aspects of the service, from the architecture, to the ambiance, to the activity on the platform.

While the celebration service is the boldest and most complex example of ongoing project orientation, Mosaic's focus on projects is also evident in small groups. Small group leaders in early 2002 became focused on hosting their own four-to-six-week series of gatherings, which they advertise. In these gatherings they concentrate on the topics and themes of the celebration services, using customized curricula. Also, small groups increasingly create multiple outreach events that take place as often as every other week for the purpose of cultivating friendships with unchurched and unbelieving friends.

Project orientation is also evident in larger, church-wide special events. *Pulse,* a play produced around Easter in April 2000, was perhaps the most ambitious project ever attempted. The play was performed at a theater in downtown Los Angeles before over two thousand people and was reviewed on the front page of the Metro section of the *Los Angeles Times* (Ramirez, 2000). Over 150 writers, actors, sound engineers, and backstage workers contributed. Projects like *Pulse* create a dynamic context in which a variety of people from different backgrounds working in teams can get to know each other and build a deeper sense of community while fulfilling the ongoing mission of the congregation.

Because there are many project teams, working in both short and long time frames, there are many ways and opportunities for people to participate in the congregation, contribute to the goals of the church, and, in the process, build relationships with people from different ethnic backgrounds. Short-term mission trips provide another opportunity for building cohesion. Ramon, a Mexican American, told me he has seen these trips bridge the cultural gap between whites and Hispanics in the congregation:

> Many of us were never exposed to white people. So it was a learning
> experience together to meet someone who shared the same faith, had

the same genuine motives, and was from a different place and culture on top of it.

By participating in projects, people at Mosaic cross ethnic boundaries to find commonality and, often, friendship. Blake, an African American, discussed his own experience on the tech team:

> One of my best friends is Craig. We work together on the tech team, and it's all good, but Craig has the same last name as I do. And I realized that at some point there's a possibility that his people used to own my people. The fact that we get along and it's not even an issue is something to celebrate.

Zack, a leader of one of the bands at Mosaic, said, "Through Mosaic I've definitely had an opportunity to learn about other cultures." Brian's participation in a small group led him to become friends with Victor, the leader of the group. When I asked him if Victor was his first Asian friend, Brian, who is Caucasian, said, "I never thought about it that way. I would say he is. He is the first person who is Asian that I would call a good friend." Over time, Kevin realized the diversity of friendships that grew out of working with different people at the church:

> One's from Hawaii; one's from Japan; one's African; a bunch of them are Latino; one's Cuban; one's from El Salvador. And I just started realizing that amongst the people that I am friends with and serve with there is probably, out of thirty people, twenty different nationalities represented.

Diverse relationships flourish in the teams. Mosaic's experience affirms intergroup contact theory, which holds that intergroup contact is easiest and most fruitful when groups have equal status and common goals, depend on each other in pursuit of those goals, and have the support of overarching authorities as they work together (Pettigrew, 1971, 1975, 1997a, 1997b, 1998). Mosaic's project teams fulfill the conditions for contacts between ethnic groups to result in mutuality rather than exclusion. People engage intimately with people of different social backgrounds and are forced to work through relational issues in pursuit of organizational goals.

Both Connect with Popular Culture

Another affinity between the entertainment industry and Mosaic is the emphasis both place on connecting to popular culture. As Balmer and

Todd (1994:665) state, "Evangelicalism has demonstrated its malleability throughout American history, its responsiveness to popular tastes and prevailing cultural norms." The public services connect to popular culture in an attempt to tap directly into the everyday experience of attenders. Mandy recalled the videos and dramas she saw on her first visit to Mosaic, saying, "I thought it was neat that a church was not afraid to be, not like the world, but able to have things people understand and that relate to our generation, you know, growing up on MTV kind of thing." Film clips are often used in celebration services, since popular movies provide a shared semantic space for talking about broad themes explicitly addressed in Pastor Erwin's messages. Popular music creates another connection. Not only is a recognizable top hit occasionally played, but the ambient music before the service, during the offering, and after the service is most often drawn from the rousing scores of blockbusters such as *The Lord of the Rings, Gladiator,* or *Braveheart.* The move toward what is fresh, new, and popular is intended to increase the sense that any message heard at Mosaic is relevant to people today.

Connecting to popular culture is grounded in a congregational core value: Relevance to culture is not optional. Erwin has said many times, "As long as we are talking about relevance, we are only talking about catching up to culture. Relevance always lags behind culture; it does not contribute new things into the culture." I asked David, the creative arts director, if the use of videos, dances, and dramas was a gimmick. He replied,

> Yes, it's a gimmick. We believe it is entertainment; entertainment is getting people's attention. We use that tool—we use that gimmick—to gain their attention. And it's okay. [...] Entertainment doesn't describe Mosaic, but it's part of it. If it's well done and it'll get them here, it's a hook.

Charles, an artist, commented on this, saying, "We do commercial art here in terms of dance or video, kind of the MTV, Pepsi generation–style stuff, that always influences people. I think that's a draw."

Mosaic's striving to connect with popular culture motivates members to invite guests. People are open to, and even enthusiastic about, inviting guests to the celebration services. As Mike, a Chinese American, commented, "They're not going to come and say, 'Oh, man, this is boring,' and put them through torture. If I go and invite someone, I can ensure that they are going to have a good experience here."

The desire for relevance gives high priority to aesthetics. Providing a pleasant and welcoming ambiance is important, although the use of rented facilities for Sunday celebration services can make it difficult. A dedicated team of five to twenty-five people brings into the celebration services attractive accessories like flowers, comfortable chairs, decorative tables, and original artwork. The aim is to create the feel of a living room, something between an artist's loft in downtown L.A. and the latest styles of furniture in new model homes. This contemporary ambiance is intended to convey that Mosaic relates to "here and now" rather than long centuries ago.

The importance of connection to popular culture is consistently noted in Pastor Erwin's weekly messages. Ralph, who was not a Christian when he first came to Mosaic, remembered his response to the message:

> I recognized what he's sayin', and it was real. It wasn't Christian-speak. It was conveying a message, telling a story, in what seemed to be the way I experience life on a day-to-day basis. [. . .] The message I heard seemed like something I could walk out into my world and work with.

Adam shared, "Somehow it seems like he knows what we're going through at the time and is able to relate to us at that level." Jerome talked about his first experience hearing the messages, saying, "I could relate to him. It seemed like Erwin had come from the world and then was a Christian. I just couldn't relate to people who had grown up in the church their whole life." And Dan said, "When the pastor speaks, he speaks like a regular guy." Through the arts incorporated in the celebration service, in the ambiance, and in Pastor Erwin's messages, Mosaic incorporates popular culture, changing with it, in order to lend credibility to its overall message and draw people into this community of dedicated followers of Jesus.

Both Have a Rapid Work Pace

Relevance and change are tightly connected in the ministries of Mosaic, especially in a pursuit of relevance within the constantly shifting local culture of Los Angeles. The rapid pace of change translates into a rapid pace of work by people in the ministry, similar to a Hollywood production schedule. Ralph's experience demonstrates the high flexibility and high intensity in the creation of weekly celebration services. He recalled coming early to Urban Mosaic with his friend Mark, who was on the lighting crew:

> It was kind of exciting, ooohh yeah, seeing what goes on behind the scenes. What struck me was the amazing amount of activity. You had

the band setting up. You had your sound people doing this, your video people doing that. They were working on the lighting. You had the people coming in and setting up the chairs. You got the café over there. It was just like an anthill or a beehive; there's so much activity going on.

Ralph got involved in the sound ministry on his second Sunday at Mosaic and commented on the flexibility his volunteering requires:

> It's pretty fluid. I don't see a lot of ruts in the organization. . . . I know that there are people somewhere meeting, talking about these things, and really trying to keep things churned up. It seems to be a very dynamic organization. It definitely does not have the feel of "that's the way we do it," 'cause I think we mostly make this up week to week. [laughter]

Flexibility, resourcefulness, and quick response are demanded from every person in the celebration teams every week.

The project-driven nature of Mosaic's ministry, combined with its desire to connect to popular culture, demands quick responsiveness. According to Kevin,

> You just expect things to be different each and every week in and out. After a while change goes from being different to being the norm. In ministry, you just learn to go with it. There are a lot of people here in the Hollywood industry and music industry. It changes so fast you just have to keep up. *So when you get into a church that's changing about the same speed, it's just like what I do at work.* I can figure it out here. [emphasis added]

The rapid pace of work means that there is little time to prepare or perfect. Instead, the public ministry of Mosaic is characterized by constant improvisation. This was articulated by Adam and Samantha when our conversation turned to contrasting Mosaic with another large church they had attended in Los Angeles. Here's an excerpt:

> ADAM: When we would go to [this other church], you sit down, and right when he says, "Turn to John 1:13" or "15," voom it's right up on screen. Or when we're singing the songs, the lyrics are always there, it's always on—
> SAMANTHA: It's too polished—
> ADAM: —too polished. They've been doing this for years. It seems very polished. Not to say our celebrations are not polished—
> SAMANTHA: —It's not! And I love it. [laughter] [. . .] We're human.

> We make errors. Have you seen the TV show *Whose Line Is It Anyway?*
> That's very unpolished, but it's great! [laughter] It's improvisational.

The weekly celebration services have become less like assembly-line productions and more like continuous innovation. This shift is comparable to one happening overall in the American economy. As Reich (2000: 106) notes, "About three decades ago the American economy began to shift out of stable large-scale production toward continuous innovation. The shift has been accelerating since then."

The flexibility and intensity of a production encourages resourcefulness. At times, proper procedures are abbreviated or even ignored. Abby related her work producing dramas and directing services at Urban Mosaic to the tight schedules she faces in the entertainment industry:

> If you need to do something, there's laws and there's unions (there's this, there's that), but if you need to put up lights in the industry, just do it. Forget about structure, forget about other stuff, and just do what you need to do.

The rapid pace of work at Mosaic is characterized by intensity, flexibility, improvisation, and resourcefulness. While the rate of change that results from such work is astonishing to respondents with experience in other churches, such change comes from a project-oriented desire to connect with popular culture, and, in the effort to get things done, continuous innovation occurs.

BOTH PRIORITIZE READY DEMONSTRATION OF TALENT

Since competition is so intense, the entertainment industry requires people to demonstrate their value quickly. You must sell your talent in five minutes or you won't get hired. The priority of ready demonstration of talent has entered the culture of Mosaic. What do you bring to the set? Since new people are constantly being recruited into ongoing projects, Mosaic leaders place a high priority on understanding who is available and what skills each could contribute to the congregation.

For example, one Sunday morning in April 2002, I met a young college student named Jonathan who introduced himself as an artist. He was enthusiastic about painters creating art in front of the platform throughout the celebration service and wanted to know how he could get involved. I introduced him to the artist who was painting that morning. She proceeded to invite him to share his artwork at the church in a gallery show being assembled to open the following week. Jonathan was not only excited, he was mobilized. On his second week at Mosaic,

Jonathan became one of the Mosaic artists, representing the community and entering a new set of relationships. Jonathan's readily demonstrated talent was his ticket into an arena of ministry.

Jonathan's story is not unique. Rapid assimilation on the basis of readily demonstrated talent is characteristic of Mosaic. Dancers see other dancers and know who to connect with if they are interested in dancing in the congregation. Musicians do so as well. Zack, a very gifted creative artist whose talents include music, drawing, special effects design, costume design, dramatic writing, and acting, talked about connecting to Mosaic:

> I had to be part of it. It wasn't a question of me thinking about it. It was like the one yellow Lego block that you always looked for, to, like—cush! snap in; it fit. I felt like, that that's where God wanted me to click, immediately, that it was a place that I could use the gifts he had given me.

Creative people whose skills are less immediately visible, such as writers and graphic artists, are publicly recruited. For example, the search for and purchase of a permanent location for administrative offices and celebration services has created a whole new arena of ministry activity requiring such skilled people as certified commercial appraisers, architects, licensed structural engineers, building demolition engineers, environmental engineers, and commercial lending officers. Other skills I have seen publicly recruited have related to moving tech equipment ("We're not leaving until we have ten volunteers!"), playing in the band ("We need a bass player!"), and working with children ("Who loves holding babies?"). In early 2002, the worship leader publicly said, "I would love to have an accordion player as part of the band." Three months later, an accordion player appeared on the platform. Wish fulfilled.

Over the past five years, Mosaic has experimented with ways to categorize the talents of the congregation to make them more readily recognizable. Spiritual gifts assessments, Myers-Briggs temperament indicators, and the StrengthsFinder assessment created by the Gallup Organization (Buckingham and Clifton, 2001) are used most often. "What are your strengths?" has become a common question at Mosaic and serves to highlight recognizable talent in every person. The most comprehensive attempt to place people according to their gifts, talents, and strengths is a ministry called Imprint, a coaching ministry taking people through a three-month assessment process. People are encouraged to contribute their skills to the church and are directed into ongoing projects that fit their interests and talents. One-on-one coaches mediate between the skills of the people and the needs of projects in the congregation.

Imprint is an explicit application of Mosaic's belief that every person is unique and can uniquely contribute to the church's mission. Rather than standardizing congregational involvement into a few roles, Mosaic attempts to channel the distinctive skills and interests of every person into activities that extend the values and objectives of the congregation. Emily contrasted this respect for individual uniqueness with her experience in her previous church. She came from a Chinese American church where the expectation was that everyone would serve. She experienced this as an obligation: "Everyone must serve." In contrast, she and other members who have come from Chinese American churches say that in their ministry involvement at Mosaic they do not feel coerced to take responsibility in a bureaucratized role but are encouraged to apply their unique skills through an organization that is working with God to accomplish his purpose in the world:

> With the arts and creativity and everything I feel like we're freeing people to do things that they didn't think possible or that maybe were stifled because my previous church would not receive that. As we open the door for people to express the God-given talents that they have, it's really affirming and releasing for a person. It may have been repressed for so long.

Joseph, a Hispanic man in his fifties, told me, "The church doesn't confine you. It helps you grow, and it sends you off." Mosaic mobilizes people around readily demonstrated talent. The affirmation of talent is ideologically motivated by the church's commitment to the uniqueness of every individual and its desire to help each person use that uniqueness for the overall purposes of the congregation.

Both Rely on Relational Networks

According to Florida (2002:30), "Hollywood is a place where social ties are notoriously tenuous and contingent." He goes on to describe "Hollywood rats" who hug and kiss their associates before stabbing them in the back. Relationships of trust at Mosaic are a welcome contrast to the exploitative relationships often experienced in the industry. Relationships at Mosaic are perceived to be real and authentic as opposed to fake and hypocritical. Mandy, active in the entertainment industry, asserted, "[W]e're just real people. We talk about brokenness. We're kind of messed up, but it's because of Jesus that we can actually function." Lindsey, an actress and photographer, said her experiences working in the industry caused her to see a need for the close friendships she found at Mosaic:

> I would say it took a huge knee scuffing and breaking of legs to find out how important it was. I knew I was in the big bad city of L.A. I was afraid to move to L.A., yet it was where I wanted to be, all these dreams and potentials, and in this place, this power place, you can see how central the city is, you can talk your way into being scabby or get anything, sleep with anybody and get anything, or get closer to something and sell yourself out. I wanted more than that. I wanted to be myself, and I didn't want to sell myself out. So, I committed. I committed to be out here, to be involved, having relationships, and being committed, being plugged into the church.

While relational fulfillment is regularly portrayed on film, people who work in the film industry rarely have great experiences in relationship with their co-workers. Intimacy is hard to find. Mosaic fulfills people's desire for intimacy by providing a place where they can have genuine community, something that they long for when they see it on film and want in their own lives, but have failed to find in Los Angeles.

Mosaic values healthy relationships, and this valuation is felt and evidenced in the welcoming atmosphere of the church. People are encouraged to cultivate healthy relationships in the church, which they are often motivated to do, since many have difficulty finding authentic friendships in urban Los Angeles. Mike shared that through Mosaic, "I realized that people are actually important. That's profound, because I used to think that Christianity was about knowing the Bible." Jerome, a thirty-two-year-old African American, told me, "Everyone is so welcoming here. They ask if you're in a small group and invite you to things. They want to make sure you're connected." He repeated several times how comfortable he felt with people at Mosaic, saying, "I felt comfortable right away. I've always felt comfortable here." He contrasted his experiences at Mosaic with those at a former congregation, saying, "They were very nice people, always treated me well, but there was always something there. It seemed forced." Jerome added about Mosaic, "If it's a weekend and you don't have anything to do, it's because you're not looking."

For many, joining a small group is the path to relationships. In any given week, about 30 percent of the congregation attends a small group.

While that may seem low, the figure conceals turnover, since small group leaders regularly report that the number of visitors in a month's time far exceeds the number of regular attenders; between eight and ten people may be in a group on any given week, but the total number of unique individuals who attend over a month could easily be twenty or more. In addition, many groups host events such as dinners, movie nights, and concerts, to which guests are invited, so that a group with eight regular members will mushroom to over thirty on a particular night. The consistent marker of engagement with a small group is the feeling of having friends. Cole told me,

> I thought they would study the Bible and stuff like that. And that's what some people do. For us, basically our small group is the time to get together and share our lives with each other. I think of it as us friends getting together like any other friends I have. . . . It's not like the church setting. It's more like just being with friends.

Small groups provide a means to forge relationships, which are a base for joining a project team, since people often recruit friends in their small group to a service team. This next level of involvement beyond attending the celebration services involves a purposeful initiation of friendships and, eventually, service in the congregation.

Like the entertainment industry, Mosaic places a great importance on networks in the constant, informal recruitment for projects. Work in the entertainment industry is mostly obtained by referrals, and success often requires cultivating a good network of referrals. At Mosaic, the pressures of working quickly and resourcefully require an extensive network of relationships so that whatever materials are needed for the moment can be pulled together. Brian says that almost everyone on his ministry team is from his small group, and half of his small group is on his team. Whenever a new project emerges, leaders think first of who they can already count on, and, when they feel unsure that they have the right people, they ask other leaders for "referrals" of those who would work well on the project. Full-time staffers make an earnest attempt to stay relationally connected, in order to know who to recruit for new and ongoing projects. Every week they actively cultivate their relational network through meeting visitors, hosting meals, encouraging team members to invite guests, and participating in nonchurch social gatherings. These kinds of activities allow them to connect with potential volunteers. In each interaction, they consider how the person they are meeting could be mobilized in a current or new project that would fulfill congregational objectives. Pastor Erwin uses the visibility and credibility he gains from the platform to network people into ministry projects. I have seen him guide many people into the band, into participating in dramas, into working with children and students, and into creating several new projects.

A Difference: Pursuit of Transcendent, Altruistic Ends

Finally, the entertainment industry encourages self-promotion. The branding of self boosts one's chances for career success. Fulfillment is found in fame: an envy-inspiring recognition of individual talents and achievements. Unlike the entertainment industry, Mosaic challenges people to find personal fulfillment in the pursuit of transcendent, altruistic goals, to concentrate not on their own careers but on evangelizing the masses through the creative media accessible to them. Many at Mosaic came to Los Angeles with a sense of mission. For example, Mandy calls being in the entertainment industry her ministry and has mobilized a group she calls Mosaic Hollywood to pray weekly for the entertainment industry. Paige, along with two other Mosaic members, established a production company called Sodium Entertainment, a reference to Jesus' admonition to be "the salt of the earth" (Matthew 5:13). These and others view being in the entertainment industry as a lever of influence for evangelization.

The call to serve transcendent, altruistic ends is not limited to those in the entertainment industry. I found many working within the ministries of the church who gave themselves to such goals. They see themselves as part of a catalytic community that calls people to become dedicated followers of Jesus Christ. Mike, a young Asian man who is part of the multimedia team, called this visionary network at Mosaic "the core":

> There's a core of Mosaic that has really sold out to Jesus. They go out of their way to serve someone so they can hear about Jesus. That's the core I'm talking about. [...] When someone brings someone, and this person isn't a believer, and everyone is mindful of that, that's valuable. That is worthy of our time. That is not something to be overlooked or neglected. That is why we're here doing it.

I asked Mike who was in the core. He replied, "The people who serve." People in the core express the mission of Mosaic, just as did the members of Mt. Hebron interviewed by Flynt (1994:144): "Members defined the primary function of their congregation as winning people to faith in Christ and enrolling them in his church." The core takes ownership of the values and objectives of Mosaic, spending time and effort on them in all their actions. Mike illustrated his membership in the core, saying,

> I'm on multimedia, and I know why I do what I do. It's not because I want to put on a good show; it's because I want someone to hear about Jesus and to experience God's salvation. [...] I feel empowered to do it when I'm with the community of people who believe the same thing and believe the same God, and they're willing. They're not disbelieving it; they're willing to do it. I'm very impressed. It's the best thing that's happened to me. [...] The vision of reaching L.A. and reaching the world through L.A., that excites me. [...] It's something that I'm willing to die for.

Service at Mosaic is made significant by tying it as concretely as possible to God's activity in the world and to the thrill and joy people feel in fostering another's conversion. For example, Mandy said,

> A lot of people I connect with understand the arts as being a tool or a vehicle of reaching out to people. ... The people I connect most with at Mosaic have the same idea. I want to reach out to people and want to reach out to people together.

Dylan, an African American musician who became a dedicated Christian at Mosaic, said, "If I can help somebody else find out who Jesus Christ is, hey, then I'll serve." He added,

> Mosaic is very unconventional; so, I figure if that's what caught me, then other people can get caught the same way. So, whatever I can do to help them keep this thing going, that would be a great thing; because whoever walks in the door at Mosaic, they're going to come back.

Kevin, who is white, was also enthusiastic, saying,

> This place has such a high value for mission that I honestly feel that there are times where I'll be doing something or maybe I'll just be reading passages in Acts and I actually feel like I'm involved in an apostolic first-century church. That it's got that same kind of focus, that kind of sense of excitement to it. Why not commit to that?

Eric, a pastor on staff, joined when he was looking for a deeper level of engagement in the Christian faith. He told me the priority Mosaic places on evangelism was significant in attracting him:

> I was really tired of being around all white people, all of these people who grew up in church but didn't really follow God or acted one way on Sunday and differently all during the week. It just seemed that people had been inoculated with Christianity and [were] immune about getting serious about their Christian faith, and I wanted to go where people had never heard the gospel.

Respondents contrasted Mosaic's passion for reaching the world with other churches' uninterest, and said that that passion was a point of attraction and even affinity.

People regularly spoke of being attracted to the congregation through vivid encounters with strongly missionary-minded members of Mosaic. Brooke, a white Southerner, talked about her first ministry leaders, saying, "They were so passionate about seeing people come to Christ." Paul, Chinese American, also commented on his first leaders, saying, "They were serious about changing the world," and added, "I was captivated. I wanted to change the world." Stephen, Hispanic, said of one of the pastors, "I loved [his] intensity. . . . He was the evangelist. Boom, already I'm interested in this guy. I had dinner with him, and again he was very serious. I loved the zeal." Trevor, another white Southerner, also commented on this:

> I noticed Erwin had a similar heart to mine. He believes he can change the world. He believes that Mosaic can be an integral part of being a change agent. What we have as our core value is to reach the city of Los Angeles and then the world—The city of Los Angeles! Gerardo! It's the second largest city in America. And in 2020, it will take over; it will become the largest city in the country. It's the—what's the— [clapping hands] Hello! Los Angeles? We're going to reach ten to twenty million people? Are you out of your mind?? Yeah, we're out of our mind. But we really believe that we can do it.

In a variant of like-attracts-like, Blake, African American, asserted that in his five years of attendance "[t]here's a constant group of people who are looking for passion in a church who already have this inner passion." According to Blake, people come to Mosaic and "stay for the passion. I think this is what makes Mosaic different from other churches." Todd, reflecting on the fervency of commitment he found at Mosaic, said, "I'd never been to a church like this, but this is the church I've always wanted to go to all my life." Zeal is a magnetic quality that has attracted many people to Mosaic who have, in turn, become zealous themselves. The passion they describe fires a vision-driven movement in pursuit of transcendent, altruistic ends that extend Jesus' original call to serve and evangelize the world.

Many generalize the visionary core and project it onto the whole congregation. For example, Stephen concluded on the first day he met people in the congregation that every person in the celebration service was part of the vision-driven community: "Everybody I met I wanted to sit under their feet and learn from them." Paul, a young Asian, told me, "What I recognized at Mosaic, which I had never seen in any other congregation that I had been to in my life, was a straight across-the-board passion for whatever they were doing." Similarly, Kevin said, "Everyone here thinks huge. No one ever thinks we're going to reach ten people. It's like we're going to reach all of L.A., the world." Derek, who is white, spent a summer as an intern with Mosaic and listed many who impressed him then with their intensity for mission. He said, "In servanthood, vision, evangelism, and missions, I felt that one member of Mosaic had more vision for the world in their pinky than a lot of pastors in other churches have in their whole bodies." He concluded that relocating to Los Angeles after college would allow him the opportunity to grow into this visionary community. He did make the move and went on to be commissioned as an overseas missionary.

The ultimate transcendent, altruistic goal is to sacrificially leave the country with a vision of making dedicated followers of Jesus Christ all over the world. This makes overseas missionaries key members of the vision-driven community. Derek and others always spoke of friends from the congregation who had gone overseas as role models. Mike talked about "the core's willingness and desire to go overseas, to basically give their lives for Jesus." Giving up a comfortable suburban life to go to the Third World challenged Mike, as the son of Chinese immigrants:

> You can't really go beyond when someone says, "I'm not going to live the American dream; I'm going to spend my life in some Third World nation telling people about Jesus." That really goes against why Chinese people come to this country. Chinese people come to this country because they want to fulfill the American dream. Wow. How weird that you abandon the American dream and go to a Third World nation to serve Jesus Christ.

For Mike, "When Mosaic is out there on the mission field, that's when you get the pure Christianity, the raw Christianity." Paul, another Chinese American, told me,

> What really made an impression on me was just a short few months [after my first visit], Violeta was leaving for missions. Jasper was also one of the first people I met at this church. [. . .] These are the first people I met coming to this church. These are the kinds of things that were happening all the time. There's no sense of stagnancy about this. That really drew me.

Dan, African American, also talked about one of Mosaic's missionaries:

> I remember when I first got to know Irma, who says, "I just feel God is calling me to be a missionary," and she's off on a ship around the world. And as everybody is unique, even though not everyone has been called to be a missionary, everybody has that reckless abandon, that whatever God asks me, that's what I'm going to do. People want to be in line with what God says here. That's what I want for my life, and for my wife, and for my family.

The pastors of the church were uniformly attracted to the global vision of the church. Pastor Erwin remarked that when he first met with the leaders of the church, "I liked their sense of passion and their vision for the world, very global." Walt recalled his first experiences at Mosaic, saying, "It felt like it was on the edge of the world. It had people overseas; it had a big global vision." Dave remembered his disbelief as a college student that a world-encompassing, vision-driven community could exist within a church:

> I was intrigued that a church had the audacity to think what they did make a difference in the world. I was very challenged by the vision of being a spiritual reference point east of downtown Los Angeles and a sending base to the ends of the earth. I told [the leader I met], "If a place like that really exists, I would lay my life down for that vision." She said, "There is." And I said, "I don't believe it."

Dave not only joined but, sixteen years later, became a pastor of the congregation. Finally, Eric came for a conference at Mosaic and remembered,

> Doug drove us every day to the church, and I was amazed by that. Here's a Latino dentist giving up his practice to go overseas. Things like that were so amazing. People were such servants. It seemed like

the whole church body was actively wanting to reach the world. Hearing this little tiny church in East L.A. talking about reaching the nations and reaching all of L.A. was so ridiculous I thought, man, I need to be a part of this and see how this is going to happen.

He moved to Los Angeles with his wife the next year, and came on staff a few months later. All the pastors on staff were initially drawn to the vision-driven community, attended the church, and became members before coming on staff.

The people I spoke with who consider themselves part of the visionary core were most influenced by personal encounters with others who were part of that core before them. The passionate involvement of the visionary core with the transcendent, altruistic goals of the congregation draws people into further involvement, often before they feel they are ready for it. As Jamie told me,

> I really enjoy Mosaic, and I want to be part of the whole essence of what it's moving toward, ministry and missions, having a whole outward focus—I really love that. And you just go, gosh, I want to reach out too. I want to share my experience, and what I can do, and how I can help and serve. Eventually, I hope to be there.

A few months later, Jamie went on to become a full member of Mosaic.

Mobilization as the Core Activity at Mosaic

Mobilization as part of the visionary community is a core task of the church. Since the mobilization of people includes the mobilization of innovative, catalytic leaders who take responsibility for the common goals of Mosaic, the next chapter will describe the innovator haven. The ongoing cultivation of catalytic leadership is an imperative within the structure of Mosaic, and understanding how these leaders are defined and recruited contributes to understanding this distinctive haven.

5

INNOVATION AND THE CULTIVATION OF CATALYTIC LEADERS: A RECONSTRUCTION OF IMPERATIVE

ERWIN: We have people who lean toward innovation, toward change, toward invention, toward risk, toward adventure. We tend to filter out into other churches people who would like stability, security, and predictability. Our clear target group is the former on that scale.

KEVIN: I love change. I love things that are different. I want something different. I want something to change. I want excitement and difference and stuff. I don't know. Maybe I have some kind of spiritual ADHD.

Reminiscent of the ruins of an ancient castle, the auditorium is decorated with large gray stones and gold-flecked tapestry-like designs painted on large canvases, creating a medieval atmosphere. A rousing musical score plays in the background (taken from a recent *Lord of the Rings* movie) as the spotlight shines on a giant obelisk, ornamented with odd writing, in the center of the platform. A "wizardly" man with a bushy white-gray wig and beard is just entering the stage, announcing, "Welcome to Quest—The Game!" Alongside him is a woman dressed as if for a Renaissance fair. They point to signs with symbols which divide the seats into a grid, and explain how the auditorium has been converted into a giant game board. Two costumed contestants emerge, attenders selected a few minutes earlier and quickly dressed. The woman is now a plump, helmeted, red-bearded dwarf, and the young man has been transformed into a wood elf with a green and tan cloak and a bow and arrows. The hosts reveal a large six-sided die. The players will roll it to move about the board, among the audience, and the symbols they land on throughout the auditorium will determine what happens in the service. Will a survey question about spiritual experiences be solicited from the congregation? Will a controversial theological question be answered by three pastors dubbed "The Council of Wisdom"? Will there be special music from the band? Perhaps a film clip? At each turn the hosts ask the players to predict audience responses to each element; the players must answer correctly in order to roll the die again and progress around the board. "Will you accept your quest?" prompts the jovial wizard. The dwarf and elf accept the challenge, heft the giant die onstage for their first roll, and proceed in two different directions. The randomness of their rolls leaves the hosts, the contestants, the multimedia crew, the band, the pastors, and the congregation uncertain of what will happen next. As the service proceeds, the flow of events elicits various thoughts and questions from the players and the audience, which Erwin, the lead pastor, draws together into a multipart message throughout the hour. At the final roll of the die, the contestant who has won by moving fastest around the board approaches the obelisk, lifts a golden vase, and smoke, lights, and thunder conclude the service.

"Quest—The Game" was a celebration service with an unpredictable progression. Its elements were planned and prepared, but much of its actual content was unknown. The day's three services were all different. How contestants would respond, how pastors would answer questions, and how the crowd would answer survey questions were a mystery. The risk involved in rolling the die, allowing the entire service to be shaped by unpredictable interactions, created tension and eagerness to see what would happen next. The immediacy of unfolding events and ongoing interaction drew the whole crowd into the experience. Almost the entire service (including the initial idea, design of the space, multimedia elements, costuming, and original songs) was designed and implemented by volunteers. The design of this service promoted a spontaneity not only welcomed by attenders but also reproduced in future original contributions throughout the year.

Mosaic's ability to respond to rapid change and leverage ambiguity goes beyond the context of a celebration service. It was tested in early 2003 with events that began in the east. On February 17, a stampede occurred at a Chicago nightclub when a security guard used pepper spray to break up a fight. Patrons panicked and fled for the doors, trampling each other as they struggled to leave through a single exit. Twenty-one people were crushed to death, their bodies stacked up against the glass front door. Three days later, on February 20, a fireworks display by a heavy metal band ignited an inferno in a Rhode Island nightclub. Fire and panic overcame the crowd as thick black smoke filled the room, hiding the exit signs and obscuring doorways. People scrambled for the main entryway in almost total darkness. Fifty-one people were injured, and ninety-eight others were burned, trampled, or suffocated to death. The National Fire Protection Association ranks the Rhode Island nightclub fire one of the deadliest fires in a social assembly in the history of the United States.

Ripples of these two tragedies were felt in Los Angeles two weeks later, on a Sunday afternoon when the tech crew of Mosaic was setting up for an evening service in a nightclub. The city's fire marshal came to the door and abruptly shut down the club. Everyone was to leave immediately, leaving supplies, chairs, and equipment inside. Local news media were on the scene, and fire officials gave sidewalk interviews for the cameras. Rumors were that there were no actual violations; rather, the city needed to demonstrate its vigilance in ensuring nightclub safety. The practical result was that Verve, a multimedia church event with roving video, special lights, multiple mini-venues, and a disc jockey mixing music, had to be scrapped. A crowd of over four hundred people was expected, including many invited guests, and, at that moment, there was nowhere to meet and no program to implement. Standing on the sidewalk ninety minutes before the service, the leaders quickly assessed their options. One half-block down the street was an empty parking lot. The lot had no lights, no power, no seating, and no shelter, but it had an excellent view of downtown Los Angeles. And it was close. Several full-time staff were arriving and contributing ideas while the tech team scrambled for equipment. The band looked at what instruments were available. Within fifteen minutes, a plan was made, a new order of service constructed, and the thirty or so people on hand knew what to do.

That evening, church was held in a parking lot. Attenders walked curiously down the block, and greeters at the driveway handed out bulletins as people milled on the asphalt. Two cars aimed their headlights toward the center of the lot. A tech guy jerry-rigged power converters using duct tape from the battery of a third car for amperes which powered a microphone and a pickup for a guitar. Just after six o'clock, two songs were sung with everyone standing. Pastor Erwin announced that four stations had been set up for everyone to visit; they were to split up into even groups, each beginning at a different one. "Ready, go!" One station led a group in interactive prayer; another played music while a speaker talked about being on mission; a third was run by two creative arts people who directed a group in improv skits; and the last station featured Pastor Erwin talking about living in uncertainty. Groups stayed at each station for about ten minutes. At the end of the evening, people left a bit cold, but seemingly satisfied. Many spontaneously said they wanted to meet in the parking lot again next week. Several first-time visitors I spoke with indicated that they had never experienced a church quite like this.

Mosaic leaders are accustomed to unexpected change, disrupted schedules, and lack of resources for ambitious projects. The most sought-after resource is not money, but a particular type of person. Catalysts, leaders who take ownership of the organization's goals and purposes, are the most valued resource at Mosaic. They pursue creative thinking and ongoing problem solving as they lead others in aggressive pursuit of the church's mission. The innovator haven at Mosaic is created out of the discovery, development, and deployment of such catalytic leaders.

Exploring Mosaic's Innovator Haven

Pastor Erwin defined for me what he considers to be the common characteristic among the diverse people at Mosaic:

> They're on the far left of the adapter categorization. Our target group is people on the left side, the innovators and early adopters. That's our people. We tend to capture a certain dynamic in the way people address change, innovation, and risk, and draw people who are highly intuitive. . . . We have people who lean toward innovation, toward change, toward invention, toward risk, toward adventure. We tend to filter out into other churches people who would like stability, security, and predictability. Our clear target group is the former on that scale. [. . .] I think that's our secret.

People at Mosaic are innovation-friendly. The concept of an innovator that Pastor Erwin uses is drawn from the innovation curve constructed by Rogers in his classic *Diffusion of Innovations* (1995). In this work, he categorizes people into "ideal types" located at various points on the innovation curve, which represent their relative willingness to innovate or to adopt the innovations of others. While most people clump in the middle of the curve (the "early majority" and "late majority"), it is the curve's extremes that are most interesting. At the far left are the innovators, 2.5 percent of the population who are actually inventive, creating new ideas, products, and processes that soon catch on with the 13.5 percent of the population who are "early adopters" (262). While there is no precise way of measuring where a particular group lies on the curve, it appears that most churches are places for those on the right side of the curve ("late majority" and "laggards"). Mosaic appears to be a haven for those on the left side. The church provides a haven for innovators, people who initiate and enjoy change.

Shelters Change-Friendly and Change-Initiating Individuals Escaping Change-Resistant Churches

Mosaic is a refuge for catalysts, change-friendly and change-initiating individuals interested in making a distinctive mark through their personal contributions to the world. In other places they have been called mavericks, rebels, or freaks. Among them are people who have chafed at the traditions of other churches or left other churches out of frustration at their own inability to change them. Trevor, a white Southerner, described his experience in other congregations, saying, "In other churches we've faced opposition, we've faced doubters, we've faced other people telling us we're heading on the wrong path." Eleanor said, "In other churches, I was the radical. It feels weird to be normal." As Rogers (1995:26) explains, "The most innovative member of a system is very often perceived as a deviant from the social system, and is accorded a somewhat dubious status of low credibility by the average members of the system." Potential innovators are suspect and therefore unlikely to garner enough influence for change. Since Mosaic as an organization is oriented toward change, they find in this church a home for their ideas.

Many respondents said that constant change, variety, and flux were part of their experience of Mosaic. Zack declared, "It's changing so fast and so quickly you never know what's going to happen." New worship songs are continually introduced in the services; the great majority of the music is original and written by members of the congregation. The structure of the programming varies from week to week. Twenty-three-year-old Kevin said, "You just expect things to be different." Abby said, "What I love about [Mosaic] is that it does change. And that's Mosaic, it changes a lot. If it doesn't work, you just try something else." Lindsey told me, "I like how we try to do things different and not like every other church. With the sketches or our praise and worship, we are not afraid of trying things. I like that." Change is normative at Mosaic. Full-time staff assignments have changed many times over the years. New dramas, shows, and special events occur at various times and in various venues throughout Los Angeles. The places and times of celebration services shift often, sometimes significantly. Molly, a member for six years, said, "In our church nothing stays the same."

Despite such frequent changes, people were thrilled (several enthusiastic) about the future of Mosaic and filled with eager anticipation. Brian, a twenty-seven-year-old Caucasian, said, "I'm excited about the vision. I don't know where God's leading, but I want to ride the train." Dan, African American, also spoke with anticipation, saying, "I feel like something is going to happen here. At any moment, I don't know if the roof is going to explode, and Jesus is going to come right down right here, but I want to be here to see it. I want to be here." And Ralph, another Caucasian, told me, "I can't wait to see what's next. Where else is this gonna go? What else is gonna happen? I definitely want to be a part of it."

In change-oriented systems like Mosaic, innovators are not only welcome but given influence. As Rogers (1995:27) notes, "When the social system is oriented to change, the opinion leaders are quite innovative" (see also 295–299; Herzog et al., 1968). Trevor said, "We have a lot of crazy people in this church. [These are] individuals who want to change the world, who want to make a difference; when I say crazy, they actually believe that they can change the world." According to Mandy, "Mosaic says, 'Yes, be creative.' I've never been to a church that said, 'Be creative; think of ideas. . . . ' It's crazy." A new attender at Mosaic who had just started a film production company said to me, "We're all dreamers around here." Another respondent added, "Hey, we want to change things. We want to make things radical. We want to make things different."

People frequently mention a sense of empowerment and camaraderie engendered by corporate activity in the congregation. Not only are creative, "edgy" endeavors in media and creative arts embraced, but Mosaic fosters an atmosphere of working together toward change that will impact history. Mike told me, "I feel I'm joining hands with everyone to impact culture, to impact the world. It's big." Kevin admitted, "Part of me just gets so excited to think that a small group of people who are determined can actually change the world." Trevor shared a comment from his roommate:

> "I can't explain it," he said, "but there's something about Mosaic that's special. It makes me feel like I can change the world, that we can actually make a difference." And I just laughed my head off. I said, "You know what? I feel exactly the same way."

Participation in Mosaic encourages attenders to believe they can change history.

Mosaic is oriented toward the future, and new projects that explore new arenas of ministry work against the inertia of tradition in favor of untried experiments. Trevor was explicit about this, saying, "A large percentage of our member base is people of vision, people of destiny, who dream big dreams, who are going after it in whatever fields." Comparing Mosaic with other churches, he said, "I have never in my life been around so many visionaries. Never." He believes this is one of the most attractive aspects of Mosaic. "[W]e welcome people of vision."

DETERS PEOPLE WHO DESIRE STABILITY AND HIGHLY STRUCTURED PROGRAMMING

While there are those who embrace change at Mosaic, others perceive *too much* change. Difficulty with change often emerged as a reason why people left Mosaic. When I asked Emily why people leave, her first response was, "Sometimes it's a little bit *too* fluid." Trevor said, "Any time we do really crazy things, there are those few people who aren't very crazy, and they get scared, and they end up leaving." Molly, answering the same question, said people felt that "we're getting out of tradition. It's okay to change, but stay with tradition." One of the best examples is the music. The worship team introduces new songs almost every week. One senior adult summarized his perspective:

> We do anything to get away from the tradition of the church. We can't even have standard music or a standard hymn, not even once in a while. Everything has to be a now thing. "Okay, we've got this song. We just made this up last week for today, and next week we're going to have another song. So don't try to memorize this song because we're going to make up another one next week."

Although this man stays at the church, he said others have left specifically because of the music.

Another frequently discussed example of change is the fact that celebration services have changed significantly about every six months over the last five years. For example, in 2000, the growth of the church made it worthwhile to start a third celebration service. This Loft service grew to over two hundred attenders. Within a few months, the Sunday morning service moved close to it, which prompted the decision to end the Loft. The change was announced one week; the next week chairs, tables, tech equipment, and other materials were moved out at the conclusion of the service. Kevin remembered, "The entire structure shifted radically in one week." Derek also emphasized the people displaced, saying, "Every time we move the service we lose people." According to him, people leave because "their tolerance for change diminishes," and "something they highly value changes."

Changes in service times and locations accompany changes in staff structure and ministry relationships. While leadership roles emerge, they sometimes also disappear. A core leadership challenge is keeping up with people who have meaningful and fulfilling roles and making sure they transition into new roles. Derek explained,

> We're always moving services; we're always moving locations. We end up moving who's in charge of it and the leadership, and at the same time try to grow. Pastors' relationships over people that they've been with switch around. Finding who to work with is difficult. Last week I was under one; this week I'm under another. Who am I supposed to get this approved by?

The pace of change requires an active attentiveness to what is happening and how to fit in at the moment. Kevin commented,

> Shift and change really knock people off track. It even knocks me around every once in a while. What are we doing? How do I fit into that? What on earth is my role?

Kevin said, "If you're a 'wait-er' at this church, you're going to have a hard time surviving because it moves so fast." And so, according to Kevin, some leave "because they feel lost." Another respondent said that in the context of so much growth and so many leadership shifts at Mosaic, "Some people feel like they're not needed anymore."

Discovery, Development, and Deployment of Leaders

The haven for innovative people emerges from the discovery, development, and deployment of catalytic leaders who take ownership of the organization's cause. Rogers (1995:264) says that an early adopter is "generally sought by change agents as a local missionary for speeding the diffusion process. Because early adopters are too far ahead of the average individual in innovativeness, they serve as role models for many other members of a social system." In the strategic mobilization of Mosaic, those who are early adopters help to bring the entire congregation along by means of the esteem with which others regard them. Rogers explains,

> The early adopter is respected by his or her peers, and is the embodiment of the successful, discrete use of new ideas. The early adopter knows that to continue to earn the esteem of colleagues and to maintain a central position in the communication networks of the system, he or she must make judicious innovation-decisions. The early adopter decreases uncertainty about a new idea by adopting it, and then conveying a subjective evaluation of the innovation to near-peers through interpersonal networks. (264)

In short, the most important job of leaders at Mosaic is to attract other catalytic leaders, because this is an excellent way to foster a fluid organization that can pursue missional opportunities in the rapid-paced urban context of Los Angeles.

Continuous Innovation through Active Experimentation

Active experimentation became a pervasive characteristic of Mosaic with the coming of Pastor Erwin. One of the most interesting arenas of experimentation is ambiance, the creation of an aesthetically pleasing environment despite the use of rented facilities. The focus on ambiance began with the creation of Café Mosaic in 1993. Two women transformed the main auditorium from a "church sanctuary" into a "coffeehouse/living room." Plants, rugs, and vases were placed everywhere. Rows of straight chairs were suddenly and almost completely replaced with couches, beanbags, futons, love seats, and overstuffed chairs. Coffee tables and end tables were placed alongside free-standing lamps. And there were candles, lots of candles. A network of cozy spots for sitting, talking, and listening was fashioned to make the space feel more like a home than a church. Cole remembered this from his first visit to a Mosaic service:

> It wasn't like stepping into a cold building; it was like stepping into someone's living room, with the couches and the way it was set up. It had that comforting feeling. It was such a warm feeling to step into.

The arrangement became characteristic of the church as a whole in 1997. The decisive leap of creativity in transforming the "church sanctuary" to a "living room" was the result of the work of innovative lay leaders in the congregation. Martha told me, "I don't know if we had total freedom before." What changed? "It was in the year that Pastor Erwin came. . . . Pastor Erwin started preaching differently." She recalled Erwin's preaching at the time, saying, "He called us to live on the edge. Rather than just thinking what we were going to do, he called us to act on it." Martha saw that the church was now willing to create new activities and risk their failure in the pursuit of innovative projects. Church culture had shifted, and "people were now willing to take a chance."

Active experimentation keeps the organization flexible, allowing it to do whatever is needed to fulfill its mission in ever-changing circumstances. And the organization can only be flexible if its members are flexible. Crystal told me, "Mosaic is constantly pushing you to be flexible and to not get rigid and to not be able to [not] change or move forward." She added,

> If something's not working, then change it. So there's no reason to say, "It will never happen, so leave." It's moldable. It's changing all the time, so you'll never know what you're gonna get.

Crystal's comment echoes several other respondents' willingness to stay at the church because they are confident that things can change at any moment. Things they are unhappy with could be shaped more to their liking. Change is so continual that structures of ministry are considered disposable. This gives rise to the idea that Mosaic can be "customized"; if people are willing to create something that would be better for them and others, then they should do it. Listen to Zack:

> We're very sensitive to the Spirit, but at the same time very sensitive to people. If people aren't growing or if something just isn't working, then we're very quick to say, "Okay, that's not working; let's get something that is working." It's not so much a change in learning from our faults: "Oh, man, we really messed up, and we need to change this." It's more, "All right, the tide is shifting. Let's go over here now. That's where the light is right now. That's where the wind is blowing. This is where the action is, over here. We're going in the wrong direction." That kind of change.

Change as described by Zack is not reactive but proactive, even opportunistic. Any change that allows the goals of the church to be accomplished is encouraged.

For Kevin, the distinctive marker of a person at Mosaic is change. He described this as meaning "that you're willing to change, that you're willing to take on radical new things and move in completely different directions just in order to follow Jesus." The phrase "in order to follow Jesus" is important. Judging from the words of Kevin and others, change at Mosaic always means following the dynamic leadership of Jesus, who is perceived to be living and active, moving from one situation to another. Trevor told me, "Every other conversation is about how somebody's been called to do this, and they're going to do that," and added, "God says to them, 'I'm putting you on this path,' and they say, 'Yes, I'm going at it whatever the cost.' " Several respondents mentioned the personal discomfort that this willingness can give rise to. Listen to Paul, a twenty-five-year-old Chinese American:

> There's no sense of stagnancy about Mosaic. That really drew me. That made me say, "This place is going to rub me the wrong way. I'm not going to be comfortable here. It's going to force me to open up into things that I would not be forced to do if I was someplace else." And that was it. Once that conclusion had been drawn in my head, I wasn't going any place else.

People introduce change personally and corporately out of a sense that God has spurred them in a particular direction.

In recent years, new arenas for dance, the visual arts, and cross-cultural ministries have provided opportunities to create without the "burden" of tradition. These opportunities were created by innovative leaders within the congregation. Abby, a young Korean American, and others emphasized the receptivity of full-time staff to creative input, exclaiming, "Wow, leaders are just open to new ideas." Lindsey said, "If someone has an idea, share it; you have it, then share it. I like that." Dave, a longtime member and now pastoral staff, talked about his early efforts at building a drama ministry, saying, "We started expanding into areas of ministry that the church didn't have a history with, so there weren't any 'we've never done it that way's." Crystal said, "Mosaic leadership looks to the future instead of staying in the past, so it's not all about tradition, and it's not all about 'this is how we do it' and 'this is how it's always been done.' " Leaders able to take initiatives that move the church into the future are embraced; often these initiatives allow a complete side-stepping of tradition.

Introducing the Catalytic Leader

Most activities are organized under three-person leadership teams consisting of a pastor, an assimilator, and a catalyst. At Mosaic these leadership titles are more important than ethnic labels. These three roles encompass specific leadership functions. Pastors are concerned with personal care and counseling. Assimilators are logistically oriented, primarily concerned with communication, proper placement of people into ministry teams, and follow-up of guests and those who indicate a desire to talk more about Jesus, be baptized, join a small group, or become Mosaic members. Catalysts, however, focus on their fervent commitment to bringing people into "a relationship with Jesus." The triad structure is intended to make sure all aspects of church leadership (i.e., pastoral care, logistical organization, innovative evangelistic ventures) are addressed, since few individuals can take on all three roles simultaneously. Its unintended result has been to legitimize the catalytic element of leadership and introduce fluidity, innovation, and change in a formerly hierarchical structure. Instead of paid church staff shaking up a rigid system whenever change was necessary, this triadic structure provides internal forces of continual change, and catalysts embedded in the organizational structure of the church provide sympathetic ears to innovations whenever they are introduced by full-time staff. Catalytic leaders at Mosaic affirm Foster's (1997) conclusion that multiethnic congregations are characterized by transformative rather than managerial leadership; they are focused on nurturing change in the congregation, not maintaining the status quo.

Catalysts are those who are especially effective in bringing non-Christian people to church and inspiring others in evangelism. Catalysts are the most action-oriented leaders at Mosaic, expressing the church's urgency in evangelistic outreach. They solve problems and seek opportunities for outreach, with the practical result that the church grows. Catalysts are those most explicitly affirmed, given influence, and held out as models for others. Erwin has called catalytic leaders "Alka-Seltzer," comparing the fizzy bubbles filling the water to the influence that catalysts have on their social networks. Catalysts are the innovators and thus often the most disruptive of effective organizational functioning. Catalysts focus on whatever people or projects serve their goals best, and that focus often conflicts with the assimilator's ideal of smooth organizational structures or the pastor's burden of caring for the overwhelming personal needs of Christians.

Catalytic Leaders and the Promotion of Catalytic Change

Through catalytic leaders, Mosaic can utilize the strategy of "audience segmentation" (Rogers, 1995:275), so that the most innovation-friendly people get information on changes first. Catalysts are then mobilized to communicate the news through their relational networks before any public announcements are made to the congregation as a whole. "The opinion leader's interpersonal networks allow him or her to serve as a social model whose innovative behavior is imitated by many other members of the system" (Rogers, 1995:27). The annual Leadership Advance is the most prominent example. Held over a weekend, this meeting introduces new plans, goals, or initiatives for the year, which are given to the leadership base of the church before being announced to the wider congregation. Sometimes direct communication is targeted to these catalytic leaders and further communication of changes occurring in the church is left entirely up to the informal effort of these leaders. This is what happened after the September 11, 2001, terrorist attack, when three different homes were opened across L.A. County for prayer gatherings. Informing people of the times and locations of the gatherings was left entirely up to the informal networks. This communication strategy is comparable to the "two-step flow model," in which information is communicated to opinion leaders, and these leaders in turn communicate it to the slower-moving, less attentive members of the population (Lazarsfeld and Menzel, 1963:96; Lazarsfeld, Berelson, and Gaudet, 1968.) It also reflects Max Weber's (1978: 48–49) characterization of organizations as consisting of a class of leaders he calls staff at the core, who lead a larger class of people in the rest of the organization. While this two-step flow is not an efficient mode of communication, it seems to be effective enough at Mosaic, since news of significant shifts, such as changes in celebration service locations, new expenditures, bids on property, staff changes, and so on, is disseminated through the congregation relatively quickly through these less formalized networks.

The influence of catalytic leaders is consciously leveraged by Mosaic leadership in order to incorporate different ethnic groups. For example, David, the creative arts director, consciously tries to keep the public platform of Mosaic diversified. "Obviously, I'm valued [as a Hispanic] because I'm up there," he said, and then added, "I want Asians when they walk in to feel valued by this church." He went on to discuss how other ethnic groups were also included and represented on the platform "instead of just being taught here by the white men, or be [used as] entertainment by them." David was quick to say that he did not want to exclude white people ("I want Caucasians to feel the same thing"); he is motivated to bring diversity to the platform so that all those who experience the celebration service will feel like they belong. Does that mean he compromises on the quality of talent? He related an experience:

> I remember somebody coming up to me and saying they felt like a token, and I said, "No, if you weren't talented, you would be a token. You actually *have* talent, and so I'm making my judgment based on that. But I'm not afraid to tell you that I use you because you're Asian over someone who is Caucasian because of your ethnicity, because I want this representation here, and because I have this value."

Beyond the platform, Erwin took the role of lead pastor with the goal of diversifying the leadership of the church in every arena. "I consciously found people who were different minority expressions and put them in leadership. As soon as I found people, I would try to highlight them and bring them up." Thus, conscientious efforts, not only by Erwin in hiring paid staff but also by team leaders in lay ministries, have served to diversify the leadership. Catalytic leaders from different ethnic backgrounds have made it possible for more people to find affinity with the core leadership of the church.

The power of these catalytic leaders is affirmed by research on the nature of homophilous and heterophilous networks (Lazarsfeld and Merton, 1964; see also Tarde, 1969). Homophily describes the degree to which people are similar; heterophily, the degree to which they are different. Research has demonstrated that people in heterophilous communication networks seek opinion leaders who are more innovative (Rao, Rogers, and Singh, 1980; Rogers, 1995:286–290). The heterophily of Mosaic's communication networks contributes to its structural embrace of innovative leaders. Certainly the multiethnic nature of Mosaic alone would characterize the organization as heterophilous. Moreover, in heterophilous communication networks, people seek opinion leaders who are more cosmopolitan and more exposed to mass media; as discussed in chapter 4, Mosaic has many ties to the Los Angeles entertainment industry. Catalytic leaders provide an organizational base for promoting change in the church. How are these catalytic leaders discovered?

Questions in Search of Catalytic Leaders

Two core questions are commonly asked to draw out catalytic leaders. These questions are "Will you fix it?" and "What is your passion?" These two questions, asked both by the organization and by individuals, move catalysts to take responsibility for accomplishing congregational objectives. The first question solicits help in arenas recognized as needing improvement, and the second assesses not only what people desire most but also how urgently they will work to fulfill it.

"Will You Fix It?"

Mosaic prompts catalytic leadership by asking, "Will you fix it?" At Mosaic, every imperfection is an invitation to participate. On his first visit, Zack thought about how the music could be improved. "I remember this overwhelming [thought], 'Gosh, they could have done that with that song.'" He told me that he perceived an attitude of "Instead of just complaining about it, if you can do it better, we need you to make it better." Now Zack leads one of the bands and has written several songs used in the celebration services. Other respondents had similar stories of helping Mosaic create things in arenas they saw as weak. When people suggest that something should be done a particular way, they are invited to take responsibility and make it happen. "Maybe God is calling *you* to do that" is the comment. Some people may be hesitant to complain because, as Crystal said, "If I complain about something or say that something should exist, I might be in charge of it. So I'm careful *not* to complain, because if I do, I might be the head of it." Others I spoke with see this expectation as reasonable. As Adam shared, "If it's clumsy, well, okay, then you make it better." The result is that congregants either get on board and begin solving problems, or they back down and say that it's not their responsibility. So Mosaic members feel that problems are not the fault of leadership but rather of people in the congregation who have failed to "step up" to the need.

Conversely, when people have the impression that things are running smoothly, they are reluctant to volunteer. Paige, who directed an evening service for several months, is not serving anywhere now. Although she is busy with the production company she recently founded, essentially she is not involved because she doesn't see anything that needs to be fixed. She said to me,

If I'm not needed, I don't have time because other people need me doing other things. And I'm not needed right now. There are a million people in tech doing what I used to do. They have enough people doing it.

Many respondents like Paige indicated that ownership of ministry projects comes when the need is significant enough to justify taking time and energy out of a very active life.

"What Is Your Passion?"

Mosaic does not have a list of open ministry positions; no listing could summarize the various interests people bring with them. Rather, out of relationships and dialogue in project-oriented teams, leaders get to know people in order to understand their distinctive contributions to the church. Crystal told me that this is often not the case in other churches:

> When [another] church tries to get people to fit a need, they're not basing it on whether that's a passion of that person or whether they would enjoy doing it. Instead of looking at their strengths, seeing where they would be good, placing them there, and letting that flourish, they end up stuffing people into all the areas they need. And it doesn't work very well. People get angry and burnt out and bitter. They feel pressured to get into something. "You need to serve, so serve here," and it's the church forcing a service onto people when they should be serving from their heart, from what they're good at and what they're passionate about.

In asking people what their passions are, Mosaic seeks to draw out enthusiastic leaders who will sacrificially give themselves to pursuing their dreams and, simultaneously, accomplish the mission of the church. Tapping into people's passions is a primary way of motivating them to become involved with the congregation. In much the same way, in the current business climate companies appeal to intrinsic motivation rather than simply money. Eric Raymond, a successful software engineer, says, "You cannot motivate the best people with money.... The best people in any field are motivated by passion" (quoted in Taylor, 1999:200; see also Raymond, 1999). Talking with Dylan about music, with Trevor about film, and with Charles about painting, I found many examples of how Mosaic utilizes the internal motivation that people bring into the ministry to channel them into activities that support the values and mission of the church. Zack told me,

What's kept me here is when I look at the gifts that God's gifted me with and the level that I truly desire to carry out these gifts, I see they can only be reached here at Mosaic. [. . .] Mosaic encourages me to use these gifts and take them as far as I want.

The encouragement to live out their passions is what has kept Zack and others in the congregation.

Initiative and resourcefulness in pursuit of a passion are rewarded at Mosaic. Kevin, a college student, said, "Leaders are willing to change for my idea if I run with it." Leadership tends to be rewarded with more leadership. In 1994, Charles began working with Christian artists. While his personal vision was "starting fires, letting people know that people could use their talents to propel the kingdom of God," it wasn't until 1997 that Erwin McManus approached him and other artists about using their skills in the church. Charles said,

I totally felt it was God-designed . . . to see Christians and non-Christians mingle in the same forum because it was comfortable for non-Christians, and then through that process they could become believers. And that's the main goal.

Charles began networking with artists who might work on projects for the Sunday services, the Lord's Supper celebrations, and church-sponsored conferences. These projects involved a tremendous amount of time and some measure of artistic talent. His networking included friends and co-workers who were not professing Christians, yet they were willing to help complete an artistic project. Dedicated artists found their place in the ministry of Mosaic. In 2000, Charles joined an artistic team painting a mural for a coffee house in the Middle East run by missionaries to reach young adults. Overseas workers are now inviting artistic teams to join them in other parts of the world. In 2002, Charles and his wife were commissioned as overseas missionaries, called to use their artistic passions to evangelize outside the United States.

The shift from program-driven to passion-driven ministry is recent at Mosaic. Before Pastor Erwin's leadership, people would serve in ministry as they were needed and "moonlight" in their areas of passion. For example, Dave arrived in the late 1970s with a theater and arts background and is a central figure in all of the artistic activity at Mosaic: "I envisioned God doing amazing things through the arts, drama and dance and music and all of that, with a kingdom direction, which I had never seen any local church connect together."

But he did not get involved in the arts right away. According to

Dave, when the church leadership of the time heard his vision, they said, "Okay, that sounds interesting. Any *other* interests or skills?" He told them he enjoyed teaching. They informed him that the church had "a very pointed need" in junior high ministry. "Now I already made it clear where my heart was, where my passion was, but that's where the church had a need." He committed to working with students for the next seven years, "because that's what the local church needed." In the beginning, Dave's contribution in dramatic arts was not so much encouraged as merely allowed. Dave wrote, acted, sang, composed, directed, produced, built sets, purchased materials, and, almost single-handedly, mentored an entire congregation in theater arts over the next ten years. "All of the drama and the staging and the sets and the costuming and the props were all done in house," he reported. What began as a side project alongside his assigned ministry became one of the greatest strengths of the church. Similar stories came from other long-time members. Sam, for example, was in a rock and roll band. His heart was in music, but the need was in preschool. So he served in preschool in the morning, but, as he told me, "I would do worship in the evening too." Mosaic has shifted from mobilizing primarily around need to inviting people to participate on the basis of their passion.

Longtime leaders at Mosaic have seen the leadership base of the church expand in scope and have come to expect new ministries that reflect the new skills and interests brought into the church by new catalytic leaders. Molly summarized this in saying, "I honestly believe that if you come with gifts and talents and you're ready to use them, then Pastor Erwin will put you in place." Luis, Hispanic and a longtime member, also said people are systematically asked about their passions: "Is it poetry? Is it singing? Is it dancing? Is it skits? A play?" For Joseph, a leader in the Ensenada business team who has had other leadership roles in the congregation, pursuing one's passions is at the heart of the church. "Pastor Erwin really teaches us to step out and pursue our dreams. I never thought Christians were allowed to do that." Joseph spoke confidently about the way Mosaic encourages people to participate according to their passions. "I know that if I wanted to do something, and if God really touched my heart, that I have an opportunity there." He stated that the purpose of full-time staff is not to create things; instead, "Mosaic's responsibility is to help the people create." Full-time staff at Mosaic support initiatives brought by catalytic leaders for projects that contribute to the mission of the church.

Catalytic Networks of Influence

I found catalytic leaders to be rich in relational networks. Catalysts use relational influence to accomplish church goals, and they occupy the center of Mosaic's social networks. Rogers (1965:27) states that "[t]he most striking characteristic of opinion leaders is their unique and influential position in their system's communication structure. They are at the center of interpersonal communication networks." The fact that Mosaic's ministries are relational and project oriented requires innovation-friendly opinion leaders to act as network nodes, guiding and shaping activities.

Rather than imposing a positional leader on a team, Mosaic tries to identify the informal relational leader and formalize that role. This fits with Foster's observation (1997) that leaders in multiethnic congregations are relational rather than paternalistic. This pattern of singling out and promoting relational leaders is particularly evident in the actions of small group leaders. Small group leaders are constantly assessing their group's members, identifying those who are bringing in new people and building healthy relationships with others, and recruiting them to take on functions of leadership. They will be asked to facilitate group meetings, and their group leaders will spend time with them, finding out where they stand in relation to the values and objectives of Mosaic. If necessary, the leaders will spend time in dialogue, alternately teaching and persuading, to guide them to Mosaic's positions on various key issues. If all goes well, they are asked to become co-leaders and, eventually, take a few people and start a new group.

Harnessing Catalysts

Finally, catalytic leadership is channeled through expectations regarding the character of a dedicated follower of Jesus Christ. One of the distinguishing marks of Erwin's teaching is his understanding of character development. For Erwin, "character" has a specific meaning, which he has articulated in a developmental flow-chart (see McManus, 2003). The essence of the model is that dedicated followers of Jesus Christ move from self-centeredness to servanthood.

All members of the congregation understand that leaders must pass certain tests of character. Mosaic requires, at a minimum, evidence of humility, faithfulness, and gratitude in people's lives before giving them influence in congregational leadership. Eric shared that this is one reason why some Christians who have had leadership in other churches have left, saying, "They start to move in our process and want influence over people, and we don't give them those opportunities based on character." Humility encourages potentially disruptive leaders to be responsible to the leadership of the church. The willingness to submit to authority is essential if decentralized, highly empowered leaders are to be governed within the project-oriented structure of Mosaic.

Since catalytic leaders are entrusted with influence over people, pastoral leadership seeks to ensure that they see ministry as serving others rather than themselves. Brooke asserted,

> I don't feel like my character was ever addressed until I got here and I saw people who led by their character. They may not have had what people consider to be outward leadership abilities like very charismatic or whatever, but they led through their character, and . . . it was very selfless.

Other multiethnic churches also concentrate on such attitudes toward leadership. In particular, Foster (1997:123) described humility as an essential quality for leaders in multiethnic churches. For Foster, humility promotes understanding between people of different cultural backgrounds and avoids attitudes of exploitation.

Ministry and recruitment in the creative arts ministry show how humility, faithfulness, and gratitude are promoted and measured among artists. An artist who desires to be on the platform (performing music, dance, or drama) first participates in ministry activities offstage, working behind the scenes. A singer will work in tech, set-up, administration, or some other area before singing on stage. These labors promote humility by requiring would-be performers to put the needs of the community before their own ego. They promote faithfulness by requiring people to work steadily and follow through with their assigned tasks. And they promote generosity by assigning people jobs that highlight others rather than themselves. Overall, potential leaders earn the respect of their peers, and thus influence, by demonstrating servanthood in their collaborative work on these projects.

Mosaic's focus on character includes attention to honesty, authenticity, acceptance, and openness. For example, people are encouraged to recognize their "brokenness." Brokenness signifies that they are not perfect, but carry with them hurts, difficulties, and unresolved conflicts. This recognition of their own brokenness nurtures integrity among catalytic leaders so that they will not fail to address potentially disruptive behaviors within themselves, which would risk invalidating the legitimacy of their spiritual leadership. Brooke moved from Mississippi to Los Angeles, and found the emphasis on character at Mosaic to be very different from that in the Southern Baptist culture she came from. Mosaic had an honesty and vulnerability that was unknown to her: "I thought, 'Why are you telling me all of this? This is really personal.' And they were just like, 'Pass the potatoes, and I'm an alcoholic.' I was blown away by the lack of fear to be real." In her first year at Mosaic, "Sin issues came up in my life . . . and I was terrified because my concept was you don't share what's wrong with you because then that makes you less valuable." Her leaders "saw some of the deepest brokenness in me that I had spent years trying to hide." One night, they set up a meeting with her. In anticipation of a bad result, she had already packed and called U-Haul, ready to move back home:

> I remember leaving that meeting just crying [. . .] I expected to be scolded, and excommunicated, and to become the church's gossip. I was astounded. [. . .] They acknowledged that I messed up, but they still loved me. And I felt that, and it wasn't about being perfect. And I remember thinking that as hard as this may be, if somebody can love me after this, then why would I leave this place?

While not everyone survives an intensive focus on personal character, those who do, like Brooke, show a great loyalty to Mosaic and give themselves deeply to the church. In several other instances, people have worked through similar processes and have channeled their energies to fulfilling congregational objectives.

Diversification and Innovation through Catalytic Leaders

Dedicated followers of Jesus Christ are cultivated among the ethnically diverse population of Los Angeles partly by progressively involving people in congregational activities, until they take ownership of Mosaic's goals and purposes. Mosaic centers communication, project activities, and influence on catalytic leaders. These leaders take ownership of the church's mission and cultivate communities to embrace and work toward that mission. Catalytic leaders are culled out from the congregation by asking people about their passions and their willingness to help fix problems they perceive. Informal leaders are often called into leadership so that leadership can be essentially relational rather than positional.

Catalytic leaders from various ethnic backgrounds are empowered to carry out Mosaic's goals by supervising diverse, creative, engaging activities that continue to draw even more people into its organizational sphere. The next section will describe how Mosaic fits the emerging culture in a way that promotes the overall youthfulness of the congregation.

6

MOSAIC AND THE EMERGING

AMERICAN CULTURE:

A RECONSTRUCTION OF

AN INSTITUTION

DEREK: The thing that attracted me when I first came was that the church places a value on twenty- and thirty-year-olds and gives them a chance at responsibility towards leadership. Other churches just wouldn't.

DELA: For me, age is more important than race. In a lot of black churches, there aren't a lot of young people. But Pastor Erwin says things that really relate to people in their twenties; the whole service does.

Through experimentation, Mosaic has become a church appealing to the cultural framework of a new generation. The flow of people in and out in the past few years reversed the age hierarchy found in most churches. Mosaic is a congregation primarily composed of young adults, because Mosaic appeals to an emerging culture most represented in younger cohorts. Mosaic succeeds because spiritual leaders tap into changing ethnic demographics, a desire for active religious participation, the rise of creativity-based occupations in the region, and people's recognition that change is an essential aspect of everyday life. The activities and beliefs of Mosaic create an age haven, a set of beliefs and practices attractive to a younger generation.

This age haven did not always exist. When the "Mosaic" Sunday night service, aimed at young adult singles, started, several influential college leaders protested against moving their worship service from Sunday morning to Sunday night. They said they didn't want to be involved in a service focused on younger people. Consequently, no one from the college ministry attended. Nevertheless, attendance at the new service grew rapidly over the next six months, from twenty to over three hundred people. Younger college-age people were gaining more and more influence in the congregation. Soon both morning and evening services began attracting more young collegians.

These young collegians formed a new young adult ministry. At that time, the "college" ministry was really more of a "postcollege" ministry. Half of the leaders had graduated some years before. Many were fifth- and sixth-year students slowly making their way through the system. Several had quit college and gone to work, with no immediate plan of returning. The college ministry had become a close-knit social group, aging together, and most of the new, young collegians and high school seniors in the church did not get involved. I remember one college student, a twenty-one-year-old Hispanic, who was pressured by several in the college ministry to join a college small group. He was adamant that he wanted to remain in the young adult ministry. "I'm not like them," he would say, noting that most in the college ministry were older and many were not even enrolled in classes. He and his girlfriend instead started a new young adult small group. Several more sprang up, with leaders who were around twenty, several years younger than those in the college ministry. College ministry leaders realized that their intended ministry was happening in another section of the church. The college ministry eventually merged with the young adult ministries in 1998.

The church kept growing younger. By 2001, the Mosaic service had drawn so many people in their twenties that the entire church became a young adult ministry. In less than five years, the congregation changed from predominantly middle-aged marrieds, with some older singles, to predominantly young adult singles, with an increasing number of married younger couples.

Exploring Mosaic's Age Haven

The average age of visitors to Mosaic's celebration services is twenty-six, and 80 to 90 percent of them are twenty-five or younger. The average age is at least two to four years lower at the Urban Mosaic evening service, held in a nightclub in downtown Los Angeles. My respondents accept as obvious that Mosaic is a young congregation. Joseph observed that since 1998 "the new people that are coming are young people. [...] That's what really makes us unique: the youth." One senior adult and longtime member simply stated, "We've become more youth oriented." The youthfulness of the congregation is a publicly recognized aspect of the church and part of the context of all of my discussions of Mosaic.

Shelters Young Adults Escaping Churches Dominated by "Old People"

I noticed that whites like Jamie frequently discussed being tired of traditional, white churches run by older generations. Jamie said that Mosaic "wasn't a church of a lot of old white people." She contrasted it with her previous church, saying, "That was nice, and it was a good time, but there was only so much time I could spend being a grandchild." Similarly, Brian described how he and his wife, both Caucasian, were pleasantly surprised at the number of young couples like them at Mosaic, saying, "It was great; we met mostly people our own age." Their first friends in the church invited them out for dinner, and they continued attending Mosaic from that night forward.

Blake, an African American, told me that more blacks are "coming from the massive upwelling of young people because more and more African Americans, young African Americans, are basically coming with their friends." Blake told me young African Americans are "much more multicultural" and that "they tend to be bonded and have friends that cross cultural boundaries." So in Blake's assessment, African Americans come because they are younger. "It's all about the age group, because there's nothing in Mosaic that even says 'black,' culturally speaking."

Young people at Mosaic are looking for relationships with people their age and for opportunities to get involved, to contribute, to have their voices heard. They spend less time complaining about older people and more time talking about their own hopes and ambitions. Zack, a twenty-six-year-old Caucasian, told me,

Mosaic encourages me to use these gifts and to encourage me to take them as far as I want. [. . .] I don't know of any other church that lets [young people] write or act or do music or write music and have it be heard and bless people.

Full-time salaried staff members who had been at Mosaic for a long time said that it was Pastor Erwin's leadership that led to young adults' being given so much responsibility. One woman said he took risks to bring on younger people who were not seminary-trained and were less experienced leaders. "He went with his intuition," she remarked. Tony said that for most of his twenty years at the church "leaders had to be 'spiritually mature,' and that meant older people." Now, he said, "[y]ou don't have to be in your thirties and forties; you can be a part of something right away. Before you felt like you used to have to prove yourself; now, you can do it right away." The willingness to allow young adults to have responsibility is part of what made it possible for artists and dancers to become part of Mosaic's public expression. According to Tony, if that willingness had not existed, Mosaic probably would not have a dance ministry, a visual arts group, or many of the other creative projects in which young adults of the congregation are so important today.

DETERS PEOPLE WHO FEEL THE CHURCH IS TOO YOUTH ORIENTED

The "youth orientation" of Mosaic deters people who see it as marginalizing older adults. A senior adult explains, "The feeling was that things are going to the youth, and older people that had once been the leaders were being discarded." Peggy told me her concern:

What I'm not comfortable with, and it isn't only me but other people who are also in the same age bracket that I am in—I'm fifty-one—is that the emphasis seems to be on the younger people, and the older ones, it almost feels like they're being pushed aside. And I have heard that from other people.

One senior adult said that older people "felt they were just there and that nobody really cared."

Respondents often discussed age and music together. One senior adult told me that older people have left the congregation specifically because of the music. Carl said that "some of the really good specials are overwhelmed by the band. You can't hear. It might be a beautiful song, but you don't know that. That's—well, you're talking to the old guys now." Besides being loud, Carl believed, the content of the music was becoming "less reverent." In his view, "The music is a little rhyme, a single verse sung five or six times." Clara added, "We're speaking on behalf of the senior group. They have been yearning for a hymn for years. Just *any* hymn." The way that music is performed on the platform can be offensive to some senior adults. One senior adult said to me, "It's kind of irreverent when the leader yelps and jumps. There are other churches where people are dancing in the aisles and listen to that, but I don't think that's for us." Another senior adult talked about an evening of artistry and musical performance held at the church. The crowd was rowdy, the atmosphere more like that of a concert:

> [W]hen we went last time, there was a group of people sitting together who were fans of one particular person on the stage. They were calling out that name and yelling from their seats. Nobody, *nobody* went to them and asked them to please be quiet that I could see. We had to move over on the other side. Why isn't there somebody taking charge? Why are we becoming that kind of a church? Because I'm sure that's not something anybody wants, including the pastor. So, I don't know what happened that night, but I'm afraid to go to the next one because I don't want to go to that sort of thing where people are out of control in the church.

A flamboyant musical style, exuberant performances, and interaction with the crowd seem to engage younger people, but distress at least some of the older adults and keep them away from such events.

One staff member described the music and atmosphere of performances at special events as an aspect of Mosaic's responsiveness to the young adults already coming to the church. As he sees it, Mosaic accentuates the aspects of the ministry that appeal to the group that is coming in the largest numbers, and that group is currently young adults in their twenties and thirties. "I think many times we make decisions based on who's being reached. We're not reaching fifty-year-olds." He conceded that "we've suffered in some ways in terms of reaching families," and added that this was "because our priorities are reaching L.A. What we see in L.A. as our niche turns out to be young adults, many of whom are single. And that group is very [ethnically] diverse." Because Mosaic effectively reaches single young adults, it concentrates on areas and forms that appeal to them.

The irony of age is that complaints about being too "youth oriented" have come from people still in their twenties. Adam originally connected to Mosaic through the Sunday evening nightclub service, but has since moved to Sunday morning. "When they start talking about their majors, that's when I'm outta there." For him and others, Urban Mosaic has become *too* young. Lindsey said, "I'm getting to feeling like I'm too old for Mosaic." She feels marginalized especially in the Sunday evening service:

> I feel like everyone's getting young. When I started going to Urban, I wasn't a college student. I'm giving my age away; I've been out of school for a few years. I'm twenty-nine, but honestly it seems like most of the people are nineteen, twenty, and twenty-one. So maybe there isn't that big a difference between twenty-one and twenty-seven, but it seems like the college mentality.

Abby, Korean American, shared similar thoughts, saying, "Since I'm getting older, Urban is getting younger. It's weird being the old person in the group. I'm, like, I'm only twenty-eight; I don't like being the old person in the group." I have spoken with others in their late twenties, both single and married, who have moved from the evening service to the morning service because Urban is "too young." So the youth orientation that initially attracted young adults to Urban Mosaic can be distressing as they get older and the downtown nightclub site continues to attract people of the same age. Attenders who connected to Mosaic through the Urban service and are moving into their early thirties are not choosing to leave Mosaic; instead, they are shifting into the Sunday morning service where the age range is broader. Aging singles find other single adults there, and young couples having their first child are finding programs for children during the celebration services. The orientation of the church has not changed, but their concerns have.

Not every person over thirty is put off by the youthfulness of the congregation. Many older adults, while standing outside of the youth culture, appreciate the energy and participation of young adults in the church. When I asked Miwako, a seventy-six-year-old Japanese American, if the congregation was too youth oriented, she said, "I love it. I think it is great. My friends love it too." And while Peggy was critical of the church's youth orientation, she valued young adults' taking on important roles and responsibilities:

> Personally, I think that, like anything, you can't stagnate. You've got to bring people in; you have to reach the very young ones. That's why we invest in children: because these children are going to grow, and they're going to come in, and they're going to take over.

And so she explained that while she is uncomfortable with a youth orientation that may seem to exclude those who are older, she is not against having younger people in the church taking responsibility and leadership in the congregation. She described her admiration for the young adults, saying, "The wonderful thing about the younger crowd is that they're so lively. It's just animated. It's a wonderful, wonderful creative group, and I'm very comfortable when I see that."

Reversing the Age Hierarchy

What makes Mosaic so predominantly young? Mosaic's youthfulness is a result of factors operating both inside and outside the church. Among the internal factors is the fact that young people remained in the congregation while older ones left. "We kept the kids but lost their parents," said one member. In addition, more young people arrived. Such dynamics are similar to those described by theorists of organizational demography and internal labor market flow. The external factors involve broad cultural trends in taste, opinion, and income and spending among different age cohorts. Mosaic reflects and concentrates on cultural patterns that appeal more strongly to the younger generation.

Intra-organizational Departures and Promotions

The most important factor in reversing the church's age hierarchy was the opening of vacancies in the first five years of Pastor Erwin's leadership. Between 1993 and 1998, five (over half) of the full-time staff, two (one-third) of the elders, and at least a dozen significant lay leaders were commissioned to initiate new church-planting ministries, both locally and overseas. Moreover, when Brother Phil left in 1998, many members and attenders left as well. This created many vacancies in such areas as small groups, overseas missions, music, sound, tech, and multimedia. Pastor Erwin and other ministry leaders had an opportunity to place new people into places of influence. They filled these empty slots predominantly with young adults in their twenties. For example, a well-respected twenty-nine-year-old leader on his way to the mission field with his family became the youngest elder in the history of the congregation. Although young, he and the other new leaders were not necessarily new to the congregation. Elders and those hired as full-time paid staff had at least three years of experience in and around the church and were thoroughly committed to the ideological orientation of the congregation.

At the same time as existing ministry positions were being filled, new positions were created. New ministry projects explicitly recruited young adults. The most important new initiative was the creation in 1997 of the Sunday night Mosaic service, run by a team of people in their twenties (except for one woman in her thirties). Almost all attenders were in their twenties and thirties, and many came from west of downtown Los Angeles. Attendance surged. This service became the seed of the downtown nightclub service, which became another magnet for young adults.

The 1997 Genesis series also created many volunteer positions and allowed young adults to get involved, invite friends, and create experiences that would appeal to people "just like them." Pastor Erwin and David Arcos, the creative arts director, called every writer, dancer, actor, painter, and any other creative artist available to a special weekend meeting at Pastor Erwin's home. Over eighty people came, most in their twenties, and most not members of the congregation. Pastor Erwin shared his idea for the sermon series, which would use metaphors drawn from nature to describe theological principles and spiritual living. The metaphors of wind, water, wood, fire, and earth became a playground of creativity. The group brainstormed, planned, and designed material for the celebration services on the spot; what they created that day became dramas, videos, and original music for the whole year. Several of these artists became team leaders for this year-long project. Although the church already had a dance ministry, started by a physical therapist, the Genesis series galvanized a group of professional dancers, all in their twenties, into becoming a committed core team. A new band was formed, made up mostly of twenty-year-olds, that played rock and roll and alternative rock, appealing to a younger age base. And a new group of young writers were brought together to construct a series of sketches supporting Genesis's overarching themes.

The sermon series initiated a more intensive use of multimedia technology in the services, which automatically reduced the age of the tech-oriented ministry teams that create and support the celebration services behind the scenes. Stan, an elder of the congregation, said, "Commitment to technology means commitment to a younger age." Multimedia ministry attracted young adults interested in computers and electronic equipment. Incorporating multimedia technology in the celebration services also attracted more young adult attenders. Carroll and Roof (2002:80) write that generations after the baby boom "are much more likely to be involved in a congregation that makes use of media such as popular music, video, and art, thereby offering culturally current and engaging opportunities for sharing and worship." At Mosaic, this is as true of those who run the equipment as it is of those who enjoy multimedia in the celebration services.

The flow of staff and leaders at Mosaic reflects the observations of organizational demographers (Brüderl, Preisendörfer, and Ziegler, 1993; Rosenbaum, 1981, 1984; Stewman, 1988; Stewman and Konda, 1983). Organizations are often seen as hierarchical pyramids, but this is not the best way to understand the mobility and promotion of people within them. Instead, the probability of an individual's promotion depends on the number of available jobs, which attributes managers prefer among those whom they promote, and the degree to which the individual displays those attributes in comparison with competitors. Specifically, the departure of staff and the creation of jobs in response to organizational growth initiate a chain reaction of promotions (see Chase, 1990; White, 1970) and bring new people into the organization. Staff departures and rapid growth have the potential to radically alter the age structure of an organization, especially when leadership prefers to hire younger people. At Mosaic, those leaving were mostly middle-aged, ranging from mid-thirties to fifties. Many of them were leaders with formal positions in the congregation. Those arriving were younger, ranging from early twenties to mid-thirties. These movements I summarize as two simultaneous flows: first, vacancies created by the departure of older adults were filled by young adults in the congregation, and, second, new positions created by Pastor Erwin and other ministry leaders were also filled by young adults.

Ultimately, 1997 saw the creation of a new internal culture which oriented Mosaic's theological framework still more on creativity, innovation, and young leadership. As church projects grew in size and complexity over the year, they served to recruit yet more young adults. Most new people found the church through friends, but others discovered it through rumors in evangelical circles of this "cool" church. Ministry involvement gave many young adults new relationships, opportunities to learn about the congregation "backstage," and ownership of congregational goals. Activities that happened "behind the curtain" gave many unchurched young adults suspicious about the nature of "church" a chance to see how the congregation exercised their beliefs, and to determine their true level of authenticity. Volunteer opportunities were given to those who had not made an explicit commitment as followers of Jesus, and their contributions were increasingly welcomed. These opportunities to engage people were leveraged by spiritual leaders, who used them to urge people to reorient their identity around the church's mission.

A Church for an Emerging Culture

Beyond the intra-organizational factors that promoted younger people into arenas of influence and responsibility, several extra-organizational trends contribute to making Mosaic predominantly young. The church's public activities in 1998 placed ever more value on relevance to popular culture. Derek, along with several others in the congregation, told me Mosaic changes because "there are cultural changes. We want to be relevant. We're following our core values." Acting on these values, young adults were encouraged to create art forms and activities that would appeal to people they knew from work and school. Mosaic co-opts elements of culture that appeal to younger ages. Some observers of Protestantism, like Laurence Moore in *Selling God* (1994), are critical of such co-optation and see it as an attempt by churches to compete in the marketplace for survival. Lyon (2000:85) observes that "Protestantism . . . learned early to make strategic concessions to cultural developments, such as the use of drama or music hall tunes." At Mosaic, the drive for relevance is less a reactive attempt merely to survive as a church, and more a strategic, proactive effort to co-opt and then influence the culture as a whole. In this section, I highlight four trends with which this congregation connects: ethnic diversification, religious individuation, the rise of the "creative class," and the increased pace of social change.

ETHNIC DIVERSIFICATION AND THE NEED FOR PERSONAL IDENTITY

Ethnic identity will certainly become more diverse and complex in the future. According to Root (1996), the number of biracial children is increasing faster than the number of single-race children. The increased heterogeneity of ethnic designations and the increasing number of multiracial children also mean that constructing an ethnic identity will become increasingly problematic. Everyday categories of race and ethnicity are already unsatisfactory among social scientists seeking to understand children of mixed heritage (Christian, 2000; Debose and Winters, 2002; Parker and Song, 2002; Root, 1992; P. Spickard, 1991) and among the children themselves (Arboleda, 1998; Chideya, 1999; Gaskins, 1999; Kaeser and Gillespie, 1997). The designation most often used today is "multiracial," and both the number of people who are working through the meaning of this identity and the number of groups advocating rights for multiracial people is increasing (Wijeyesinghe, 2001). Much research presents the conflicts and ambiguities of having a multiracial identity (Philip Brown, 1980; Gibbs, 1997; Logan, Freeman, and McRoy, 1987; Bradshaw, 1992). And as multiracial categories and children of immigrants continue to increase, the number of people whose ethnicity is fluid is likely to grow. The practical result of being multiracial is often a persistent sense of ethnic ambiguity. As ethnic diversity expands in metropolitan regions like Los Angeles, ethnic loyalties become increasingly problematic. In response, individuals of mixed heritage often seek a more stable base of personal identity. They look beyond ethnic identity to some other cohesive identity that will integrate who they are.

Mosaic is able to become multiethnic in part by offering an alternative to the growing fluidity of ethnicity. Wijeyesinghe (2001:143) asserts that the process of finding an identity "is influenced by personal spiritual beliefs, traditions, or experiences" and that "spirituality can create a sense of connection between people that transcends racial labels and differences." She also states,

> [A]lthough some Multiracial people have concerns related to their racial identity, others may not feel the need to explore racial identity issues at all, or may feel that other social identities such as their ... religion ... are more pressing in their lives. (145)

Therefore, the ambiguity of racial identity may be superceded by other forms of identity, a religious identity being one such option.

Another reason that multiracial identity may be superseded by an overarching religious identity is that younger generations are downplaying ascriptive labels such as race and ethnicity (see Roof, 1987:49). Instead, individuals are renegotiating such demographic categories to pursue more holistic bases of identity. Ascriptive loyalties and social identities are being set aside in favor of more "authentic" expressions of the self, and new religious identities are often considered such expressions. Becoming a dedicated follower of Jesus Christ is a way to consolidate personal identity without relying on ethnicity. Religious identities are not created in isolation, and congregations like Mosaic are likely sites for such identity work.

Finally, people can choose to adopt different kinds of religious identities. Lyon (2000:90), developing ideas from Castells (1997), describes two ways of constructing a personal identity when "social narratives seem beyond our control." The first is "resistance identity," which defines itself against the surrounding social context and preserves the past. This leads to "fundamentalism that tends to be backward looking and retrenching," an orientation that can be prominently seen among many churches. The second is "project identity," which looks forward and often takes on causes tied to social movements. Instead of reactive resistance, it is oriented toward proactive change. Rather than attempting to reestablish a nostalgically viewed past, a project identity catalyzes a new, even unprecedented future. In contrast to other possible forms of Christian engagement, Mosaic does not encourage a fundamentalist reaction to contemporary culture. Those who encounter fundamentalists experience them as narrow-minded, racist, bigoted, arrogant, and intolerant. The identity constructed at Mosaic, that of a dedicated follower of Jesus, is experienced as more open and forward-looking.

Since ethnic identity is becoming less stable among the emerging generation, people of this generation may take on the religious identity offered through Mosaic as a more central and more reliable base for personal identity. Mosaic encourages its participants to cultivate this new identity by pursuing a positive, proactive engagement with culture such that each person makes a personal creative contribution toward fulfilling God's mission in the world.

Religious Individuation and the Need to Affirm Individual Involvement

The younger generation today does not wish to passively receive religious performances, but desires to be individually engaged. Carroll and Roof (2002:89) describe the emergence of a participatory model for congregational life:

> [T]his congregation designs its programs to meet the needs of an increasingly diverse and well-educated laity—different "audiences"— who are self-conscious about their participation and choose to be involved on their own terms and not necessarily those set by a leadership elite. Lay initiative and participation in all aspects of congregational life, including decision making and corporate worship, are emphasized.

I will call this desire for participation in religious activity "religious individuation." "New paradigm" or "posttraditional" churches are deliberately designed to respond to religious individuation (Miller, 1997; see also Carroll, 2000; Carroll and Roof, 2002:90), and several indications suggest that this individuation is increasing.

Carroll and Roof (2002:77) state, "Over the past several decades, there has been a movement within religious communities to recover the personal and experiential—as spiritual style and as mode of religious knowing—and many Americans, including young Americans, seem to be rejuvenated." The "New Voluntarism" discussed by Roof (1987:40) emerged in the 1970s and 1980s, when the rise of consumerism offered myriad choices, as part of a quest for personal fulfillment. This voluntarism is characterized by individuals' taking religious journeys that they themselves control and emphasizing personal choice in religious acts and expression. According to Roof, "Religion became essentially an individual matter, something to be 'worked out' on one's own terms" (50). The emerging generation sees congregational involvement as instrumental to personal fulfillment, and remaining involved in a congregation is dependent on the individual's belief not only that the church is "good" but that it is "good *for me*." Moreover, Roof states that individual decisions concerning religious belief and practice are now made "on the basis of genuine religious preference" (50). Believers make stronger commitments to congregations, if they bother to make any commitment at all, since that commitment is based on authentic allegiance to the beliefs and values of the congregation.

In such an environment, churches like Mosaic that welcome individual contributions and direct involvement can flourish. While traditional religious authority may be declining, there is still room for charismatic leaders who point the way to individual fulfillment through religious activity. Significant lay involvement has always been important in the history of Mosaic, and the leadership of the church increasingly allows people to shape their participation. At Mosaic, people, even young adults, have considerable influence on the creation and execution of ministry activity. As Pastor Erwin explains, any member of Mosaic may reflect that "there are cultural values I may have to work from, but it doesn't mean that I can't put my fingerprint, my own style and flavor, on things."

THE "CREATIVE CLASS" AND THE NEED FOR OWNERSHIP

In the past few decades, economic systems have shifted from a dependence on manufacturing and bureaucracy to a dependence on creativity and symbolic management. For example, Reich (1991) describes "symbolic analysts," who are people in problem-solving, opportunity-seeking, and strategic negotiating occupations. Rather than working with standardized products or procedures, symbolic analysts are creative people who work with "data, words, oral and visual representations" (177). The "new economy" (Reich's term) is dependent on skillful knowledge handlers because this emerging economy is "replete with unidentified problems, unknown solutions, and untried means of putting them together" (182). The bulk of symbolic analysts' time is spent conceptualizing problems, devising solutions, and planning their implementation. Information is not valuable in the new economy, because it changes too quickly and vast domains of knowledge are increasingly available at one's fingertips through globally interconnected computer networks. "What is much more valuable," says Reich, "is the capacity to effectively and creatively use the knowledge" (182).

Symbolic analysts represent one segment of what Florida (2002) calls the "creative class." By his estimate, 30 percent of the American workforce (about 40 million people) belong to this new class, whose employment depends solely on creativity. Florida asserts that creativity "has come to be the most highly prized commodity in our economy" and "is now the decisive source of competitive advantage" (5). Winners in today's economy will master creativity. Members of the creative class include artists, musicians, professors, and scientists. They are people "whose economic function is to create new ideas, new technology and/or new creative content" (28). Florida asserts that corporations are now "taking people who would once have been viewed as bizarre mavericks operating at the bohemian fringe and setting them at the very heart of the process of innovation and economic growth." According to him, innovators are not marginalized but are "the new mainstream" (6).

And members of the creative class don't live just anywhere. According to Florida, "They cluster in places that are centers of creativity and also where they like to live" (7). Los Angeles, especially Hollywood, is one such region. Members of the creative class gravitate toward cities like Los Angeles because, according to Florida, they "offer a variety of economic opportunities, a stimulating environment, and amenities for every possible lifestyle" (11). Similarly, Reich (1991:235) describes Hollywood as a critical place for symbolic-analytic work. These centers draw both established symbolic analysts and those in training. Mosaic benefits from being affiliated with Hollywood, absorbing people who work in the symbolic-analytic parts of the industry.

Mosaic is a church suited to the creative class because it is located in a geographic center where members of this class cluster, it is structured to embrace their creative contribution, and it appeals to them by providing ethnic diversity, artistry, and continual change. According to Florida (2002:15), "Creative people have always gravitated to certain kinds of communities. . . . Such communities provide the stimulation, diversity, and a richness of experiences that are the wellsprings of creativity." The communities sought by the creative class offer "experiences, an openness to diversity of all kinds, and above all else the opportunity to validate their identities as creative people" (218). Members of the creative class most desire the opportunity to express "creativity in building something, to experience the whole cycle of having ideas, putting them into action, and seeing the rewards" (103). Mosaic provides this opportunity in the context of a local church. Lindsey, a twenty-nine-year-old actress and photographer, told me,

> Creativity is a natural result of our spiritual life. It's the essence of God. It is in us. And we need to express that. We should do it in a place that is safe, and we should do it in a place that's impactful, and that would be the church.

"You have an empowerment to be creative with your thoughts and ideas," said twenty-five-year-old Chinese American Paul. The diversity and youthfulness of Mosaic are also attractive. Ethnic diversity is attractive to the creative class because such diversity indicates tolerance for difference. As Florida states, diversity "is a sign that reads 'nonstandard people welcome here' " (21). And for many who are older, youthfulness is attractive because, according to Florida, "middle-aged and older people I speak with may no longer hang in nightspots until 4 a.m., but they enjoy stimulating, dynamic places with high levels of cultural interplay" (296).

Challenge and responsibility remain key factors in motivating the creative class. Creative work is often pursued even when it offers no financial gain. Members of the creative class value the intrinsic rewards of creativity. This suggests that congregations that thrive will move beyond individual affirmation to a creative involvement that elicits ownership and collaboration. Churches that harness their members' imagination to create public events that effectively communicate in the service of the church's ends are availing themselves of one of the most valuable tools for mobilization and growth. Mosaic provides opportunities for innovators in a challenging environment to meet the ambitious goals of the congregation.

RAPID PACE OF CHANGE AND THE NEED FOR A CHANGE-FRIENDLY IDEOLOGY

The pace of social change has quickened in the past century, and many observers argue it has accelerated still more in the past decade, due to innovations in computer processing, especially relating to the Internet (Brockman, 1996; Broderick, 2001; Cetron and Davies, 1997; Gleick, 2000, 2002). People feel the pace of change in almost every sphere of everyday life, and the rapidity of such change is likely to continue.

To the degree that a church is sheltered from social change, it becomes a foreign experience. Since eternity is perceived to be static, "timelessness" and a "slow pace" in church are often assumed to be the norm, and even beneficial. For Mosaic, such a pace simply means the church is woefully out of touch with culture as a whole. The theological emphases at Mosaic (described in chapter 3) incorporate societal change rather than isolating the church from change, by assuming that a living God is active in the work of history, that human beings are part of shaping that history, and that change in society can be leveraged to craft a gospel message that can reach people in ever changing cultural circumstances. Change-friendly frameworks give individuals a sense of personal agency rather than letting them feel swept away as victims of an aggressively unfolding history.

Has the pace of social change accelerated? If so, churches that thrive will be those that learn to take advantage of changes in culture rather than isolating themselves from such changes. And ideological frameworks that acknowledge rather than ignore social change seem likely to appeal to the emerging culture.

Cultural Appeal in the Coming Century

The youthfulness of the congregation is an indication of Mosaic's tapping into the themes of an emerging culture. Mosaic appeals to a younger generation because it appeals to an emerging culture that is most concentrated in that generation. It is possible, then, that, as the characteristics of emerging culture highlighted in this section spread to all age groups, Mosaic will appeal not just those who are younger but to all ages. The next chapter will explore the bearers of ideology, the dedicated followers of Jesus Christ who are on mission as members of a catalytic community, and how this identity is shaped out of the ethnic fluidity of people who become part of Mosaic.

7

BECOMING A MOSAIC OF
BELIEVERS: A RECONSTRUCTION
OF IDENTITY

MIKE: I'm excited about Mosaic because these are all followers of Jesus Christ. I feel at home with God's people. And I believe I'm one of them.

CARL: People in the church have a common goal: the Lord. Introducing the Lord to other people, praising the Lord, worshiping the Lord. And it doesn't make a difference if you're a honky or anything else.

It was early summer, 2002, and I was sitting in the living room of Pastor Erwin's home listening to Eric, one of the pastors of Mosaic, address a group of potential members. The class is held about every six weeks and is the most focused opportunity for understanding the inner workings of the congregation. In the middle of his talk, Eric caught my attention. Emphatically, he told us, "Mosaic is *not* multicultural." Given what I knew about this church, I wasn't sure what he meant. My entire research agenda was built on the fact that Mosaic was ethnically diverse. Then he added, "Our church is not multi*cultural;* it's multi*ethnic.* We have many ethnicities but only one culture. We are all dedicated followers of Jesus Christ." Mosaic appears multicultural. Yet all my respondents, regardless of their ethnic heritage, stated with Eric that they considered themselves to be the same thing: dedicated followers of Jesus Christ.

This chapter highlights the way church leaders, jointly with the people of Mosaic, construct a new, shared identity. In the introduction, I discussed how ethnic identity is selectively emphasized or obscured depending on social context; Mosaic is a place where ethnicity is more often obscured, making way for a shared religious identity. The strategic management of a constructed and negotiated religious identity is the central work of charismatic authority within this multiethnic congregation. While the people of Mosaic embrace a religious label, they consistently avoid ethnic labels. They express a desire to escape ethnic entrapment. Most have experienced a great deal of ethnic diversity; the remainder expressed an earnest desire to do so. The wish to escape ethnic enclaves and experience ethnic diversity was fulfilled at Mosaic. Mosaic creates a multiethnic space of shared religious identity where ethnicity is respected, not buried, and where, most importantly, ethnic enclaves are avoided. Leaders at Mosaic are attuned to the fluidity of ethnic identity among immigrants and children of mixed ethnic backgrounds and make intentional, proactive use of this fluidity. Whites are nurtured to view ancestral background as far less relevant than specific religious commitment. In the end, participants at Mosaic co-construct a new shared identity as dedicated followers of Jesus Christ.

Exploring Mosaic's Ethnic Haven

Churches have historically served as an ethnic haven for recent immigrants, helping them assimilate into and acculturate to their new home (Burns, 1994; Ebaugh and Chafetz, 2000; Gordon, 1964; Papaioannou, 1994; Shaw, 1991). Certainly Los Angeles has immigrant congregations that are mono-ethnic, e.g., Korean, Japanese, or Armenian, and intended to be "a refuge from an alien culture" that surrounds them, providing an "alternative community" (Holifield, 1994:40; see also R. Warner, 1994:57–58). The children of these immigrants are now finding their way into a more broadly Americanized setting. Their schools and their workplaces are diverse, but their churches are not. Mosaic provides a haven for second- and third-generation ethnics escaping from mono-ethnic home churches and the ethnic enclaves of their parents and grandparents. And whites find a place to experience diversity within a culturally familiar setting.

SHELTERS SECOND- AND THIRD-GENERATION ETHNICS ESCAPING ETHNIC ENCLAVES AND CAUCASIANS SEEKING DIVERSITY

Pastor Erwin McManus described the nonwhite population of Mosaic, saying, "What we have are second- and third-generation expressions; they work cross-culturally, they tend to be more global in their orientation anyway, but their church life is homogeneous." While their parents and grandparents have often been part of a mono-ethnic, immigrant church, these second- and third-generation immigrants feel they do not fit there and begin the process of leaving as soon as they enter college. They chafe against the demand to not just respect but also represent their ancestral culture. Erwin said, "We are definitely a third-generation church: people whose parents speak English but their grandparents came from another country, or their parents came from another country but English is the more preferred language." He added, "Mosaic is that refuge for people who are bicultural." I found this to be a very accurate assessment. Erwin also describes himself in this comment. Although he is a first-generation immigrant from El Salvador, he adapted as a third-generation immigrant might. "I speak English as my primary language; I don't speak with an accent," he explained, and his value system is "more from the American ethos," which represents the shared popular culture many consider to be the generalized American worldview.

Overall, people I spoke with at Mosaic sought to avoid ethnic entrapment. At Mosaic they find refuge for "being" ethnic without having to "act" ethnic. Desire for such a refuge was especially prominent among Asian Americans. For example, as a Chinese American who had been in both Asian churches and Asian parachurch organizations, Mike found himself tired of constantly being around Asians. "I lived in a bubble world when I was in college." His social network was almost entirely Asian and Christian. Mike describes an experience with his college roommate:

> My roommate George was a white guy. He was coming up on an elevator, and came out. He's a little taller than me—I could see his chest—but I could tell that he was a white guy. I walked right past him because in my mind if he's a white person, I don't know him.

That's how I was in college. I was part of a Christian fellowship, and that's how I thought. There's a white guy, I don't know him. But he goes, "Mike?" And I go, "George! I'm sorry. Hey, man."

He began asking himself, "How do I get connected to the real world? Or how do I get connected to the more diverse world? You find Mosaic, *ahhhh,* breath of fresh air." Mike told me, "I'm really happy after Urban Mosaic when we go to dinner and we show up in a restaurant and it's a diverse crowd. I'd never been in a diverse crowd like that in all my life." The diversity in the church was a new, exciting experience. Mike exclaimed, "They speak different languages; they come from different backgrounds. That excites me. Blond hair? Blue eyes? They're my friends?! That amazes me."

Most respondents mentioned that they strongly valued diversity. Dan, a thirty-five-year-old African American, repeatedly said enthusiastically, "I love diversity." He continued,

> The diversity at Mosaic breaks down racial stereotypes when you come here. Most definitely. Because you're sitting there and you'd be talking to a Chinese guy one minute, and you think, "Well, he's not that bad." And over here you got a Mexican guy, and he's like my brother. He's as loud as all get-out. Or you got the white guy over there. He's real cool.

According to Dan, "We're reaching everyone; that means there's something relevant to every person and every race here." Manuel, a thirty-six-year-old Hispanic, described his first experience at the church, saying, "Right away I noticed people were here from every color. I grew up in El Monte. I was never in gangs but was around gangs and grew up racist: *la raza.* But when I came, it actually attracted me. Something about seeing that every color was here, that attracted me." He added, "My first Asian friend was here." Another African American, twenty-year-old Janet, said, "I noticed that when I looked around you could not tell if it was an Asian church or a Hispanic church or a white church; it was so well mixed. I thought, 'I like this church.' " Abby, a twenty-eight-year-old Korean woman, said her desire for diversity was affirmed in the music: "As soon as I walked through the doors, they were playing Latin jazz, and I said, 'This is my church!' That was it; it was over. I said, 'They're playing conga drums? That's it.' "

Christians who were second- and third-generation ethnics talked about having formed friendships with people from other ethnic groups but never feeling comfortable bringing them to their home churches. Emily, Chinese American, said, "It was harder in the Chinese American church context to invite a Latin person or a Caucasian person. They would feel like the odd one out." Eleanor, a Chinese American also coming from an all-Chinese congregation, wanted to bring friends to church but knew they wouldn't fit because the atmosphere was so culturally Chinese. "I wanted to invite people but couldn't." Several Asians said that non-Asians feel stigmatized in Asian churches, which keeps them from ever committing. But at Mosaic, another Chinese American said, "[h]ere all of a sudden you have a church that enables you to do that and do it more freely."

Why do Caucasians come to Mosaic? The answer lies partly in taking pleasure in inviting diverse friends. Jamie, twenty-six years old, told me,

> I feel like I can invite people and not be like, well, everyone here is white or everyone's this or that. It's a place that feels like it's really inclusive of everyone; there are only different styles from different backgrounds. It makes it a lot of fun to invite people.

The public experience of diversity fulfills a core belief: that people connect to the same God all over the world. Jamie echoed other Caucasians in the congregation when she talked about heaven, saying, "It's going to be everybody. So it's nice to see some of that reflected in a congregation here. We don't have to wait until heaven to experience the diversity." Eric, who grew up in Texas, said he "went to a predominantly Anglo high school and a definitely Anglo church." Eric began to be concerned for nonwhites after encountering racism in a ministry that involved serving African American students. He moved with his wife to California to leave behind such racist attitudes and experience greater diversity. Jamie, Eric, and other Caucasians sought to escape their all-white ethnic enclaves and find a refuge of ethnic diversity at Mosaic.

Many Caucasians also come to Mosaic in search of cross-cultural preparation for overseas mission work. Eric and his wife initially came because they wanted to train as missionaries to Spain. They hoped to learn about Hispanic culture and become skilled at building interethnic relationships. For Eric, the ethnic haven at Mosaic provided a safe place to pursue relationships with various peoples and cultures without the excessive burden of constant cultural adjustments. Other Caucasians I interviewed who relocated from the South and the Midwest also came to the church with intentions to go to places like China and the Middle

East. In this way, the ethnic haven at Mosaic serves whites planning to go overseas and hoping to gain cross-cultural experience before being commissioned.

People find Mosaic to be welcoming of mixed friendships, relationships, and marriages. Erwin said, "We're one of the few places where people can have a bicultural marriage, bicultural relationships, bicultural friendships." According to Erwin, if you are Japanese and marrying a Chinese, or if you are Caucasian and marrying an Asian, "Mosaic is where you feel normal. Any other context that I know of, you're aberrant." At the celebration services, especially the Sunday morning Metro service that includes student and children's programming, white-black marriages, black-Mexican marriages, Korean-Chinese marriages, and others are evident. A Chinese woman and her Korean husband both left their home churches to attend Mosaic because neither felt fully accepted at the other's church. One couple I met explicitly told me that one of the main reasons they attend Mosaic is that their relationship is accepted without comment and they sense no prejudice.

What is the ethnic "culture" of this multicultural church? Mosaic's culture is the American acculturated center. Second- and third-generation ethnics at Mosaic describe themselves as "American" or as "hyphenated-Americans" ("Asian-American," "Cuban-American") who are not competent in their ancestral culture. Many do not use their birth names, instead going by a popular American name. Kyle, a Japanese American who grew up in Idaho, described how his mother was more committed to his being Japanese than he was. He spoke no Japanese himself and considered himself a novice in his parents' culture. Kyle married a Caucasian woman from Minnesota in a ceremony that celebrated both Japanese and Norwegian culture. He told me that even though there was diversity at Mosaic, he thought there was a lot of a similarity between people like him and his wife. Both were born in America, do not speak the language of their parents, and are not committed to their ancestral culture. Blake, an African American, labeled Mosaic's ethnic culture "pan-Anglo," meaning that it embodied the middle-of-the-road, generalized American culture. With a few exceptions of people who broke away from tight ethnic groups (e.g., former gang members from East L.A.; Chinese Americans from Chinatown), almost all of the ethnics at Mosaic grew up in suburban, Anglo neighborhoods. While these ethnics have not abandoned their ethnicity, they are in the process of renegotiating it toward an Americanized center. And if they are single, they intend to marry someone who occupies that same cultural center regardless of ethnic ancestry.

Deters Ethnically Committed Immigrants and African Americans

Mosaic's ethnic haven is not attractive to all people who visit the church. For example, families of recent immigrants do not come together to Mosaic; their acculturated children do. Eric, a pastor working with student ministries, told me he has seen Hispanic students come to Mosaic in the last three years and, more recently, Asian students, but their parents do not attend. According to Eric, these parents are not fluent English speakers, and they don't bother even visiting. The church has made several attempts over the last fifteen years to build an international ministry among first-generation immigrants, usually those coming to study at one of the local colleges. But the language barrier was always a hindrance. Kyle told me about international students who were brought to the church through a campus ministry in the late 1980s, but who would not stay because the English used from the pulpit were too sophisticated for them to follow. Unless they have been well acculturated, first-generation immigrants are unlikely to stay in the congregation long-term.

Similarly, Mosaic does not provide an ethnic haven for African Americans. This does not mean that there are no African Americans at Mosaic; it means that they do not relate to Mosaic on the basis of ethnic affinity. African Americans equate Mosaic with assimilated "white" culture. This was forcefully demonstrated to me in September 2001, when an African American woman made an appointment to meet with me at the church office. After a few opening remarks, she told me she was leaving the church. She was bright, articulate, and very gracious in our conversation. She told me Mosaic was a "white evangelical" church emphasizing values that were not compatible with the African American experience. She talked about reading Emerson and Smith (2000), saying that white evangelicals are individualistic rather than systemic, and that Mosaic was unwilling to work with broader cultural issues. She said, "The mindset is not sufficient for racial reconciliation," and "diversity does not equal racial reconciliation." She worked with a parachurch organization active in racial reconciliation. Since her understanding of racial reconciliation was not likely to be implemented, she did not perceive Mosaic as a place she could consider home.

Several African Americans talked about the difficulty of leaving settings that were predominantly black. For example, Bridgette spoke of being an obvious minority, saying, "When you take a black person from being around a lot of blacks, and they're not used to that, and you put them in a situation where they truly are the minority, then they will work through issues of self-esteem." Bridgette also described African American friends who saw her as a racial "sellout." "[Y]ou don't want to see yourself as a sellout. You don't want to be called an Oreo. They think you're trying to be white, even if you're not." Another African American, Dela, shared with me, "The fact this church isn't a black church has been an issue regarding whether I should join this church. At times I definitely feel like I don't really fit in and that I don't have much in common."

Music was the site of a specific culture clash between African Americans and Mosaic. Almost every African American I interviewed talked about the different music styles of Mosaic and black churches. Bridgette said,

> If someone is used to black music and black culture, then it's tough to make a shift into a church like this because the music is basically pop-ish. We call it "Vineyard music." It's not gospel. It's not real soulful. You can sing it that way; we just don't sing it that way. It's uphill for a person who likes or is used to hearing a soulful gospel sound.

Among the reasons Dela has considered leaving the church, she mentioned music, saying, "In most black churches you're going to hear gospel music. You won't hear people playing guitar. There would be a choir. So a difference in worship style is one thing I've thought about." Blake told me African Americans "often find themselves just visiting [rather than staying] because the music is not as passionate." An African American who left and then returned said, "I love Pastor Erwin; I hate the music."

Not all African Americans in the congregation felt this way. Two African American men who grew up in white communities both enjoyed the music at Mosaic. Jerome commented that it was only in the last three years that he had come to enjoy rap and soul and to get in touch with his musical "black heritage." Dylan, a musician, described his first visit to Mosaic:

> I sat down and Pete was up there singing, and I was like, "This is church?" And he was singing a Creed song which at the time I didn't know was a Christian song. And I was like, "Why are they playing this kind of music in church?" And later on I found it was a Christian song and Creed was a Christian band, but *the music which caught me when I was a kid was the first thing that grabbed me.* I thought, "Okay, I can get into this." [emphasis added]

So while African Americans can find a place to belong at Mosaic, it helps if they have been raised in an Anglo-based American culture. As Dylan indicates, "When I go someplace I never really think about there being no black people because this is what I'm used to." Musical compatibility may have contributed to the assimilation of Jerome and Dylan, since each made a commitment to dedicate himself as a follower of Jesus only a few weeks after first coming to Mosaic. Other African Americans I met who like the music at Mosaic have no commitment to gospel, rap, hip-hop, or other styles of music associated with African American popular culture.

Blake suggested that age has much to do with how African Americans relate to Mosaic.

> It's all about the age group. My age, *pffft*, forget it because there's nothing in Mosaic that even says "black," culturally speaking. And unless you're connected in some other way, there's no way that you're going to get more middle-aged black people in here or older black people here unless they're looking for a break from some janky [i.e., crappy] congregation [they] used to go to. And that's a lot of the reason why they came, if you ask them. The congregation they came from was so bad that this was just a wonderful relief.

Blake sees a difference between African Americans whose attitudes were formed before and after the Civil Rights Act of 1964. According to him, "The younger culture is now much more multicultural, and they don't have a problem celebrating cultures. As a matter of fact, they love it. They tend to have friends that cross over cultural boundaries." He expects Mosaic to include more African Americans in the future simply because those who are younger are more amenable to diversity.

The ethnic haven centers on a broadly Americanized culture that deters ethnically committed groups like immigrant parents not fluent in English who experience the church as "foreign" and African Americans who experience the church as "white-dominated." The more highly committed people are to a single ethnic expression, the less likely they are to come to and stay at Mosaic. As ethnicity is certainly a potential source of honor, it is logical that it can also be a source of dishonor, disloyalty, and disunion. This creates challenges for leaders who wish to create and sustain solidarity among diverse ethnic groups. I believe that leaders at Mosaic enact their authority both personally and structurally in ways that allow ethnic identity to be renegotiated and transcended. The unique potential and challenge of charismatic authority addresses this issue.

Charismatic Authority and the Strategic Management of Ethnic Identity

At Mosaic, leaders expand and articulate charismatic authority within an ethnically diverse congregation. An essential question in race and ethnicity studies is when ethnic identity is enacted and when it is obscured. Doornbos (1972) suggests that since ethnicity often lies dormant, it is fair to ask why ethnic relations are inactive in some circumstances and active in others. For example, Jackson (1982:6) states that "modern sociologists, following Weber, should be more involved in trying to determine the conditions under which ethnicity does or does not transform into action." Weber did not explicitly address the relationship between ethnic identity and charismatic authority; however, an examination of his writings reveals several important connections that can be used to do so. Thus, this chapter expands on Weber's conceptual framework, first discussed in the introduction, to understand the relation between ethnic identity and charismatic authority.

As a revolutionary and disruptive force, charismatic authority renegotiates the identities of its followers, enhancing anything that will allow followers to perceive a connection between themselves and the leader. Weber implicitly asserts that charismatic authority is capable of abolishing or transforming ethnicity. Transformations come through a renegotiation of ethnic identity. Jackson (1982) shows that Weber says that while ethnic relations are maintained because they are legitimated by traditional authorities and their followers, they can be changed or transformed under charismatic authority. Ethnic groups are alternative forms of status groups, so charismatic authority can transform the standards by which status is earned. In a multiethnic organization, especially a church whose context is already affectively charged, ethnicity cannot be ignored by charismatic leaders. It is at least acknowledged; it is at most co-opted. Ethnic status is regularly co-opted or renegotiated under the guidance of the charismatic leadership of Mosaic.

For Max Weber (1978), religious authority is rooted in charisma within the confines of the group's concern. While Finke and Stark (1992) assert that religious leaders come from social locations similar to those of their followers, so that they understand the social location of their followers and speak their language, Weber's assertions are broader. Charismatic leaders must be able to communicate to people's felt needs and embody religious solutions to those needs. Similar social locations may facilitate the ability, but they certainly do not guarantee it. Charismatic leaders must find a base of connection for leadership wherever they can. This is because, as David Smith (1998:35) argues, "Charisma is an ulterior, socially constructed reality, the result of popular faith rather than its cause." This conception of charisma is different from a more popular understanding that charisma is a mystical force that compels people's obedience. Smith corrects this notion, saying, "The parameters of leadership, in other words, are set by public opinion" (33). Smith shows that Weber says that followers choose to accept charismatic authority: rather than being a miraculous power, charisma is conferred by people on leaders.

I affirm with Smith that for Weber the "spark" of charisma must be recognized and valued by followers in order for them to be attracted and devoted to the charismatic leader. Any authority, including charismatic authority, must find ways to bolster and strengthen its base of social status. Ethnicity is a possible base of status. Indeed, Weber believed ethnic groups to be conceptually related to status groups. He is clear on this point: "The conviction of the excellence of one's own customs and the inferiority of alien ones, a conviction which sustains the sense of ethnic honor, is actually quite analogous to the sense of honor of distinctive status groups" (M. Weber, 1978:391). Being a member of an ethnic group conveys a sense of ethnic honor. Again, Weber states, "All differences of customs can sustain a specific sense of honor or dignity in their practitioners" (387). Ethnic honor "is accessible to anybody who belongs to the subjectively believed community of descent" (391). Weber hoped to articulate the relation between ethnic honor and status honor, but failed to do so.

Different social circumstances make different types of status available to an individual; more specifically, leaders maximize bases of status according to their immediate audience. In a multiethnic setting, ethnic identity may be a base of status. If it is not, it is obscured and another base of status accentuated, limited only by the performative repertoires available to an individual. As Okamura (1981:455) states, "the actor may consider it in his interests to obscure rather than to assert his ethnic identity in a given situation so that the relationship recedes in terms of other social statuses he holds."

All leaders at Mosaic must ground their claim to legitimacy. In order to do so, charismatic leaders access aspects of their identity that are likely to enhance their status. A critical way in which charismatic authority is exercised is by managing, through personal contact, the ways that impressions of ethnicity are formed. Ethnicity can interfere with a sense of affinity; these charismatic leaders acknowledge this, and they negotiate (or manipulate) what they can control: the presentation of their own ethnic identity. Ethnic identities are assets, resources from which different repertoires of identity can be constructed. Leaders engage in the "tactical use of ethnicity" to serve the ends of the organization (Royce, 1982:11). Indeed, "[e]thnicity is a strategy adopted to fit a particular situation" (26). Ethnic identity is negotiated to foster affinity, a connection that will authorize and justify for charismatic leaders the kind of authority that allows for working with people's understanding of themselves and their relation to other people.

How is a person's inner life to be renegotiated by charismatic leaders at Mosaic? When charismatic leadership asserts itself within a religious organization, it is guided by what Max Weber called "value rationality" (*Wertrationalisierung*). Value rationality is a conscious enactment of values that heightens awareness of the interpersonal dynamics involved in enacting those values. Weber (1978:24–25) defined it as "conscious belief in the value for its own sake of some ethical, aesthetic, religious, or other form of behavior, independently of its prospects for success." As a revolutionary force, it transforms the affectual or instrumental bases of action into a higher standard of "ultimate values" and overcomes "unthinking acceptance" of attitudes and behaviors stemming from habit or custom (30). In Weber's writings about charismatic leadership, especially in religious contexts, the exercise of charisma is most closely related to value-rational action. When charismatic leadership is exercised, it "is distinguished from the affectual type by its clearly self-conscious formulation of the ultimate values governing the action" (25). That is, affectual action is motivated by emotion or feeling, often fleeting or temporary in nature and aroused spontaneously rather than consciously. In contrast, according to Weber, "pure value-rational orientation would be the actions of persons who, regardless of possible cost to themselves, act to put into practice their convictions of what seems to them to be required by duty, honor, the pursuit of beauty, a religious call, personal loyalty, or the importance of some cause no matter in what it consists" (25). In an organization guided by charismatic authority, ideal interests overcome antithetical material interests.

What this means is that in multiethnic congregations leaders use the complexity of ethnic identity to serve their value-rational goals. At Mosaic, the value rationality of charismatic leaders includes beliefs, duties, and values concerning the role of ethnic integration in evangelizing Los Angeles. The leaders consciously manage not only their own ethnic identity but the ethnic identity of others. Theorists of instrumental and situational ethnicity address only the manipulation of ethnic identity for material ends, which means that they see the shifting of ethnic identities as work done by subordinate groups who are maneuvering for power (e.g., Eriksen, 1993). At Mosaic, ethnic identity is manipulated for value-rational ends. When the ends pursued are not material (political and economic) but instead transcendent (spiritual and other-worldly), charismatic leaders can use the flexibility of their and others' ethnic identities to accomplish value-rational goals and purposes.

Assuming, then, that charismatic authority can transform ethnic relationships, multiethnic religious communities must be a product of a distinctive (and rare) type of charismatic authority that changes the nature of ethnic identification and ethnic relations. Value-rational purposes can emphasize the overcoming of ethnic categories and fuel the renegotiation of ethnic identity and ethnic membership. "Doing church" in an increasingly multiethnic society calls for charismatic authority to be exercised in such a way that ethnic identity is mobilized to achieve value-rational goals.

On the basis of my observations and interviews, I see ethnic identity as instrumental for purposes of charismatic authority. Ethnic identity is a resource utilized by leaders in multiethnic groups to increase their chances of achieving organizational, value-rational ends. Leaders ask, "Is my ethnic identity a help or a hindrance in accomplishing my goals?" If it is a help, they accentuate it as a base of affinity, connection, and status. Ethnicity will be expressed if it serves instrumental ends. If ethnic identity is a hindrance, then it is obscured in favor of other social statuses. The most important maneuver is to transform the initial base of status away from either ethnic or secular honor to a religious honor within a broad community of people on mission with God. Charismatic authority at Mosaic has as its fundamental goal to have people adopt a new shared identity as dedicated followers of Jesus Christ. The three strategies discussed below summarize my observations of leader-follower interactions, accentuating the means by which ethnic identity is alternatively emphasized or masked by leaders at Mosaic.

ETHNIC CONNECTION: APPEAL TO ETHNIC AFFINITY

In interacting with potential followers, spiritual leaders in multiethnic churches like Mosaic will appeal to ethnic affinity first. Leaders in multiethnic contexts attempt to create a connection by "ethnic signaling" (Plotnikov and Silverman, 1978), a subtle giving of verbal and nonverbal cues indicating their ethnicity. Weber (1978:390) wrote that "the intelligibility of the behavior of others is the most fundamental presupposition of [ethnic] group formation." Signaling is a discreet but deliberate advertisement of ethnic identity intended to establish both the other's ethnic identity and one's own.

Signaling is delicate and risky work. One must successfully signal membership in a group; according to Royce (1982:187), "An individual who is unable to do so may be relegated to the periphery of the group or even be discounted as a group member." I found that, at Mosaic, people selectively access pan-ethnic designations, such as Hispanic or Asian, in order to signal ethnic affinity and avoid being rejected on the basis of ethnic identity. Leaders at Mosaic often avoid exclusive identification with a specific ethnic identity. Instead, they selectively use pan-ethnic, poly-ethnic, and symbolically ethnic designations to signal ethnic affinity. For example, as a Cuban American, I am often faulted for not speaking Spanish as fluently as a native speaker. I have met several other Cuban Americans at Mosaic in the last several years, and I fumble in talking about Cuban celebrities, local Cuban cultural events, and local Cuban restaurants. I have been told that I am not truly *cubano*. Royce explains my situation by saying that "cultural illiteracy is as crippling as illiteracy in a language" (212). She writes,

> Ethnic cues and clues form the basis from which identities are negotiated. Cues are the features over which the individual has little or no control—skin color, hair type, body shape, and any other physical characteristics that can be used to categorize a person. Clues, in contrast, are identifying marks that people reveal during the course of an interaction in order to establish a specific identity. They may include language, dialect, origin, patterns of nonverbal communication, and in-group knowledge. (212–213)

Nancy, a leader at Mosaic, uses several pan-ethnic labels for herself. She varies her ethnic connections so that sometimes she is "Japanese-Hawaiian," other times she is "Hawaiian," other times she is "Japanese," and other times she is just "Asian." She told me explicitly that the choice depends on which will best connect her to a person with whom she is trying to establish affinity. Pan-ethnic designations such as white, Hispanic, and Asian represent high levels of abstraction. Leaders strategically select their level of ethnic abstraction in each interaction. Among Hispanic leaders, at times being Hispanic is enough; at other times being specifically Mexican American, Brazilian, or Peruvian is more advantageous. The same applies to being Asian, which often subdivides into being Chinese, Japanese, Korean, or Vietnamese.

The poly-ethnicity of many leaders at Mosaic increases the potential bases for signaling. Many leaders are aware they fit into two or more ethnic designations. The lead pastor of the congregation is a good example. In his first book (McManus, 2001), he chose to present his full name, Erwin Raphael McManus. "Erwin" is a German name assigned by his grandfather, and "McManus" is an Irish name received from his stepfather. Yet he is neither German nor Irish. He is from El Salvador. To accentuate his Latin roots, he inserted his middle name, "Raphael," even though until that point he had not done so on business cards, letterhead, résumés, or any other public document. Using his middle name on the book allows him to make a connection on the basis of Hispanic identity with readers, who cannot judge his ethnicity from his appearance. Mosaic has other hybrid ethnicities in leadership: Asian-Cajun and Chinese-Peruvian are two of the more interesting.

The use of symbolically ethnic designations is also important since the idea of ethnicity is powerful even without actual ethnic interaction. Studies have shown people can organize their identity around ethnicity without even interacting within an ethnic group (see especially studies of white ethnicities in Gans, 1979, 1994; Alba, 1990; Waters, 1990). Gans (1994:577) writes,

> Symbolic ethnicity—and the consumption and other use of ethnic symbols—is intended mainly for the purpose of feeling or being identified with a particular ethnicity, but without either participating in an existing ethnic organization (formal or informal) or practicing an ongoing ethnic culture.

An individual can be a "symbolic ethnic" without actively sharing the habits or customs of a particular ethnic group. This is especially true among whites. "Italian" or "Swedish" may be "little more than a label they recall when asked the right interview question" (Gans, 1994:579; see also Gans 1979). At Mosaic, symbolic ethnicity allows Caucasians to have a "real" ethnicity; I gather from my interviews that many Caucasians feel that they have no ethnicity at all, yet feel the need for one. It also allows fully acculturated ethnics, especially fourth- and fifth-generation Mexican Americans with a long history in Los Angeles, to still claim to be ethnic long after they have lost all traces of their ancestral culture.

Regardless of ethnic designation, a strong commitment to a particular ethnic identity seems to hinder leadership in the multiethnic context of Mosaic. Christians who have been strongly committed to a particular ethnic identity (e.g., white Southern, Korean American, or Mexican American of East L.A.) have been known to leave for another congregation that is more affirming of their specific ethnic background. Cornell (1996:278) discussed this, saying, "The more involved our membership in the group—the more of our life that the membership organizes or embraces—the more likely we are to see the world through that particular frame as opposed to any other, and to interpret our circumstances accordingly." As Stryker (1981:24) states, "Commitment affects identity salience which, in turn, affects behavioral choices." Drawing on Ann Swidler's (1986) notion of a "tool kit," I suggest that those whose cultural resources are centered in only one ethnicity find themselves limited in their ability to connect deeply with others.

In sum, leaders at Mosaic selectively signal ethnic designations to appeal for ethnic affinity. Yet it is important to note that most leaders at Mosaic are not strongly committed to an ethnic identity. The selective use of pan-ethnic, poly-ethnic, and symbolically ethnic designations reveals the malleability of ethnic identity among leaders at Mosaic. Spiritual leaders at Mosaic use ethnic signaling as a means of establishing a connection with potential followers. The connection is a stepping stone to the development of a new shared identity as dedicated followers of Jesus Christ. However, if connection through shared ethnic identity fails, another claim for status will be substituted.

ETHNIC SUBSTITUTION: APPEAL TO OTHER STATUS GROUPS

If the appeal to ethnic affinity fails with potential followers, spiritual leaders in multiethnic churches like Mosaic will appeal to other status groups for affinity and legitimation. Losing ethnicity as a base of affinity weakens the base of charismatic authority; so another base is presented.

This observation is supported by social theorists discussing the malleability of ethnic identity. For example, Okamura (1981:460) writes, "The individual actor has the option, on the one hand, of emphasizing or obfuscating his ethnic identity, or on the other, of assuming other social identities that he holds." In other words, if leaders do not find status on the basis of ethnic group to be an option, they will use another basis. According to instrumental and situational ethnicity theorists, individuals "have the option of asserting either their primary ethnic identity or other social identities, such as that derivative of class or occupation, that they legitimately hold" (Okamura, 1981:460). Royce (1982:211) points out, "Obviously, persons with a large repertoire of statuses will have an advantage over those with more-limited repertoires." Spiritual leaders building a multiethnic ministry bring a different awareness and skill-set (perhaps not consciously acknowledged) to their negotiations and interactions with a variety of ethnicities. Their sensitivity to context includes awareness of the stereotypes to which they are subject and "the content of these different sets of stereotypes" (Royce, 1982: 167). Charismatic leaders not only understand the nuances of their own ethnic identity, but are also able to be accepted as members of an ethnic group. This limits their ability to manipulate their ethnic affiliations. Leaders of multiethnic churches are not only more likely to understand and use the advantages of their ethnic identity but also limit and circumvent any possible disadvantages.

Applying these insights to Mosaic, we can see that leaders within the congregation are likely to draw on a large number of repertoires to enhance their status when interacting with people of other ethnicities. They have access to symbolic materials that can be assembled to emphasize an aspect of their multiple identities that they believe will earn recognition from followers. Leaders access appropriate aspects of their identity, moving past ethnic affinity toward whichever bases of affinity are likely to enhance status and thus confer legitimacy.

Pastor Dave Auda is an example of a leader who regularly uses status honor rather than ethnic honor as a base of legitimacy. Dave is Caucasian, and often refers to himself as ethnically Italian. In our own conversations, Dave conceded that there are many ethnic influences in his background, but he chooses to call himself Italian for the sake of giving his children some form of ethnic identity. At Mosaic, his greatest base of status is not his ethnicity but his artistry. As a painter, set designer, writer, and actor, Dave creates many of the design elements for public celebration services. He often steps in at the last minute to do anything that is needed. Using the base of artistic mastery, he effectively builds tight, relational, multiethnic teams around his projects. Adding to his status repertoire, Dave drove a delivery truck for United Parcel Service for fifteen years. Delivering for UPS is known to be a sweat-inducing, labor-intensive, blue-collar job; Dave quickly connects with those who labor with their hands in physically demanding jobs. Those who are not artistic but understand what it means to work hard, especially those from a working-class background, connect well with Dave and are willing to take vital roles on his project teams. Dave usually builds affinity based on his artistry and his work experience, not on his ethnicity.

The experiences of Dave and other leaders suggest that if a connection is not established on the basis of ethnicity, leaders will draw on a repertoire of other bases for status. Moreover, it appears that the more repertoires for identity leaders have, the more able they are to lead in a multiethnic setting like Mosaic. One base, for example, is a broad, liberal arts education. All but one full-time staff member has a bachelor's degree, half of them have a master's degree or at least some graduate education, and two teach at the college level. This creates a range of educational experience; each level can appeal to others with similar education and accomplishments. Another base is social class: leaders at Mosaic often have experienced both relative wealth and poverty in their lifetime. The lead pastor, all of the elders, and most of the staff come from working-class to lower-middle-class backgrounds and have risen to upper-middle or even lower-upper-class status. Many have worked with people in the working class and the underclass in ministry or previous occupations. These experiences allow leaders several bases from which to relate to people of various social classes. Other status experiences include international travel, a broad range of occupational experiences, obtaining a professional certification, and success in some form of creative arts, such as writing, composing, or performing music.

Because Mosaic is a multiethnic congregation, it must be able to appeal to a non-ethnic status. People at Mosaic are not strongly ethnically committed; they may remain connected to their ethnic roots, but they are also acculturated to be more generically "American." Because of this, ethnicity is not the most salient base of social status among attenders. Also, seeking status solely on the basis of ethnic identity will alienate those not sharing that ethnic identity. For spiritual leadership to be exercised among diverse congregants, a base of status recognized by ethnically diverse people is essential. Therefore, leaders at Mosaic regularly substitute another status-building identity, which helps to legitimate their authority, for their ethnic identity. Such substitution is, again, a stepping stone to the establishment of a new shared identity as dedicated followers of Jesus Christ.

ETHNIC TRANSCENDENCE: CONSTRUCT A NEW SHARED IDENTITY

At Mosaic, I consistently found that religious identity was more important than ethnic identity. Building on the appeal to ethnic affinity (or, in its absence, building on other status groups), Mosaic leaders most consistently and most publicly utilize the strategy of transcendence. While Mosaic has no majority ethnicity but multiple dominant ethnicities, it is in the category of "dedicated follower of Jesus Christ" and being "on mission with him" that the leadership of Mosaic offers an alternative base for constructing identity in this multiethnic context. Mike, Chinese American, emphasizes, "We don't say Christians; we say followers of Jesus Christ." Here I wish to appropriate the conclusions of Williams in his study of a black Pentecostal congregation. He (1974: 157) states that the church "allocates social status" and "provides for social mobility and social rewards within its confines." A status system exists within every congregation, and in this place, away from the varying and competing bases of social status, a particular hierarchy is created and enforced. Spiritual leaders provide opportunities for individuals to identify and acculturate themselves as dedicated followers of Jesus Christ, gaining status and rewards on that basis. Being a dedicated follower of Jesus Christ at Mosaic has five significant elements. These elements or practices create a shared identity as they are enacted in the presence of others under the guidance of spiritual leaders.

Common Confession as Follower of Jesus

First and primarily, people at Mosaic express a common connection to others based on their common confession of being dedicated followers of Jesus Christ. The confession is a visible declaration of allegiance that precedes the rituals and actions described below. Mike, Chinese American, gushed with enthusiasm for the congregation during our interview. I asked him what he was excited about:

> I'm excited about Mosaic because these are all followers of Jesus Christ. I feel at home with God's people. And I believe I'm one of them. And it's fabulous. It really excites me to be with God's people. It's about God. It's this idea that I am a world Christian; I'm connected to people outside of this little world in this big world, and they may speak another language, but they love the same God, they worship the same Jesus, they will live and die for him. That excites me.

Joseph, Hispanic, stated, "I see a lot of people who love God; that's what we all have in common." And Paige, a Caucasian woman coming from a white-dominated and racially tense background, expressed her belief that the only point of commonality within the congregation was their common identity as followers of Jesus. She even suggested that going to a multiethnic church is evidence of being a true follower of Jesus, saying,

> You go to a white church and you spend like a year trying to figure out who the Christians are. You don't walk into Mosaic and spend a year trying to figure out who the Christians are. You kinda, like, you see it, it's just there.... All the ethnics coming together, it could only happen because God is moving, God is at work and that people are really Christians and feeling the Spirit.

[173]

All of the respondents, regardless of their ethnic background, participated in a common confession of being a dedicated follower of Jesus Christ and seemed to value the connection this confession formed with other true followers regardless of their ethnic identity.

People at Mosaic have the opportunity to initiate becoming dedicated followers of Jesus in various ways, such as by turning in response cards at the end of the service; by coming forward at occasional "altar calls," which summon people to the stage to publicly accept Christ; by meeting with a member of the guest reception team after service; by participating in a small group designed for people interested in learning about being a dedicated follower of Jesus; and by talking with a member of the congregation. Most often people declare themselves to be followers of Jesus in informal interactions with others at Mosaic. Having made this declaration, they are immediately, or very soon after, encouraged to be baptized by immersion.

Common Rite of Baptism by Immersion

Mosaic, like all churches, has rituals designed to engage a new shared identity (Toulis, 1997). These rituals affirm an alternative identity as one who is under the submission of Jesus Christ and also affirm the status of those who act on his behalf in performing them. Among them, baptism by immersion is prominent and important.

In deciding to be baptized, the individual completes a "baptism class" that presents the biblical meaning of baptism. The actual baptism usually takes place in a swimming pool or the ocean. Before entering the water, those being baptized are asked three questions: "Have you made a focused commitment of your life to Jesus Christ?" "Do you believe he has forgiven you of all your sin?" and "Are you saying before all of these witnesses that you are following Jesus and there is no turning back?" They answer yes (often very enthusiastically) to all the questions. The baptizer then states, "It is my privilege to baptize you, not under the authority of men, but in the name of the Father, the Son, and the Holy Spirit as my brother [or "sister"] in Christ." Then, while submerging them in the water, the baptizer proclaims, "Buried with Christ in baptism, and raised to walk in the newness of life!" The final proclamation emphasizes the death of an old identity (buried with Christ) and the taking on of a new one as a follower of Jesus (raised to walk in the newness of life).

This ritual engages the baptizer, the baptizee, and the witnessing community. The physical act of baptism affirms the belief of baptizer and baptizee, demonstrates the religious commitment of both, and asserts that they are both members of the same community. The ritual also serves to remind those previously baptized of their own baptism and the significance of their commitment, and to further acculturate the unbaptized to an aspect of being a follower of Jesus that they may not yet have grasped or still be negotiating. And in Mosaic's multiethnic context, it also affirms an almost familial connection between diverse peoples that supersedes ethnicity, as well as social class, educational level, and gender.

Common Commitment to Membership

New members are received monthly at Mosaic. Yet before new members go through this ritual, they complete two classes which acculturate them into the language, values, and priorities of the congregation. "Life in Christ" is first, consisting of five sessions, usually held before Sunday services or in members' homes. The first session begins with the mission statement of Mosaic ("To be a spiritual reference point throughout Los Angeles and a sending base to the ends of the earth") and is followed by presentation of a gospel message. Lessons follow on several aspects of life as a follower of Jesus, including baptism, prayer, Scripture reading, growth in character, involvement in the local church, and guidelines for sharing one's faith.

"Life in Church" is the second class and takes place at Pastor Erwin's home. It consists of one three-hour session that provides a chance to speak intensely and intimately with Erwin and one or more full-time staff members, in order to gain a clear understanding of the philosophical underpinnings of the church before committing to membership. Because "Life in Church" is the final step toward membership, most who come are well acquainted with the church, have many friendships within it, have joined a small group, and, often, are actively involved in an ongoing ministry team. People seem to enjoy spending time with their lead pastor, meeting others who are also becoming members, and hearing their church's philosophy articulated clearly and concisely. What they hear is a concentrated introduction to the practical theology of the church: for example, why small groups and serving in a ministry are important, five core convictions that supplement the church's doctrinal statement, and five core values that guide decision making. The session ends with a review of four commitments asked of every person joining Mosaic: (1) to keep a close relationship to God; (2) to actively participate in the life of the congregation through weekly celebration services and a smaller community such as a small group or a ministry team; (3) to tithe 10 percent of income to this church body; and (4) to maintain significant relationships with those who are not dedicated followers of Jesus Christ for the purpose of evangelism. The goal is to acculturate them into a shared identity as dedicated followers of Jesus Christ who take on the mission of this congregation. Pastor Erwin (McManus, 2001: 215) writes, "Becoming a member of Mosaic is a declaration that you are moving from being a consumer to being an investor, that you are joining not simply the community of Christ, but the cause of Christ."

Those becoming members face the congregation during the Lord's Supper celebrations and publicly affirm their commitments. The ritual is familiar to members. Pastor Erwin begins by saying, "No one joins Mosaic—," and the congregation shouts, "—*alone!*" This signals the beginning of what feels like a rally. People shift in their seats, the noise level goes up, and a feeling of anticipation emerges. Pastor Erwin holds up a membership booklet with a small certificate attached to the front, and the first name is called out. "Vincent Chang! Welcome to Mosaic!" The crowd cheers as Vincent makes his way to the front, and members of his small group or ministry team come with him. He gets his booklet, along with a hug, from Pastor Erwin and is then embraced by everyone from his small group or ministry team as they stand behind the pastor in front of the congregation. The next name is called; more whoops and clapping. As many as thirty-five people have been received into membership in one night. After all the books have been distributed, Pastor Erwin will turn and face the new members, repeat the four commitments that they have made, and end with a note of encouragement. These new members kneel and are anointed by an elder, leadership team member, or a spouse of one of these, commissioning them to being on mission in the world. Everyone receives a gift Bible, which is to be in turn given to a person with whom they are sharing the gospel. Pastor Erwin concludes, the crowd cheers once again, and everyone returns to their seats as the evening continues.

Several respondents describe the solidarity that comes from making an explicit commitment to the community of Mosaic. These common commitments not only reaffirm a new religious identity but also create connections to other members of Mosaic who reflect that identity back to them.

Common Meal in the Lord's Supper

The Lord's Supper is the communion service, held every month on a Wednesday night. It is not sacramental and not necessary for salvation, but a memorial or commemoration of the death, burial, and resurrection of Jesus Christ (see chapter 3). As Toulis (1997:152) explains, participants in this ritual are

> asked to examine themselves in light of the sacrifice which Jesus made for them and to consider whether they are worthy of receiving the supper. In self-examination, individuals assess their progress as "Christians," examine their relationships with God and others, and re-dedicate themselves to God.

Typically, about four hundred people participate in the Lord's Supper, less than the average Sunday attendance because it is held on a week-night and because guests do not normally come to this event. Those gathered at the Lord's Supper represent the committed core of the congregation. As Mandy said, "I love the Lord's Supper because I look around the room, and it's very diverse, and it's comforting to know that there's other people from other walks of life there at the church."

The theme of the Lord's Supper service centers on a country, usually the destination of a missionary. The ambiance, music, graphic art, and type of bread all relate to this theme. The elements of the evening are woven together into a contemporary, participatory, multisensory experience, and the service still succeeds in feeling sanctified, reverential, and consecrated.

With the taking of the bread and cup, the emphasis is on the sacrifice, servanthood, and mission of Jesus. These qualities of Jesus are to be reflected in the lives of those gathered. The common experience of eating and drinking emphasizes that everyone is part of a community under his leadership. Moreover, those gathered reaffirm their shared identity, mutually acknowledging the activities and messages occurring in the course of this evening. It is a reorienting experience that aligns people toward their identity as dedicated followers of Jesus Christ.

Common Character in Attitudes and Perspectives

Cultivating a shared identity as a dedicated follower of Jesus Christ includes internal reorientations toward certain virtues. At Mosaic, "character" is important and has a specific meaning. As discussed in chapter 5, the virtues of humility, faithfulness, and gratitude offer a conceptual roadmap for personal growth and allow leaders to assess where people fall on the map, highlighting deficiencies as well as an indication of what their next step of growth should be.

The essence of the model is that dedicated followers of Jesus Christ are not consumed with their own selves but are servants who care about others first (McManus, 2003). People willingly identify themselves as working on specific aspects of their character, often naming particular arenas that they feel are least developed. The character of potential leaders is assessed. Leaders are not to be abusive, exploitative, or in any way self-centered. A minimum criterion for stepping into a leadership role at Mosaic is evidence of humility, faithfulness, and gratitude. In addition, this model of character growth provides ways for leaders to guide the development of others.

These qualities are more important in the community of Mosaic than ethnic identity. This pervasive emphasis on personal character substitutes the virtues of humility, faithfulness, and gratitude for the performance of ethnically specific actions. This is conceptually related to Weber's observations about sect membership: "More important than any other factor is the fact that a man must hold his own under the watchful eyes of his peers" (1978:1206). While members can "become" leaders in a process like what Weber calls "depersonalization of charisma" (1135, 1139, 1159), leaders do not keep their position of spiritual authority at Mosaic long without demonstrating gratitude, faithfulness, and humility. Individuals can become leaders, but they keep that leadership role by manifesting personal charisma.

Shared Reorientation of Ethnic Identity

Multiethnicity is achieved in part by creating a haven for children and grandchildren of immigrants who are renegotiating their ethnic identities by moving from their ancestral culture to a more broadly Americanized culture. Within this overarching cultural context, charismatic leaders strategically manage their own identities to move others to take on an identity as a dedicated follower of Jesus. Summarizing theoretical insights gained from Weber and contemporary ethnicity theorists, I suggest that these spiritual leaders use three strategies in managing ethnic identity. These are connection, substitution, and transcendence. An ethnic connection grants status to leaders on the basis of a shared ethnic identity. Since ethnic bonds are more affectively based, they are powerful, and therefore such connections are pursued first. If an ethnic connection is not possible, then another status affinity is substituted. Ethnic transcendence is the third strategy. Status and legitimacy are granted on the basis of bearing a leadership role in a pre-established sacred realm. Those taking on an identity as a dedicated follower of Jesus participate within this sacred realm and consequently are apt to honor the authority which has been established within it. These leader-follower roles transcend ethnic affinities. Activities and rituals enacted by spiritual leaders within Mosaic serve to cultivate a shared identity as dedicated followers of Jesus Christ and reinforce status claims by spiritual leaders. The conclusion of this book will summarize the overall findings of this study, indicate several implications for congregational diversification, consider the future of this particular church, and explore the implications of Mosaic's organizational practices for the religious experiences of emerging generations in America.

CONCLUSION

TREVOR: I really think Mosaic is on the cusp of something. We're moving with momentum, and God is moving in people's lives.

ERWIN: We don't call ourselves a contemporary church; we call ourselves an experimental church. We see ourselves as the R&D department of the kingdom of God.

This study began as an exploration of how Mosaic came to be a multiethnic church. How does Mosaic attract and keep its diverse population? Ethnically inclusive communities like Mosaic are important not only because they are rare but because they may hold the key to resolving one of the most persistent social problems in America: racial segregation. When a diverse people voluntarily congregate together, the dream of integrated community is fulfilled. The value of diverse congregations is acknowledged by both religious scholars and practitioners; for example, Carroll and Roof (2002: 214) expect one of the essential qualities of successful congregations in the near future to be the ability to integrate diversity:

> Perhaps the test of a strong religious institution in times of great social change is not its diversity of theological and cultural styles, but how well it handles that diversity. The challenge ahead for the congregation is to create an environment that not only accepts and respects this internal pluralism but institutionalizes creative ways of dealing with it theologically and programmatically.

The ability to overcome the challenge of diversity reveals an important aspect of Mosaic. Here is a multiethnic congregation with three dominant groups, Caucasian, Hispanic, and Asian; yet in the end this analysis reveals that the more fundamental characteristic of Mosaic is the ability to access alternative bases of identity and construct a new corporate identity that transcends ethnicity. Mosaic did not achieve multiethnicity by selectively parceling out arenas of ethnicity ("Who's missing?") and creating segmented programs for their incorporation ("Let's get them!"). Instead of targeting ethnic groups, Mosaic became multiethnic as a by-product of innovatively creating inclusive arenas that make ethnic identity irrelevant—or at least much less relevant. Multilayered personal identities are accessed through one or more havens that emerge from innovations charismatic leaders enact in response to a changing social environment. Interpersonal interaction in the context of attractive arenas of involvement facilitates the strategic work of managing and reconstructing identity toward a common mission.

Innovation and Diversification in Pursuit of Mission

Given the complexity of the social self and the many groups a person may be a member of, ethnicity is only one aspect of the self, an aspect whose salience is variable. In a contemporary, pluralistic society, people do not base their entire identities on ethnicity alone. This can be illustrated by something as common as pumping gasoline; at gas stations, the lines of inclusion involve need for fuel, not ethnicity. On a much broader level, it is possible to define inclusion on a basis other than ethnicity so that diverse people can find themselves in the same inclusive space. The ability to cultivate and nurture these spaces is critical.

Mosaic demonstrates that social systems contain many more boundaries than ethnic boundaries. Barth's work on boundaries between ethnic groups (1969) assumes ethnic boundaries always exist—a "fence" between ethnic groups is always there—although they may be moved back and forth or rearranged. However, the community established within Mosaic does not fall neatly within ethnic boundaries, because the lines of inclusion and exclusion are multiple and selectively enforced such that ethnic boundaries may be deemphasized in favor of others.

Mosaic is a place where leaders continually construct places of inclusion whose boundaries make ancestral ethnic affiliations less relevant. These multiple havens provide multiethnic spaces of interaction and community. In these places of refuge, participants are included, find companionship, and contribute to the mission of the church. Each haven emerges out of beliefs and practices channeled by charismatic leaders within the congregation. These are multiple, overlapping, and interlocking spaces that not only accept but attract diverse peoples, incorporating them into ministry activities. Charismatic leaders create places of inclusion, multiethnic spaces that simultaneously propel the twin organizational purposes of evangelistic growth and influence.

What is significant at Mosaic is the ability to reorient identities so that people of various ethnic heritages subdue their ethnic distinctions in favor of one common religious identity within this diverse congregation. Church leaders and members co-construct a new shared identity, especially through rituals and shared practices. Although Weber did not explicitly address the relationship between ethnic identity and charismatic authority, his writings indicate the fluidity of ethnicity and the power of charismatic leaders to create new bases of affinity. The strategic management of ethnic identity is a central process in the exercise of charismatic authority within this church. Selectively emphasizing or obscuring their ethnic identity depending on social context, leaders strategically manage their charismatic authority to construct a base of mutual affinity among ethnically diverse peoples. They may connect with potential followers on the basis of common ethnic status, or substitute another basis to transcend ethnic identity and create a new base of shared identity as dedicated followers of Jesus Christ who are on mission.

Mosaic fits the profile of what Ammerman, Farnsley, and Adams describe as a "niche congregation." They (1997: 130–131) write,

> [N]iche congregations do not serve a specific locale. They reach beyond an immediate neighborhood to create an identity relatively independent of context. While many forces still bind congregation and · community to each other, making parish-style congregations a recognizable part of the religious landscape, there are also strong forces creating a larger urban religious ecology with many choices not tied

to residential neighborhood. The implications of a mobile, cosmopolitan culture, where congregational choice is the norm, make such specialized religious sorting more and more likely. . . . The community that is operative for any given congregation, then, may not fall neatly within geographic boundaries, being defined instead by the social niche it has established.

Mosaic has become a "niche-embracing" church that accomplishes diversity through its culture and purpose, creating attractive spaces for people with particular desires and preferences (Emerson and Kim, 2003; see also Stark and Finke, 2000: 195–198). Multiple havens allow several points of contact for people from all over the cosmopolitan region of Los Angeles. Danièle Hervieu-Léger calls these "affective parishes," which she defines as "religious neo-tribes that have lost their connection to place but none the less operate as 'community'" (see Lyon 2000: 104–105). And Warner's (1988) case study of the Presbyterian church of Mendocino, California, affirms that the "liveliest churches" are those that accommodate themselves to their community. Because Mosaic's celebration services occur on many sites, in rented facilities—are almost nomadic—they create multiple points of connection, furthering affinity, belonging, and community through multiple arenas of congregational participation. Most important, Mosaic accesses a textured, multifaceted identity found in a highly urbanized context. Social niches are created that emphasize aspects of identity other than ethnicity, that render ethnic identity moot. Indeed, perhaps Mosaic is more accurately defined as a "multiniche" congregation.

Subculture identity theory (C. Smith, 1998) helps account for the vibrancy of evangelicalism in America over the past half-century, and may affirm my understanding of the racial and ethnic diversity within Mosaic. According to Smith's subculture identity theory, evangelicals manifest great religious strength due to their faithfulness to their form of orthodoxy, their expressions of great salience and robustness in their faith, their participation in regular church activities, and their support for the mission of their churches, particularly in the winning of new converts. Smith argues that the vitality evident among evangelicals is due to the distinctive subculture they share. For example, evangelicals see themselves as distinct from mainline Christianity, as having a moral stance superior to that of mainline Christians, and as actively participating in the world around them. Some see themselves as fighting against forces that oppose them. Evangelicals thrive because they enact a distinctive subculture that has a clear mission in the midst of a pluralistic society. Mosaic, through its multiple havens, provides multiple arenas for initiating people into the broad evangelical subculture. In the end, other bases for identity are released in favor of a shared identity within evangelicalism.

Mosaic also demonstrates that there are many layers to individual identity, and each of the havens at Mosaic may be viewed as a particular subculture that accesses different layers of individual identity outside of evangelicalism. This has implications for the possibility of racial reconciliation. Specifically, racial reconciliation is possible when church leaders recognize that members of ethnic and racial groups can participate in subcultures where racial differences are relatively unimportant. However, since any particular subculture will not attract every member of different racial or ethnic groups, complete racial reconciliation may be an impossible goal. Therefore, congregational blending within evangelicalism demands a successful negotiation of the multiple bases of identity in a pluralistic society, yet a complete unity between races and ethnicities may simply be unattainable. Indeed, in order to overcome racial differences, churches may have to establish or co-opt several subcultures that will still inevitably exclude individuals on a base other than race or ethnicity.

In summary, havens at Mosaic emerge out of a sense of a mission to evangelize the people of Los Angeles. Mission is the central organizing principle in this congregation. Mission informs, inspires, and instructs all aspects of the organization. In their bold pursuit of mission in the dynamic, metropolitan context of Los Angeles, the leaders of Mosaic cultivate an innovative stance that asks, "What must be done to reach people for Jesus Christ?" Aside from global evangelistic commitments through both long- and short-term overseas mission trips, Mosaic's mission is accomplished primarily in Los Angeles. For the leaders of this congregation, evangelism in Los Angeles necessitates relevance to local peoples and styles of life. Charismatic leaders find points of affinity and leverage these toward the adoption of a new religious identity. As a result of aggressive, innovative efforts to reach out to the broad mass of people who live in L.A., Mosaic has become an innovative organization that provides multiple arenas for multiethnic interaction, companionship, and camaraderie that transcend ethnic affiliations, and, thereby, accomplish diversity.

Multiethnic Assimilation, Younger Generations, and African American Culture

This section will speculate on the nature of certain religious movements today, the significance of these movements to younger generations, the effort of white pastors to cultivate diverse congregations, the relation of these developments to African Americans, and the future of Mosaic.

Premodernism, Ethnic Culture, and the Quest for Authentic Spirituality

Many young adults are attending churches characterized by candles, liturgy, and sacred art. In turn, many churches are trying to reach younger generations by using these elements in an attempt to create church services that invoke a "medieval" spirituality. Kimball's *The Emerging Church* (2003) is one of many books, articles, and conferences for pastors describing a model for creating "alternative," "contemporary," or "postmodern" celebration services. While Kimball's book emphasizes mission and relevance, it evokes a spirituality that looks back to a more "ancient" faith. However, this ancestral memory of ancient faith, I believe, exists predominantly in the minds of young Caucasians. Young whites are attempting to access a memory of a faith supposedly older and, therefore, more pure.

Modernity is usually characterized by a comprehensive systematization, i.e., a machinelike control represented by bureaucratization, standardization, efficiency, and mass output through industrialized processes. Spirituality based on modernity is being rejected in many churches today. One dominant reaction against modernity is to reject a sterile and streamlined faith and try to move back to premodern conditions in order to access a more unrefined, unprocessed type of spirituality. In cultivating their spirituality, young whites are essentially rejecting a post-Enlightenment style of faith that grew out of fundamentalism. They reject a faith that appears to be not just mildly tainted but thoroughly corrupted by modernity. They are going back to the last popular expression of Christianity they are aware of *before* modernity and attempting to access the medieval (sometimes Roman, sometimes Celtic) church, in the hope that this premodern faith is a more authentic faith, closer to "real" Christianity. No one believes it represents first-century Christianity; it is not a primitive faith, but an attempt to re-create a premodern faith. However, it is not representative of premodern Christianity as it was actually practiced either in the exercise of ecclesiastical authority or in the articulation of theological distinctions; rather, it is a highly selective re-creation, taking a few desirable elements and elevating them to prominence.

I believe this attempt to re-create an earlier form of the Christian faith will not flourish. First, it is a reactionary response that lacks creativity in responding to social change. As other alternatives emerge and the fashion of worship styles change, it will be supplanted by something else. Second, and more important, the current attempt to build a pre-modern Christianity is not amenable to multiethnicity. It is a mono-ethnic spirituality, because it plays on popular stereotypes that exist only within white European culture. African Americans, for example, do not share this medieval European ancestral memory. And certainly immi-grants from India, China, the Middle East, and South America (despite the Roman Catholic presence dating from the conquistadors onward) are not accessing this ethnically specific historical memory either. Mov-ing into a white European ancient Christianity is a significant cultural leap for all these ethnic groups. In the minds of young Caucasians who hate their "boring" and "ugly" church, re-creating this aesthetic makes sense. But African Americans and nonwhite immigrants know this does not represent their ancestral spiritual history. They do not experience this spirituality as more "authentic"; it is yet another form of white culture to which they must acclimate.

The move toward craftsmanship is an alternative attempt to recover a valued aspect of premodern life. This second strategy is to move away from homogenization to an accentuation of difference that allows people to creatively and spontaneously participate in religious activities. Indi-vidual contribution is not only welcomed but considered necessary. Mo-saic has chosen this second response, accentuating intense, individual contributions from congregants. Members are encouraged, not to be good consumers of religion, but instead to participate as spiritual crafts-men. Mosaic encourages the use of electronic music, digital media, and urbanized ambiance while welcoming the unique contributions of peo-ple with skills, gifts, and talents in each of these arenas. Rather than rejecting all that is modern ("Turn off the lights and get out the can-dles!"), it embraces technological elements that allow new forms of art-istry and creativity.

Churches may succeed because they have many things to offer re-ligious patrons. There is a "religious marketplace" in which "church shoppers" are attempting to be good, spiritual consumers of religious experiences (for more on the "rational choice theory" in religion, see Finke and Stark, 1992; Roof, 1993, 1999; Stark and Bainbridge, 1987; Young, 1997). Yet I believe that people are increasingly seeking not merely "good choices" but authenticity in their religious experiences. In a church culture that values individual craftsmanship instead of religious consumerism of preprogrammed activities, people get to shape and put their personal stamp on their religious engagement. I believe Mosaic demonstrates that churches that create spaces for unique, individual contributions may draw more and more people in the coming century. The managerial demands of routinely incorporating creative input are quite high. Yet this adaptive response to social change may make a church more popular and contribute to its growth.

ACCOMPLISHING DIVERSIFICATION IN WHITE AMERICAN CHURCHES

My observations of church leaders outside of Mosaic suggest that creating multiethnic churches is a concern mostly among Caucasian pastors of European descent. (Nonwhite ethnic pastors seem far more preoccupied with trying to protect their ethnic heritage and keep younger generations from leaving their churches.) When Caucasian pastors describe their attempts to diversify their ministry, they adopt the perspective of a foreign missionary and attempt to cross over broad spans of culture. Pastors tell me they are "proud of their outreach to Cambodian boat people" or they are "making inroads to the Vietnamese community" or they are "creating a program focusing on [insert any Third-World ethnic group here], who recently moved into the area."

These white pastors create auxiliary ministries targeting distinct immigrant groups. They make a cross-cultural leap to reach first-generation immigrants. These groups are highly segregated. They are just as homogeneous as the white churches trying to assimilate them. Such strategies fail to substantively increase the degree of congregational diversity. Most church members do not participate in outreach ministries. Also, these ministries target small segments of the local population while neglecting the increasingly diverse population of their region.

A less popular strategy that is nonetheless frequently mentioned by white pastors is the use of ethnic music. A congregation will sing a worship song in a tribal language from Africa or incorporate a Spanish refrain. By diversifying the languages of the worship songs, church leaders believe they are diversifying the cultural experience of the congregation. They feel they are "celebrating culture" by displaying cultural differences. However, the move to celebrate cultures can unintentionally further isolate cultures from each other and create a sense of competition over which culture is being honored over another. And if a congregation contains numerous ethnicities, it would be impossible to celebrate the dozens of nationalities represented; for example, a single congregation cannot meaningfully sing in several languages of East and Southeast Asia (such as Korean, Japanese, Vietnamese, and Cantonese and Mandarin Chinese) in addition to reflecting the cadence and intonation characteristic of regions of Mexico, South America, or the Caribbean.

Rather than accentuating foreign cultures, Mosaic conducts its activity in the context of a popular American culture accessible to English-speaking second- and third-generation immigrants living in Los Angeles. This culture is already accessible to young Caucasians, and its accessibility provides the church with the opportunity to become multiethnic. The children and grandchildren of immigrants assimilate into the segment of American culture most accessible to them: white popular culture. These ethnics are socialized into popular culture through readily accessible media channels, substituting it for their identification with their ancestral history. Their American culture is formed by their most recent experiences outside their parents' culture. Churches may effectively accomplish diversification by focusing on the acculturated children and grandchildren of immigrants. If white-dominant churches keep up with popular culture, second- and third-generation immigrants will be more able to access a spirituality based on a culture they have come to understand. Additionally, success in reaching second- and third-generation immigrants could provide opportunities to reach local first-generation immigrants. An ever-expansive mission could extend the margins of a congregation to include ever more distant cultural expressions.

The experience of Mosaic suggests that truly multiethnic congregations are more likely to emerge from predominantly Caucasian churches if, instead of reaching out to a culture they have never known, they catch up to the culture of which they are already members. For a second- or third-generation immigrant (whether Asian, Hispanic, or Middle Eastern), stepping into a "traditional" church often means having to make yet another cross-cultural leap. Caucasian pastors may diversify their churches more quickly if they are willing to move their churches into contemporary culture, which is becoming increasingly globalized, and mobilize themselves not so much to reach first-generation immigrants, who are isolated from the churches' patterns of life, but their children and grandchildren, who are already in mainstream America's schools, offices, and grocery stores. The ancestral culture of their parents and grandparents is foreign to them; instead, their culture is "American" and their cultural experiences are obtained from the sources most accessible to them, i.e., television, movies, and radio. Even while they participate in many face-to-face interactions that acculturate them, the common basis of much interaction is derived from media of mainstream American culture.

In contrast to acculturated immigrant groups, African Americans in the United States have their own distinct American culture separate from white American culture (and from every immigrant culture coming into the United States). African Americans attempting to assimilate into a white culture make a cultural leap. Consequently, the culture of second-generation immigrants is more similar to young Caucasian popular culture than to African American culture. Indeed, research shows that African Americans do not assimilate well into white culture.

Yancey (2003) forcefully argues that African Americans experience an alienation that cannot be compared to that felt by other racial and ethnic groups. Drawing on the changing definitions of what it means to be "white," Yancey speculates that Hispanics and Asians have a good chance of being well assimilated in the coming century and, therefore, will be redefined as white, much as southern and eastern Europeans were in the 1900s (Alba, 1995; Kennedy, 1944). This process will leave African Americans at the bottom of the racial hierarchy, since they will never be defined as white (according to Yancey), so the persistent black/nonblack racial divide will continue into the future (see also Gans, 1999). Other research by Quillian and Campbell (2003) on friendship patterns in multiracial schools indicates an important black/nonblack segregation: friendships are more likely to form among whites, white Hispanics, and Asians, with black Hispanics and blacks clustering separately.

Given the challenge African Americans face in assimilating to white-dominant popular culture, it is not surprising that Mosaic is primarily white, Hispanic, and Asian, with a smaller proportion of African Americans. Mosaic remains committed to connecting with the dominant popular culture, what David called the "MTV–Pepsi Generation" culture, and the culture of African Americans does not fit it. Indeed, my interviews suggest that young African Americans are currently caught between cultures. While they do not readily relate to white culture, they also do not relate to their parents, uncles, or cousins in their "black" culture. In particular, they reject their parents' and grandparents' African American expressions of spirituality.

Certain cultural developments, however, may increase the proportion of African Americans at Mosaic and other multiethnic congregations in the future. African Americans have told me there are striking generational differences between blacks who grew up before and after the successes of the civil rights movement. Younger blacks are more open to multiethnic interaction and are more comfortable in a diverse society that appears increasingly to be embracing them as well. A greater number of African Americans are willing to assimilate into a diversifying culture since popular culture is becoming more inclusive of them. The coming generations of African Americans may be more willing to connect to this more inclusive popular culture. Indeed, a time may come (how soon is impossible to tell) when every ethnic group may be able to access a common popular culture that is diverse, ethnically sensitive, and globally embracing. Future research should investigate how congregations that include both blacks and nonblacks are different from each other and how the dynamics of diversification differ when African Americans form a sizeable proportion of the church (for an initial discussion see Marti, 2003, 2004).

Until then, Mosaic may involve enough young adults in artistic efforts that, even though it participates in a white assimilated culture, more African Americans will be willing to make the cultural leap necessary to join. So the proportion of African Americans may increase at Mosaic due to the existence and even multiplication of havens that attract them on a basis other than race, until a time when popular culture changes to become more consonant with African American culture.

Unanswered Questions and Unexplored Issues

Not every viable research question was answered in this analysis; many important issues were not pursued. First, this analysis did not tease out many of the stresses and contradictions evident in organizations. Since the initial research question focused on attraction and retention, respondents were asked what brought them to and kept them at Mosaic. Consequently, their answers concentrated on what they liked about the church. Mosaic is certainly not a perfect church; it has internal conflicts and contradictions, as would be expected in any associative union. But in this analysis, not all of the various tensions and contradictions that emerge from each of the "havens" found at Mosaic were explored. Pursuing the mission of the congregation surely involves strategic tradeoffs. Moreover, in the ongoing activity of Mosaic, many projects have been tried; not all have been successful. Organizational failures which distracted from or worked against the goals of the church were not explored.

Second, while leadership is a frequent theme in the analysis, many questions regarding the exercise of authority were not systematically addressed. Apart from the extended discussion of charismatic authority in relation to ethnic identity management in chapter 7, important aspects of organizational leadership, such as the mechanisms for decision making, church discipline, and negotiation of competing visions for the church, were not explored.

Third, the innovative nature of Mosaic presents interesting challenges. Will people continue to accept ongoing change? Will the rate of change decrease? If arenas of innovation increase, can the church continue to keep coherent boundaries so that all its parts move consistently with each other? In the face of continual innovation, the challenge for the church is to maintain a consistent direction so that every innovation contributes to the central mission. How the church is preparing itself for the inherent threats of innovation was not explored.

Fourth, the style and future prospects of Mosaic's lead pastor, Erwin McManus, raise several interesting questions. For example, what will happen when the leadership of the church passes to another? Innovation and Pastor Erwin's leadership have been interconnected. The previous lead pastor found his own replacement, after twenty years. Is it possible that Erwin will be patient enough to wait for his own replacement? The emergence of like-minded churches across the country and the multiplication of Mosaic church-plants mean more places where a successor could be discovered and cultivated. Perhaps in the coming years Erwin will find someone he perceives to be capable of leading the congregation better while honoring the goals and values he emphasized.

Fifth, a comprehensive description of the type of leadership necessary for leading a multiethnic church like Mosaic is lacking. Briefly, I believe Mosaic demonstrates that in order to grow and thrive in a metropolitan region like Los Angeles, leaders must shape congregations to (1) have an ideological framework emphasizing mission to the whole metropolitan region; (2) reflect the diversity of the region by diversifying leadership; (3) affirm individual creativity, talent, and skill; (4) co-opt an array of media channels (e.g., drama, music, and film) for communicating the core message and values; (5) move as quickly as other fast-paced regional organizations in embracing and pursuing innovation; and (6) target future leaders, especially nonwhites and single young adults. As lead pastor, Erwin imparts a clear sense of vision and direction that followers can easily absorb. Erwin is increasingly "hands-off," giving away large ministry projects in such a way that people have the authority and responsibility to make their own decisions. Erwin has a high tolerance for failure; he encourages experimentation. People in the congregation seem to capture this sentiment and run with it. As a result, more and more people are willing to take purposeful initiative in pursuing new projects. Overall, an analysis of his leadership and its implications for leadership of other multiethnic churches was not pursued.

Sixth and finally, many interesting questions concern the age structure of Mosaic. Will Mosaic continue to be a youth-oriented church? What happens to members as they grow older? And what happens as the leadership of the church ages? Will leadership constantly accommodate itself to appeal to youth? As the church grows, perhaps young adults will continue to be hired. And when people leave the church through natural turnover, the church may continue to favor bringing in even more young adults. Or perhaps the attraction to the young is a broad-based cohort phenomenon such that Mosaic will remain attractive both to current youth as they age and to children growing into young adults. Generational and cohort concerns were largely ignored.

Capturing a Movement in Action

In view of Mosaic's achievements and the increased attention Mosaic and its leader, Erwin McManus, are receiving from other church leaders, Mosaic appears to be part of an emerging social movement. Perhaps Mosaic is not the vanguard, but it certainly appears to be an organizational representative of an overall movement in church revitalization that incorporates artistic, change-friendly young adults in twenty-first-century churches. As Sargeant (2000: 145) states, "When innovative churches are successful, they quickly become the model for others."

Doug McAdam (1999) synthesizes the insights of contemporary theorists of social movements and presents a conceptual framework for understanding the emergence of new movements. He specifically highlights five critical processes, which I will explore in light of Mosaic and its social context. First, *exogenous change processes* indicate the role of broad social changes which destabilize customary relations within a society. Rapid technological development, the multiplication of non-Christian religious bodies, and the rise of postmodern sensibilities have certainly destabilized the traditional religious landscape of America. In a highly literate culture where information is almost instantaneously accessible, information gained in sermons and Bible study will be less and less important to Christians in the next century. The Reformation opened access to theological knowledge in the form of the Scriptures; one unintended result is the belief that the church is unnecessary, superfluous, and actually a hindrance to authentic spiritual experience. Another is an excessive focus on doctrinal articulation drawn from a scientistic approach to the Bible. The church in a literate, "information-rich" culture must offer more than good information.

Second, *interpretive processes which influence a collective attribution of opportunity or threat* are evident in an emerging stream of evangelicalism. A growing number of "new evangelicals" "reject institutionalized routines and taken for granted assumptions about the world" and are starting to "fashion new world views and lines of interaction" (McAdam, 1999: xxi). Erwin McManus's book *An Unstoppable Force* (2001) is a distinctive expression of ideas circulating among these new evangelical leaders. Dan Kimball's *The Emerging Church* (2003) and Leonard Sweet's *SoulTsunami* (1999b) are others. Church leaders in organizations like the Leadership Network and the Terranova Theological Project are questioning traditional ways of doing church and exploring new ideas and practices. These and other church leaders believe American society has substantially changed in the past few decades and are attempting to adjust their congregations accordingly. Robert Webber (2002) labels these "the younger evangelicals." They grew up in the 1980s and 1990s and are trying to accommodate evangelicalism to a new, postmodern society.

Third, *appropriation of existing organizational space and routine collective identities* corresponds to growth in the innovative use of church facilities (or the use of nonchurch facilities for church functions) as well as alternative definitions of what it means to be a Christian. Many churches are choosing to abandon traditional church buildings and rent facilities, including nightclubs, movie theaters, warehouses, and entire shopping malls. Some church buildings are being refurbished to look like coffeehouses, with lounges and decentralized seating areas. Others are prominently incorporating contemporary paintings, sculptures, and new forms of architecture. Mosaic avoids the word "Christian" and prefers "dedicated follower of Jesus Christ." At the Oasis Christian Center, another congregation in Los Angeles, believers are "Champions in Life" who have fun, build lifelong relationships, and inspire others. Brian McLaren's *A New Kind of Christian* (2001) and its sequel *The Story We Find Ourselves In* (2003) renegotiate Christian identity through a dialogue between a pastor struggling with his failing belief system and a former pastor mentoring him in different ways of thinking. The first book won *Christianity Today*'s "Best Christian Living" book award, and the second book quickly became a bestseller.

Fourth, *innovative collective action and the onset of contention* represents "action that departs from previous collective routines" (McAdam, 1999: xxxvi). Mosaic demonstrates innovation in the various activities that together construct the multiple havens at Mosaic. These innovations in theology and practice are mirrored, imitated, and echoed in churches around the country. As part of the stream of "new paradigm" churches (Miller, 1997), Mosaic has a particular constituency within this movement. McAdam and Snow (1997) address the role of organizations in movements, saying that movements cannot be adequately understood without reference to specific organizations. The civil rights movement, the women's movement, and the pro-life and pro-choice movements all have organizational representatives. Some movements are associated with particular organizations; for example, the Willow Creek Community Church is associated with the seeker church movement. Leaders of other churches look to Mosaic for ideas, direction, and a particular kind of mentoring in the framing of theological statements as well as the use of art, music, and drama to connect with younger adults. Erwin McManus is a bestselling author who speaks to hundreds of thousands of church leaders yearly at conferences and other speaking engagements. And Mosaic's Origins conference is drawing more leaders who are taking up these innovations. This innovative collective action leads to ongoing, collective contention with mainline tradition and "older" styles of doing church: both the styles of former times and those preferred by older people.

Fifth, *contentious politics* describes the interaction of "popular discontent" and the "elite discontent" that arises in response to it. Social movements are born out of the interaction between elite and popular discontent, which produces a sustained contention that carries the movement forward. With Mosaic, such an interaction is evident in the attention paid by various segments of institutionalized Christianity to the ministry of this Los Angeles church. Erwin and other Mosaic leaders are consulted by the headquarters of several denominations (e.g., Southern Baptists, the Lutheran Church, the Missouri Synod), large parachurch organizations (e.g., Promise Keepers, Campus Crusade for Christ, Fuller Seminary), and influential and innovative American churches (e.g., Willow Creek Community Church, Saddleback Community Church, the Crystal Cathedral). Christian leaders visit Mosaic, attend its conferences, and invite its staff members to speak to their organizations. Large institutions distribute Mosaic audiotapes and books to their people and create study guides to facilitate discussion of them.

In describing Mosaic, one captures a movement in action. Mosaic is an organizational representative of a vibrant religious social movement. The role of Mosaic within this movement of church revitalization may be best described as frame amplification, i.e., "the clarification and invigoration of an interpretive frame that bears on a particular issue, problem or set of events" (Snow et al., 1986: 468). Values amplified through Mosaic include the power of the local church, the concern with evangelism, the need for cultural relevance, and the priority on creativity. Beliefs amplified through Mosaic include that the church exists for mission, that leaders exist to serve others, and that every person is open to God. Mosaic is contributing to an emerging form of evangelicalism that is mission-driven, creativity-affirming, innovation-friendly, and, significantly, ethnically diverse.

APPENDIX A. METHODOLOGICAL CONSIDERATIONS FROM A RELIGIOUS INSIDER

Herbert J. Gans (1994:589) wrote,

> [T]he study of how people construct, carry out, feel about, their ethnic and religious lives, including their identities, is going to become ever more interesting. The availability of immigrant, second- and later-generation Americans of an unsurpassed diversity should lead to the flowering of joint ethnic and religious studies, and if enough ethnographic fieldwork and depth-interview studies could be carried out, proper micro- and macro-sociological analyses might finally be possible.

I had the opportunity to undertake such a study. Pursuing it allowed me to make a scholarly contribution to areas that engage my identity, my own intellectual preoccupations, and my career. However, because this case study used ethnographic methodology in obtaining data, legitimate concerns emerge regarding my status as a religious insider.

What McCutcheon calls the "insider/outsider problem in the study of religion" (1999) is under ongoing discussion. The dilemma of qualitative work is that researchers must get close to get the data; however, being close inevitably affects the data itself, since interacting with people affects their behavior. The researchers' task is to assess whether they have marred the data relevant to the research question. The study of religion poses particularly acute problems because some believe that outsiders to a religious system can never truly understand it, however close they may come. Conversely, religious insiders may be too close, as their immersion in their own religious beliefs and practices seems to make it unlikely that they will solicit, obtain, and report valid, unbiased information, especially if they think such information will undermine their religious beliefs or betray others in their religious system. Regardless of the particular study, understanding how researchers solicit, obtain, and report their information is critical to understanding the analysis as a whole.

Since all researchers have a particular social location that impacts the research process, I offer this appendix to clarify and present my own. Most ethnographers studying religion enter communities whose values and beliefs they do not share. I, however, faced an inversion of that dilemma. I found myself at the center of a sociologically significant phenomenon which other scholars were already investigating (e.g., DeYoung et al., 2003; Flory and Miller, 2000) and that involved topics of broader interest to scholars of race and religion (e.g., Christerson, Emerson, and Edwards, 2005; Emerson and Kim, 2003; Emerson and Smith, 2000). I had the opportunity to turn a sociological eye on an ethnically diverse congregation from the inside. Fortunately, scholars are openly bringing themselves more intimately into the research process and entering communities to which they are or become sympathetic. The line between "outsider" and "insider" is blurring, prompting continued dialogue on the nature of such work (Spickard, Landres, and McGuire, 2002). Below, I explore the unique challenge of undertaking qualitative research as a staff member in this congregation. In the end, I suggest a few methodological guidelines for other religious insiders pursuing such delicate work.

Qualitative Research and the Dilemma of Researcher Involvement

Qualitative fieldwork has grown significantly in the past few decades. Qualitative fieldwork operates within an interpretive paradigm which recognizes "facts" not as objective realities but as social meanings attributed by social actors in interaction with others, and incorporates fieldworkers as actors in the setting studied (Berg, 1989; Wilson, 1970). According to Robert Emerson (1983:vii),

> As field research has become more explicit about and more committed to such an interpretive paradigm, it has not only become less apologetic about field methods and findings, but it has also begun the difficult task of tracing through the full implications of this approach.

Qualitative research derives its methodology less from geography (locating oneself in a particular social setting) and more from empathetic understanding (understanding symbolic activities with intimate familiarity). This is the *verstehen* or interpretive understanding discussed by Max Weber (1978). Fieldwork is characterized by immersion in a social world and the "ability to grasp the symbolic nexus between thought and action in a particular social milieu" (Schwartz and Merten, 1971:280–281; see also Geertz, 1973). The goal in such analysis is to approach the world "as subjectively experienced" by the social actor (Goffman, 1961:ix). Qualitative research assumes that systematic inquiry takes place in the natural setting of social actors, and the observational focus is on uncovering the processes in social life (Marshall and Rossman, 1989). Such research involves scrutiny of "statements and actions for patterns, inconsistencies, contradictions, and intended and unintended consequences" (Charmaz, 1983:113).

A particular challenge of ethnographic research is gaining access to informants and establishing rapport with them. It is not only access to participants but also relationships of trust that are essential for gathering data. The quality of interview data and participant observation is almost always a function of the rapport a researcher has with the social actors studied (Douglas, 1976; Johnson, 1983). Ethnographic data collection requires the researcher to "penetrate the rational appearances of the public front of a setting" and build "relations of trust with the individuals there to obtain a truthful, empathetic, valid and reliable understanding of the actions occurring there" (Johnson, 1983:254). In studying religion specifically, Lyon (2000:18) recommends that as social researchers "we should be prepared to listen sympathetically to the accounts of believers."

My ethnographic research project required me to immerse myself in Mosaic. Such immersion is a valid method of gathering data. Gold (1958) characterized this approach as "participant-as-observer," which involves entering the lives of the people studied as closely as possible while making them aware of the research project. Nevertheless, since I was one of the members of Mosaic's pastoral staff during the time of this study, due consideration must be given to how my position affected the answers given by respondents. Such consideration is necessary in any qualitative analysis in which the investigator is immersed in the social context, has established rapport, and is actively interacting within the social environment. As Brasher (1998:6) states, "A cardinal goal of any religious ethnography, including this one, is to advance our understanding of lived religion, that is, religion as it is commonly practiced; however, the epistemological ambiguities entailed in ethnographic work are considerable." Let me begin with my base of rapport within this congregation.

My Access and Rapport within Mosaic

I began attending Mosaic in 1995 and marveled at the degree of diversity evident in the congregation even then. At that time, it was predominantly Hispanic and white, with a few dozen Asians and several people of Middle Eastern descent. A few African Americans attended, and a longtime member who was African American led music and worship.

Having come from churches that were all overwhelmingly white, I found the diversity refreshing. I was teaching sociology classes that examined issues of race and ethnicity. As I explored my own ethnic identity and observed the interaction and integration of people of various ethnicities, my curiosity continued to grow. Very quickly, my wife Laura and I formed many relationships with church members and became active in the life of the congregation. I was asked to join the pastoral staff in late 1996 and remained on staff through the time of this study.

I was able to do qualitative research largely because of the trust I had established with a broad range of participants at Mosaic since 1995. Ammerman (1987:11; see also 1982) discusses the value of being accepted as an insider:

> I am committed to the Christian faith; and I knew that I could translate much of my experience into terms this group would recognize and accept. I could speak the language of an insider, and I was willing to live by an insider's rules. [. . .] Because I was identified as saved and spoke the language of a saved person, I was accepted by most of the congregation and granted access that a complete outsider might never have gained.

When I suggested this study to the leaders of the church, they immediately encouraged me to pursue it. I was granted access in 2001 to written materials, database records, lay leaders, members, attenders, and guests for the purpose of research. My study generated curiosity among staff, elders, members, and regular attenders at Mosaic. "What have you found?" was asked often; to this I said, "I don't want to taint you before I interview you." It was a good answer that gave me time to think and to include more people in a conversation. At times I would tentatively share an observation or two as a "member check" to see if people invested in Mosaic recognized themselves in the concepts and theories I presented. Their objections or amendments to my conclusions were great occasions for more questions and further learning.

While I believe my rapport within Mosaic allowed me to gather high-quality data, my involvement at Mosaic may have had an effect on the process of data collection. I bring myself into this study. As a matter of full disclosure, I present below what I perceive as personal influences relevant to my conduct of this study.

AMBIGUITY IN MY OWN ETHNIC IDENTITY

As the son of Cuban immigrants who learned English as a second language, I have had many occasions to reflect on my own ethnic identity.

I was born in Massachusetts, raised in Southern California, and surrounded for the majority of my early life by the local Cuban community. I have light skin, appearing "Anglo" rather than "Hispanic," and have as a result benefited from passing as white. In my acculturation I have been encouraged to be white and been rewarded for doing so. This has created internal ambiguity and external social tensions in my own ethnic orientation.

I empathize with the generational tensions experienced by children of immigrants. I understand the feelings of marginality that emerge when people regularly cross vast cultural boundaries in daily life. Finally, I also understand the sense of stupidity or betrayal experienced by other children of immigrants who suppose me to be a full-blooded member of an ethnic group but find that I cannot or do not act like a "normal" member of that group (e.g., speak Spanish fluently, follow Cuban cultural mores). Many times I have been told that I am not "truly" Cuban.

As I grow older and reflect on my ethnic heritage, I find that I have choices. Do I take as my own the history of a country to which I have never been (Cuba)? Or do I embrace the history of a land in which my parents took refuge (the United States of America)? Questions about ethnic group interaction and ethnic identity construction intrigue me in great part because they are deeply personal.

SOCIOLOGICAL INTERESTS AND THEORETICAL FRAMEWORK

While I have read broadly in sociological theory, both classic and contemporary, in this study I continue my long-held interest in Max Weber as a theorist and acute observer of social processes. Much of my grounding as a sociologist comes from the historical and theoretical analyses conducted by Weber. I also continue my inclination toward social constructionism and the social phenomenological viewpoints that have grown in part due to his influence, such as the work of Alfred Schutz, who joins the interpretive sociology of Weber with the phenomenology of Edmund Husserl. I reflected a great deal during the 1990s on intersections between philosophy, theology, church history, and sociological theory. Also, during many years of teaching college courses on race and ethnicity, I took the opportunity to examine such issues as ethnic identity construction, interactions between ethnic groups, and the ethos underlying discrimination and prejudice in contemporary history. I was forming a research agenda to consider the dynamics of race, religion, and ethnic transcendence. Analyzing this congregation has been a way for me to draw together my varied scholarly interests.

EXPERIENCES WITH OTHER CHURCHES

I also bring to my study of Mosaic a comparative perspective shaped in part by my intimate experience as a participant in other local churches in Southern California. Reason (1988:12) defines "critical subjectivity" in the use of experiential knowledge as "a quality of awareness in which we do not suppress our primary subjective experience; nor do we allow ourselves to be overwhelmed and swept away by it; rather we raise it to consciousness and use it as a part of the inquiry process." Apart from my brief experience with the Roman Catholic Church as a child, I stepped into Mosaic after having been a member at four predominantly white churches. They ranged from a new fifty-member church-plant to a five-thousand-member suburban megachurch. All of these churches were evangelical; two were from different denominations (Evangelical Free Church and Church of Christ), and two were "independent Bible churches" with no connection to each other. I was a pastoral staff member at three of them. Including Mosaic, I have been on the pastoral staff at four churches, managed up to five staff people, and administrated annual budgets as low as $3,000 and as high as $1.8 million. I was involved in these churches while I was in graduate school and forming my research agenda. In addition to having been a member at four churches besides Mosaic, I have participated in dozens of churches from other traditions within Protestantism (Pentecostal, Charismatic, Methodist, Lutheran, Episcopal, Greek Orthodox) as well as many non-Protestant churches and religious assemblies (Roman Catholic, Jewish, Mormon, Hare Krishna, Islamic, Buddhist). The various roles I have played within these churches include friend, tourist, attender, and invited speaker.

TENSIONS BETWEEN ROLES OF PASTOR AND SOCIOLOGIST

In this study, I was a full insider, a native, and a complete participant. I was a pastor in this church; yet, for this research, I entered it in the role of sociologist rather than pastor. The pastor and the sociologist have different values, perspectives, and audiences.

The pastor is both a shepherd who nurtures and guides a flock and a prophet who catalyzes and cajoles the slumbering and the wayward to religiously motivated action. The pastor's perspective is shaped by a transcendent authority, a personal god who calls the pastor to go into the world. The pastor's action is inspired and guided by imperatives received from that authority, often supported by a canonical text. The pastor brings humanity into harmony with the heart of God. Toward that goal, the pastor seeks an audience among the unbelieving and instructs and exhorts the believers in the audience to adhere to doctrinal beliefs and actualize religiously motivated actions.

In contrast to the pastor, the sociologist is committed to examining life on the basis of empirical evidence, looking for social causes for behavior within the patterns of human interaction. God is absent in analysis and is either ignored or considered to be an emergent property of human interaction (for a prominent example, see Durkheim, 2001). The sociologist's perspective is shaped by a scientistic worldview emerging from the Enlightenment and, arguably, is an alternative to religious frameworks for understanding human behavior. It is further shaped by a liberal humanism committed to freedom from oppression and injustice. This humanism gives the sociologist an ethical edge, often resulting in a passion to fight for such freedom. Here lies the source of sociology's "debunking" function, a toppling of idols, a pulling back of the curtain on people and events to reveal the all-too-often base, self-serving, power-driven, and exploitative nature of social life. It seems, to the dismay of many in the profession, that the bulk of sociologists talk mostly among themselves and so constitute their own audience. As a science, sociology is practiced within a scholarly community that justifiably evaluates and judges the merits of knowledge produced by its members. However, as an agenda for social change emerges, sociologists move outside of their scholarly community toward real-world advocacy, activism, and sometimes revolution.

While it is certainly possible to be both a pastor and a sociologist, it is extremely difficult to fulfill the roles of pastor and sociologist in the same organization simultaneously. Both are all-consuming roles. To succeed, one must keep the values, perspective, and audience of each distinct. Since I was committed to being a sociologist many years before I was committed to being a pastor, I have become accustomed to the tensions in perspectives that occasionally arise. But looking back at my twelve months of fieldwork, I see that I may not have fully succeeded in operating as a pastor. In attempting to be an observer and ensure the soundness of my data, I distanced myself through a "hands-off" attitude. I wanted very much to conduct this study with academic integrity, in the hope of making a scholarly contribution to the understanding of interethnic congregational diversification. My role as sociologist became prominent, and I found myself pulling back in meetings and events, becoming more of an observer, trying not to influence situations (an admittedly impossible goal). Because of the rarity of multiethnic churches, the organizational inventiveness of Mosaic, and the attention this particular organization receives from scholars, journalists, and congregational leaders, I concentrated on my role as a sociologist until a time that I could release myself from the tension of being a sociologist and return fully to the role of pastor. (Soon after completing the study, I once again accentuated my role as a sociologist in an academic job search that culminated in my joining the faculty of Davidson College as an assistant professor of sociology in 2004.)

For this study, I operated primarily as a scholar working on behalf of other scholars to generate new knowledge about the processes of ethnic transcendence and congregational diversification. I hoped my analysis would be of use to others examining other multiethnic settings. I also hoped it would provide useful information for church leaders who desire to build integrated congregations effectively.

Seeking Validity for My Study of This Congregation

In-depth interviews with members and attenders, along with elite interviews with church leaders and longtime members, provided the most focused information, which was supplemented by participant observation. Sixty interviews (both semi-structured and unstructured) were obtained through a purposive sampling of leaders and longtime attenders, and members and attenders with varied ethnic backgrounds, ministry experiences, and length of time at Mosaic. My intention was to select categories of typical individuals yet adequately capture the heterogeneity of the population, in a process similar to maximum variation sampling (Guba and Lincoln, 1989; see also Lincoln and Guba, 1985; Patton, 1990). My participant observation consisted of attending group gatherings such as leadership meetings, weekend celebration services, and other relevant church-related activities. I attended almost all church-wide activities as well as dozens of activities centered on ministry teams or small group functions; most were advertised as being open to all, while I discovered other, more spontaneous functions through word of mouth.

The researcher's influence on the subject cannot be eliminated (Hammersley and Atkinson, 1983). Rather, it must be understood and productively used. Since I based much of my research on in-depth interview data, I was most concerned with obtaining valid data from respondents. As Balmer and Todd (1994:664) noted in their study of Calvary Chapel, Costa Mesa, "Reliance on firsthand information, particularly from people still associated with the congregation, carries with it certain perils: selective, enhanced memory and, more frequently, a rhetoric that is so cloaked in spiritual language as to constitute providential history." Beyond considerations of memories and rhetoric, my greatest fear was distortion by respondents trying to please me, whether as a pastor or as a sociologist. I was also concerned that respondents would oversimplify or gloss over information, particularly if it was not complimentary to themselves or to the church. Finally, I feared that respondents would assume that I already understood what they were talking about, since I was an insider, and that I would fail to draw out their own awareness and perspective.

In estimating the risk of data distortion, I first sought to discover how people at Mosaic perceived me. What kind of relationship had I established with them? In the time I was a pastor at Mosaic, many people were aware that I teach sociology classes at local colleges. People at Mosaic are accustomed to thinking of me in an academic, professorial role. When they learned that I was completing my Ph.D. at the University of Southern California, people were sympathetic; many were even excited about my desire to focus my research on Mosaic. They were willing to offer themselves as interviewees to provide information I might need to complete my study. Several felt "privileged" to know someone who is "so smart" and earning this kind of degree. Many respondents said that it was an honor to be part of my study. While most had not seen me outside of my role as pastor, all were willing to accept me in an additional role as sociologist.

As a pastoral staff member at Mosaic, I took several precautions in conducting this research. First, since I exercised a role of authority within the church, I was careful not to reveal my own thoughts about belief or process to those I observed or interviewed. Second, I was careful in all interactions to listen and observe rather than attempt to alter whatever was happening before me to suit my preferences or desires. Third, I was careful not to limit my contacts to people with whom I had already established personal rapport. I solicited interviews from people with whom I had no personal relationship, and I also had numerous informal conversations with guests and visitors, who were often unaware that I was a pastor on staff. Fourth, I was open and receptive to whatever respondents wished to share with me, however they wished to share it. I was accepting and tolerant of beliefs and actions even when they differed from my own. I was also careful to remain open and welcoming if aspects of the church were discussed that did not show Mosaic in its best light.

Everyone I asked to participate was willing to be part of the study; this came as a pleasant surprise given that one-third of my respondents had no prior relationship with me. I had no difficulty scheduling interviews, almost always within five days of asking the person to participate. The only interviewees who seemed nervous were two Hispanics (both Mexican American, one male and the other female), who were unwilling to have their interviews taped. The thirty-two-year-old male Chicano said, "I'll tell you everything, and you write down the truth." What made taping objectionable is not clear to me; on the basis of what I know about their lives and a few comments they made before the interviews, I believe prior bad experience with authority figures outside the church, especially law enforcement, made them cautious. Despite their unwillingness to be put on tape, they did allow me to take handwritten notes and were willing to answer any question I put to them.

I interviewed a total of sixty people, thirty-seven men and twenty-three women. Men outnumber women because all church elders and most of the full-time paid staff are male. My goal was to mirror with my respondents the ethnic breakdown of the congregation. In the end, 28 percent were Caucasian, 27 percent Hispanic, and 30 percent Asian. The last 15 percent were all African American; I intentionally over-sampled this group (which is less than 2 percent of the congregation) in an attempt to understand why it forms such a small proportion at Mosaic. The educational background of my respondents was as diverse as their ethnic backgrounds: ten had completed high school, nine had a master's or doctoral degree, and the rest had bachelor's degrees or at least some college education. Eight percent of my respondents were first-generation immigrants to America, 28 percent were second- or third-generation, and the rest had a long ancestral history in the United States. To my surprise, 90 percent of my sample were active in some type of ministry at the church. Four out of five were members. Thirty percent came from nondenominational Christian backgrounds (often multiple churches), 30 percent came from Baptist backgrounds, 30 percent came from Roman Catholic backgrounds, and 5 percent claimed no religious background at all. In terms of tenure, 22 percent of my respondents had been attending less than two years, while the majority (60 percent) had been at Mosaic five years or more. A full one-third of my respondents made their first commitment to become "Christian" at Mosaic. While the average age of my respondents was thirty-six, the youngest person interviewed was twenty and the oldest was seventy-six. In sum, my respondents demonstrated a wide range of social demographic characteristics and came from a variety of lifestyles and life experiences.

When interviewing, I attempted to make respondents comfortable being honest with me. I assured them that I would protect their anonymity, revealing no identifying information without their explicit permission. I was willing to interview them anywhere they desired. Most of the interviews were about ninety minutes long and occurred at the church office, a place they considered comfortable and familiar. Other interviews occurred at a coffee shop, a restaurant, the interviewee's home, or my home. I explained that I was working as a sociologist rather than a pastor and that their responses would help me understand what was going on at Mosaic. I emphasized that for the purpose of the study I was a researcher and a sociologist, with questions and issues that differed from those of a pastor, friend, counselor, or the like. The presence of the tape recorder was a very clear signal that the interview was somehow official. The tape recorder itself created an interesting dynamic, as people seemed to often address remarks to my dissertation committee (e.g., "We call our small groups 'life groups' at Mosaic"), as if their words weren't for me, but for another group of people who were using me only to ask the questions. I presented myself during each interview as a student of my respondent. I simply asked people to tell me their stories: how they came to Mosaic, what their lives were like before Mosaic, and what they had experienced since coming. I often asked them to give examples and describe specific incidents in answering questions. Once I had completed a substantial number of interviews, I increasingly collaborated with respondents by discussing my observations and my conclusions. These "member checks," in which I systematically solicited feedback about my tentative conclusions, were very important in eliciting more data that clarified or amended my analysis. Such conversations increased my confidence in the validity of my work.

I believe that my relationships within Mosaic improved the quality of my data. With trust established and many relationships already formed, I could ask deeper, more nuanced questions quickly. I believe that my position created more benefits than obstacles or hindrances in my collection of relevant data, and I took appropriate measures to limit the risk of data corruption and ensure the validity of my results. People seemed comfortable rather than threatened in our discussions. I did not pursue issues or topics that disturbed the interviewee. If sensitive issues were discussed, it was almost always because the interviewee introduced them. I consistently found people at Mosaic to be interested in and willing to discuss sensitive issues, including their life experiences, even ethnic experiences and prejudices.

Guidelines Offered in Hindsight

Very little is straightforward in the process of ethnographic research, not least the methodological difficulties of alternately negotiating, constructing, discovering, concealing, and reconstructing the identities of religious insiders within the communities they study. Reflecting on my experience, I cautiously suggest a few guidelines for religious insiders pursuing ethnographic research. These are drawn from my experience during twelve months of data collection and are offered by a fellow student to others considering these processes.

First, I took time to *carefully formulate a key research question* before collecting data. It was vital for me as a religious insider to determine the problem to be investigated before beginning any formal analysis. This is proper procedure for any research, but it bears repeating here because of the immediate and ongoing accessibility of the research site. Without adequately formulating research questions, a religious insider is sorely tempted to begin collecting data before specifying the problem being pursued. My dissertation committee assisted in honing one central question, "What makes and keeps Mosaic multiethnic?" This question promoted a useful form of selective perception and was critical in formulating interview questions. It was simple and specific enough to direct me toward what was to be observed and who was to be interviewed. I was spared the risk of unfocused observation, meandering conversations with respondents, and months of wasted effort.

I found it advantageous to *clearly specify the research topic with potential respondents,* especially in the in-depth interviews. Respondents were given a brief overview of my topic and asked explicitly for permission to analyze and publish their words. The issue of disclosure is rife with ethical considerations, and I am aware that much ethnographic work is done without the knowledge of others in the setting. Certainly not everyone at Mosaic was aware of my study; however, when I interacted with people specifically for the purpose of gaining data, I was forthright about my stance as a researcher. I found myself saying, "I'm doing a study about what makes and keeps Mosaic multiethnic, and your experience is important to me." For myself, I felt that it would be deceptive to be an attentive listener in conversations that the other participants considered merely personal. I did not want them to find out later that I was recording their words for analysis. My feeling that this would be a betrayal of their trust moved me to be open about my topic, soliciting their involvement while defining for them the nature and subject of my research.

Clarifying my stance as a researcher was part of my ongoing attempt to *introduce distance in familiar social settings.* I found ethnographic work to be a curious movement away from the spontaneous immediacy of social interaction. In various and subtle ways, I became an outsider in day-to-day life in order to generate knowledge that would be accessible to colleagues who could not be present themselves. In a very real sense, I repeatedly reintroduced myself into Mosaic as a researcher. In my interviews, a critical tool for introducing distance was my tape recorder. Bringing out the recorder, setting it up, and placing it in plain view was an important, nonverbal process declaring to both of us that this conversation was not strictly private. I also introduced distance by deliberately stating that I was acting as a sociologist, asking particular questions for particular reasons. The rapport I had already established allowed people to take a jump into the unknown of being interviewed, recalling experiences and articulating viewpoints both familiar and unfamiliar to me. With some distance introduced, a new relationship was formed which had no previous history and was therefore an uncharted ground for exploration.

One conscious commitment I made from the beginning was to *respect unexpected responses.* I was accustomed to the clichés, norms, and rituals of Mosaic. Because as a religious insider I presumably know what other members think, I quickly found that I could be surprised, distressed, or even shocked when other insiders introduced unsanctioned views, opinions, and experiences. I readily understood that to gloss over these unexpected responses was to lose significant data. The unexpected, once noticed, revealed patterns that were pervasive and significant. I discovered much that I did not expect in talking about why people left the church. I was uncomfortable talking about reasons why people would, in a sense, reject Mosaic as their church, but the responses eventually formed a pattern that allowed me to describe havens, "places of refuge," in the church that were not universally experienced. Differing responses to Mosaic did not mean something was wrong with the church; it meant that people have different reactions to it. Discerning a pattern to account for those responses became a substantive goal of my analysis.

By committing to research Mosaic, I found that I was ready to *embrace the problematic.* I anticipated that tensions, dilemmas, and ambiguities would undoubtedly emerge. As a member of this group, I wanted to be loyal to it and feared betraying it. I was troubled when anything seemed to threaten the good impression I wanted to maintain. It was uncomfortable for me to discuss things that might reflect badly on the group. Nevertheless, investigating the problematic was at the core of my task, and facing difficult subjects as they emerged greatly deepened my thinking.

Another critical way to create distance was to *remember that the core audience is an academic audience.* In asking questions and analyzing responses, I was guided by the interests and knowledge of my audience. What could I assume? What would they most want to know? What questions would they ask if they were here? Addressing an academic audience gave me freedom to be a scholar within Mosaic, something I had not been accustomed to doing as a religious insider.

I also found it useful to *keep in touch with colleagues.* Work on my research project required time, emotional energy, and intellectual effort. I found the work of examining a familiar setting in such great depth to be puzzling to those outside of the academic community. Colleagues frequently lent support to perspectives and questions which in turn led to fruitful lines of inquiry. These perspectives and questions did not naturally emerge from within the research setting itself. My participation in the Lived Religion workshop, an interdisciplinary discussion among a small group of junior and senior scholars at Boston College in spring 2002 organized by Alan J. Wolfe and Patricia Chang, was particularly helpful.

I chose to *read ethnographic accounts to nurture a sociological imagination.* Having been immersed in Mosaic, I was unused to translating everyday experiences into text. Yet I knew the work of scholarship was built on narrative discourse. I found it particularly helpful to spend time seeing how others accomplished this, first in congregational studies (e.g., Ammerman, 1987; Carroll and Roof, 2002; Miller, 1997; Neitz, 1987) and then in religious ethnographies more broadly (e.g., Bender, 2003; Griffith, 1997; Haberman, 1994; Orsi, 2002). Reading such works prodded me toward creative insights. It also reinforced my sense of connection with an unseen community, namely my colleagues not available for face-to-face interaction.

In the end, I found that the most basic task of a religious insider is to *embrace the role of the outsider.* Taking note of Burke's (1984:631) statement that "adherents of a religion do not necessarily understand their religion," I did not assume that as a member of Mosaic I understood the reasons for its diversification. However, having noticed a significant phenomenon, I chose to reenter as a sociological observer. I tried to thoughtfully develop the art of asking questions of familiar people and processes. The constant danger was assuming the obvious, but my role as a religious insider researching his own community was to uncover what was obvious to everyone in this community for the benefit of outsiders and, in the process, explain significant phenomena. My hope is that others will not hesitate to take up similar tasks for themselves.

APPENDIX B. WOMEN AND LEADERSHIP AT MOSAIC

While Mosaic is affiliated with the Southern Baptist Convention and holds to conservative doctrine like other churches in the denomination, Mosaic does not publicly affirm many of the statements made, or protests and boycotts announced, by national denominational leaders through their annual conventions. Such statements have been controversial among Southern Baptists, especially among church leaders, like those at Mosaic, who believe in the autonomy of each local church (see Ammerman, 1990, for a social scientific perspective on the "fundamentalist takeover" of the Southern Baptist Convention in 1979). Mosaic's leaders seldom publicly acknowledge statements that stir controversy—for example, statements regarding the submission of women and the implications of their influence and authority within the local church.

In her study of two conservative evangelical congregations, Brasher (1998:61) notes,

> In overall congregational governance, gender functioned as a unique symbol that qualified a person for, or disqualified a person from, participation. Yet here, sexual dominance prevailed. Men were privileged over women. Males retained exclusive access to key authoritative posts such as the pastoral office, board membership, and eldership.

Male leadership has predominated in Mosaic's history. One notable exception was a woman who essentially served as, but did not hold the title of, executive pastor of the church. (She is introduced as "Susan" in chapter 2.) She was neither an elder nor ordained but had a vital partnership with the lead pastor for the greater part of his tenure and supervised other male pastors on staff. Although she was subordinate to the lead pastor, she was the director of ministries, overseeing every ministry area in the congregation. Every other staff position, such as assistant youth pastor and assistant worship leader, was subordinated to hers. She modeled a high degree of commitment, involvement, and authority. Soon after brother Phil left the church, she moved out of the area and became a church consultant. Subsequently, following her model, other women at Mosaic now occupy various ministry positions under the overall leadership of the lead pastor and the elders.

Mosaic restricts the role of women in ministry in three notable ways. First, the elders of Mosaic are men, specifically, married men. While every elder's wife is held in high esteem, and all of them take on significant roles of leadership, wives are not considered elders. Second, although women occupy full-time staff positions, team leadership roles, and other significant ministry roles within the congregation, they are not publicly ordained or given the title of pastor. Third, women do not baptize believers. Mosaic practices baptism by immersion, and only men, both ordained and nonordained, perform baptisms.

Given these parameters, women take on every other leadership role in the congregation. For example, women can and do

> occupy staff leadership roles,
> lead small groups,
> mentor and oversee small group leaders and ministry team leaders,
> teach from the pulpit,
> serve the elements of the bread and the cup at Lord's Supper celebration services,
> teach classes on counseling, biblical studies, world awareness, current events, and various other topics,
> lead congregational worship,
> lead overseas ministry teams, and
> go overseas as commissioned missionary workers.

The highest lay authorities under the elders are members of leadership teams, who oversee the leaders of small groups and service teams; women can and do occupy these leadership roles. And while there are technically no women pastors, there are women on full-time staff who lead staff projects, participate fully in staff meetings, and provide input that is both solicited and welcomed. Many large and long-term jobs on projects (e.g., managing a fund-raising campaign for the purchase of new property and administering the selection and commissioning of overseas missionaries) have been and are currently given to women.

As described earlier, a woman functioned as executive pastor of the church for about twenty years; in the early 1990s a woman also functioned as youth pastor. Brasher (1998:69) notes that "it has been easier for women to obtain authority in extracongregational endeavors such as overseas mission work" and that women are readily accepted in a role that involves the care and development of children (see also Beaver,

1968; Bendroth, 1993, 1996). This is generally true of Mosaic today. At the time of this study, a woman was director of child development (from birth to junior high school), overseeing three married couples. Another woman was coordinator for international ministries, responsible for sending out and caring for overseas missionary workers, both short-term (50–150 adults per year) and long-term (well over a hundred career missionaries). In sum, while there are notable restrictions on the roles women may play, Mosaic allows and even encourages women to take on significant leadership roles under the direction of the lead pastor and elders of the church.

BIBLIOGRAPHY

Alba, Richard D. 1990. *Ethnic Identity: The Transformation of White America.* New Haven, Conn.: Yale University Press.

———. 1995. "Assimilation's Quiet Tide." *Public Interest,* no. 119:3–18.

Alexander, Claire E. 1992. "The Art of 'Being Black': The Creation of Black British Youth Identities." D.Phil. thesis, Oxford University.

Ammerman, Nancy Tatom. 1982. "Dilemmas in Establishing a Research Identity." *New England Sociologist* 4:21–27.

———. 1987. *Bible Believers: Fundamentalists in the Modern World.* New Brunswick, N.J.: Rutgers University Press.

———. 1990. *Baptist Battles: Social Change and Religious Conflict in the Southern Baptist Convention.* New Brunswick, N.J.: Rutgers University Press.

Ammerman, Nancy Tatom, with Arthur E. Farnsley II and Tammy Adams, et al. 1997. *Congregation and Community.* New Brunswick, N.J.: Rutgers University Press.

Arboleda, Teja. 1998. *In the Shadow of Race: Growing Up as a Multiethnic, Multicultural, and "Multiracial" American.* New York: Lawrence Erlbaum Associates.

Aston, Margaret. 1988. *England's Iconoclasts.* New York: Oxford University Press.

Balmer, Randall, and Jesse T. Todd, Jr. 1994. "Calvary Chapel: Costa Mesa, California." In *American Congregations,* ed. James P. Wind and James W. Lewis, vol. 1, 663–698. Chicago: University of Chicago Press.

Barna Research Group. 2004. "Religious Activity Increasing in the West." *Barna Research Online,* March 1. http://www.barna.org/cgi-bin/PagePress Release.asp?PressReleaseID=159.

Barth, Fredrik. 1969. Introduction to *Ethnic Groups and Boundaries: The Social Organization of Culture Difference,* ed. Fredrik Barth, 9–38. Boston: Little, Brown.

Batson, C. Daniel, Patricia Schoenrade, and W. Larry Ventis. 1993. *Religion and the Individual: A Social-Psychological Perspective.* 2nd ed. New York: Oxford University Press.

Baumann, Gerd. 1999. *The Multicultural Riddle: Rethinking National, Ethnic, and Religious Identities.* New York: Routledge.

Beaver, R. Pierce. 1968. *American Protestant Women in World Mission: History of the First Feminist Movement in North America.* Grand Rapids, Mich.: Eerdmans.

Becker, Penny Edgell. 1998. "Making Inclusive Communities: Congregations and the 'Problem' of Race." *Social Problems* 45:451–472.

Bellah, Robert, Richard Madsen, William Sullivan, Ann Swidler, and Steven Tipton. 1985. *Habits of the Heart: Individualism and Commitment in American Life.* Berkeley: University of California Press.

Bender, Courtney. 2003. *Heaven's Kitchen: Living Religion at God's Love We Deliver.* Chicago: University of Chicago Press.

Bendroth, Margaret Lamberts. 1993. *Fundamentalism and Gender, 1875 to the Present.* New Haven, Conn.: Yale University Press.

———. 1996. "Women in Twentieth-Century Evangelicalism." *Evangelical Studies Bulletin* 13:4–6.

Berg, Bruce L. 1989. *Qualitative Research Methods for the Social Sciences.* Boston: Allyn and Bacon.

Berger, Peter L. 1961. *The Noise of Solemn Assemblies: Christian Commitment and the Religious Establishment in America.* Garden City, N.Y.: Doubleday.

Berger, Peter L., and Richard John Neuhaus. 1977. *To Empower People: The Role of Mediating Structures in Public Policy.* Washington, D.C.: American Enterprise Institute for Public Policy Research.

Berkhof, Louis. 1941. *Systematic Theology.* Grand Rapids, Mich.: Eerdmans.

Bradley, Barbara. 1995. "Marketing That New-Time Religion." *Los Angeles Times Magazine,* December 10, 30–33, 54, 56.

Bradshaw, Carla K. 1992. "Beauty and the Beast: On Racial Ambiguity." In *Racially Mixed People in America,* ed. Maria P. P. Root, 77–88. Newbury Park, Calif.: Sage.

Branson, Mark Lau. 1998. "Intercultural Church Life and Adult Formation: Community, Narrative, and Transformation." Ed.D. diss., University of San Francisco.

Brasher, Brenda. 1998. *Godly Women: Fundamentalism and Female Power.* New Brunswick, N.J.: Rutgers University Press.

Braude, Ann. 1995. "Forum: Female Experience in American Religion." *Religion and American Culture: A Journal of Interpretation* 5, no. 1:1–11.

Brenton, Raymond, and M. Pinard. 1960. "Group Formation among Immigrants: Criteria and Processes." *Canadian Journal of Economics and Political Science* 26:465–477.

Brockman, John. 1996. *Digerati: Encounters with the Cyber Elite.* San Francisco: HardWired.

Broderick, Damien. 2001. *The Spike: How Our Lives Are Being Transformed by Rapidly Advancing Technologies.* New York: Forge.

Brown, Philip M. 1980. "Biracial Identity and Social Marginality." *Child and Adolescent Social Work Journal* 7:319–337.

Brown, Prince, Jr. 2001. "Biology and the Social Construction of the 'Race' Concept." In *The Social Construction of Race and Ethnicity in the United States,* ed. Robert Ferrante and Prince Brown, Jr., 2nd ed., 144–150. Upper Saddle River, N.J.: Prentice Hall.

Brown, Raymond E. 1979. *The Community of the Beloved Disciple: The Life,*

Loves, and Hates of an Individual Church in New Testament Times. New York: Paulist.

———. 1984. *The Churches the Apostles Left Behind.* New York: Paulist.

Browning, Don S. 1994. "Congregational Studies as Practical Theology." In *American Congregations,* ed. James P. Wind and James W. Lewis, vol. 2, 192–221. Chicago: University of Chicago Press.

Bruce, F. F. 1979. *Peter, Stephen, James, and John: Studies in Early Non-Pauline Christianity.* Grand Rapids, Mich.: Eerdmans.

———. 1985. *Paul and His Converts: How Paul Nurtured the Churches He Planted.* Downers Grove, Ill.: InterVarsity.

Brüderl, Josef, Peter Preisendörfer, and Rolf Ziegler. 1993. "Upward Mobility in Organizations: The Effects of Hierarchy and Opportunity Structure." *European Sociological Review* 9:173–188.

Buckingham, Marcus, and Donald O. Clifton. 2001. *Now, Discover Your Strengths.* New York: Free Press.

Burke, T. Patrick. 1984. "Must the Description of a Religion Be Acceptable to a Believer?" *Religious Studies* 20:631–636.

Burns, Jeffrey M. 1994. "¿Qué es esto? The Transformation of St. Peter's Parish, San Francisco, 1913–1990." In *American Congregations,* ed. James P. Wind and James W. Lewis, vol. 1, 396–463. Chicago: University of Chicago Press.

Campbell, Donald K., and Jeffrey L. Townsend, eds. 1992. *A Case for Premillennialism: A New Consensus.* Chicago: Moody.

Carroll, Jackson W. 2000. *Mainline to the Future: Congregations for the 21st Century.* Louisville, Ky.: Westminster John Knox.

Carroll, Jackson W., and Wade Clark Roof. 2002. *Bridging Divided Worlds: Generational Cultures in Congregations.* San Francisco: Jossey-Bass.

Castells, Manuel. 1997. *The Power of Identity.* Malden, Mass.: Blackwell.

Cenkner, William, ed. 1996. *The Multicultural Church: A New Landscape in U.S. Theologies.* New York: Paulist.

Cetron, Marvin, and Owen Davies. 1997. *Probable Tomorrows: How Science and Technology Will Transform Our Lives in the Next Twenty Years.* New York: St. Martin's.

Charmaz, Kathy. 1983. "The Grounded Theory Method: An Explication and Interpretation." In *Contemporary Field Research: A Collection of Readings,* ed. Robert M. Emerson, 109–126. Prospect Heights, Ill.: Waveland.

Charry, Ellen T. 1996. "Reviving Theology in a Time of Change." In *The Future of Theology: Essays in Honor of Jürgen Moltmann,* ed. Miroslav Volf, Carmen Krieg, and Thomas Kucharz, 114–126. Grand Rapids, Mich.: Eerdmans.

Chase, Ivan. 1990. "Vacancy Chains." *Annual Review of Sociology* 17:133–154.

Chaves, Mark. 1999. *National Congregations Study: Machine-Readable File.* Department of Sociology, University of Arizona.

———. 2004. *Congregations in America.* Cambridge, Mass.: Harvard University Press.

Chideya, Farai. 1999. *The Color of Our Future: Our Multiracial Future.* New York: William Morrow.

Cho, Paul Yonggi, Harold Hostetler, Yonggi Cho, and David Yonggi Cho. 1987. *Successful Home Cell Groups.* New York: Bridge-Logos.

Chong, Kelly H. 1998. "What It Means to Be Christian: The Role of Religion in the Construction of Ethnic Identity and Boundary among Second-Generation Korean Americans." *Sociology of Religion* 59:259–286.

Christensen, Michael J., with Carl E. Savage, eds. 2000. *Equipping the Saints: Mobilizing Laity for Ministry.* Nashville: Abingdon.

Christerson, Brad, Michael O. Emerson, and Korie Edwards. 2005. *Against All Odds: The Struggle of Racial Integration in Religious Organizations.* New York: New York University Press.

Christian, Mark. 2000. *Multiracial Identity: An International Perspective.* London: Palgrave Macmillan.

Christopherson, Susan, and Michael Storper. 1989. "The Effects of Flexible Specialization on Industrial Politics and the Labor Market: The Motion Picture Industry." *Industrial and Labor Relations Review* 42:331–347.

Collum, Danny Duncan. 1996. *Black and White Together: The Search for Common Ground.* Maryknoll, N.Y.: Orbis.

Comiskey, Joel. 1999. *Groups of 12: A New Way to Mobilize Leaders and Multiply Groups in Your Church.* Houston: Touch.

Conner, Brittany. 2002. "Want to Send More Workers Overseas? Give Them Mentors." *Commission* 63:28–37.

Conzen, Kathleen N., David A. Gerber, Ewa Morawska, George E. Pozzetta, and Rudolph J. Vecolli. 1992. "The Invention of Ethnicity: A Perspective from the USA." *Journal of American Ethnic History* 12:3–41.

Copeland, E. Luther. 1995. *The Southern Baptist Convention and the Judgment of History.* New York: University Press of America.

Cordeiro, Wayne. 2001. *Doing Church as a Team.* New York: Regal.

Cornell, Stephen. 1996. "The Variable Ties That Bind: Content and Circumstances in Ethnic Processes." *Ethnic and Racial Studies* 19:265–289.

DeBose, Herman L., and Loretta I. Winters, eds. 2002. *New Faces in a Changing America: Multiracial Identity in the 21st Century.* Beverly Hills, Calif.: Sage.

De Vos, George. 1975. "Ethnic Pluralism: Conflict and Accommodation." In *Ethnic Identity: Cultural Continuities and Change,* ed. George De Vos and Lola Romanucci-Ross, 5–41. Palo Alto: Mayfield.

De Vos, George, and Lola Romanucci-Ross. 1975. "Ethnicity: Vessel of Meaning and Emblem of Contrast." In *Ethnic Identity: Cultural Continuities and Change,* ed. George De Vos and Lola Romanucci-Ross, 363–390. Palo Alto: Mayfield.

DeYoung, Curtiss Paul. 1995. *Coming Together: The Bible's Message in an Age of Diversity.* Valley Forge, Pa.: Judson.

———. 1997. *Reconciliation: Our Greatest Challenge—Our Only Hope.* Valley Forge, Pa.: Judson.

———. 1999. "Racial Reconciliation and the 21st Century Church." *Clergy Journal* 75, no. 8.

DeYoung, Curtiss Paul, Michael O. Emerson, George Yancey, and Karen Chai.

2003. *United by Faith: The Multiracial Congregation as an Answer to the Problem of Race.* New York: Oxford University Press.

Doornbos, Martin R. 1972. "Some Conceptual Problems Concerning Ethnicity in Integration Analysis." *Civilisations* 22, no. 2:268–283.

Dotson, James. 2002. "Young Adults and Meaningful Faith: Pastors Tell of Strategy and Passion." *California Southern Baptist* 61, no. 5:1, 6.

Douglas, Jack D. 1976. *Investigative Social Research: Individual and Team Field Research.* Beverly Hills, Calif.: Sage.

Duffy, Eamon. 1992. *The Stripping of the Altars: Traditional Religion in England, c. 1400–c. 1580.* New Haven, Conn.: Yale University Press.

Durkheim, Emile. 2001 [1912]. *The Elementary Forms of Religious Life.* Trans. Carol Cosman. New York: Oxford University Press.

Ebaugh, Helen Rose, and Janet Saltzman Chafetz. 2000. *Religion and the New Immigrants: Continuities and Adaptations in Immigrant Congregations.* New York: AltaMira.

Ehrlich, Paul R. 2000. *Human Natures: Genes, Cultures, and the Human Prospect.* Washington, D.C.: Island.

Emerson, Michael O. 1998. "Why Racial Reconciliation Alone Cannot End Racial Strife." *Christian Scholar's Review* 28, no. 1:12–17.

———. 2000. "Beyond Ethnic Composition: Are Multiracial Congregations Unique?" Paper presented at the annual meeting of the Society for the Scientific Study of Religion, Houston.

Emerson, Michael O., and Christian Smith. 2000. *Divided by Faith: Evangelical Religion and the Problem of Race in America.* New York: Oxford University Press.

Emerson, Michael O., and Karen Chai Kim. 2003. "Multiracial Congregations: An Analysis of Their Development and a Typology." *Journal for the Scientific Study of Religion* 42, no. 2:217–227.

Emerson, Robert M., ed. 1983. *Contemporary Field Research: A Collection of Readings.* Prospect Heights, Ill.: Waveland.

Erickson, Millard J. 1977. *Contemporary Options in Eschatology: A Study of the Millennium.* Grand Rapids, Mich.: Baker Book House.

———. 1985. *Christian Theology.* Grand Rapids, Mich.: Baker Book House.

Eriksen, Thomas Hylland. 1992. *Us and Them in Modern Societies: Ethnicity and Nationalism in Mauritius, Trinidad, and Beyond.* Oslo: Scandinavian University Press.

———. 1993. *Ethnicity and Nationalism: Anthropological Perspectives.* London: Pluto.

Feher, Shoshanah. 1997. "Managing Strain, Contradictions, and Fluidity: Messianic Judaism and the Negotiation of a Religio-ethnic Identity." In *Contemporary American Religion: An Ethnographic Reader,* ed. Penny Edgell Becker and Nancy L. Eiesland, 25–50. Walnut Creek, Calif.: AltaMira.

Fenton, Steve. 1999. *Ethnicity: Racism, Class, and Culture.* New York: Rowman and Littlefield.

Finke, Roger, and Rodney Stark. 1992. *The Churching of America, 1776–1990:*

Winners and Losers in Our Religious Economy. New Brunswick, N.J.: Rutgers University Press.

Fischer, Michael M. 2000. "Ethnicity and the Post-modern Acts of Memory." In *Writing Culture: The Poetics and Politics of Ethnography,* ed. James Clifford and George E. Marcus, 194–233. Berkeley: University of California Press.

Fisk, Alfred, ed. 1975. *The First Footprints: The Dawn of the Idea of the Church for the Fellowship of All Peoples—Letters between Alfred Fisk and Howard Thurman, 1943–1944.* San Francisco, Calif.: Lawton and Alfred Kennedy.

Flynt, Wayne. 1994. "'A Special Feeling of Closeness': Mt. Hebron Baptist Church, Leeds, Alabama." In *American Congregations,* ed. James P. Wind and James W. Lewis, vol. 1, 103–158. Chicago: University of Chicago Press.

Florida, Richard. 2002. *The Rise of the Creative Class: And How It's Transforming Work, Leisure, Community, and Everyday Life.* New York: Basic.

Flory, Richard W., and Donald E. Miller. 2000. *Gen X Religion.* New York: Routledge.

Fong, Bruce W. 1996. *Racial Equality in the Church: A Critique of the Homogeneous Unit Principle in Light of a Practical Theology Perspective.* Lanham, Md.: University Press of America.

Foster, Charles R. 1997. *Embracing Diversity: Leadership in Multicultural Congregations.* Washington, D.C.: Alban Institute.

Foster, Charles R., and Theodore Brelsford. 1996. *We Are the Church Together: Cultural Diversity in Congregational Life.* Valley Forge, Pa.: Trinity Press International.

Franklin, Robert Michael. 1994. "'The Safest Place on Earth': The Culture of Black Congregations." In *American Congregations,* ed. James P. Wind and James W. Lewis, vol. 2, 257–286. Chicago: University of Chicago Press.

Galloway, Dale E. 2000. *20/20 Vision: How to Create a Successful Church with Lay Pastors and Cell Groups.* New York: Ballantine.

Galush, W. J. 1977. "Faith and Fatherland: Dimensions of Polish-American Ethnoreligion, 1875–1975." In *Immigrants and Religion in Urban America,* ed. Randall M. Miller and Thomas D. Marzik, 84–102. Philadelphia: Temple University Press.

Gans, Herbert J. 1979. "Symbolic Ethnicity: The Future of Ethnic Groups and Cultures in America." *Ethnic and Racial Studies* 2:9–17.

———. 1994. "Symbolic Ethnicity and Symbolic Religiosity: Towards a Comparison of Ethnic and Religious Acculturation." *Ethnic and Racial Studies* 17:577–592.

———. 1999. "The Possibility of a New Racial Hierarchy in the Twenty-First-Century United States." In *The Cultural Territories of Race: Black and White Boundaries,* ed. Michèle Lamont, 371–390. Chicago: University of Chicago Press.

Gaskins, Pearl Fuyo, ed. 1999. *What Are You? Voices of Mixed-Race Young People.* New York: Henry Holt.

Geertz, Clifford. 1963. "The Integrated Revolution." In *Old Societies and New*

States: The Quest for Modernity in Asia and Africa, by the University of Chicago Committee for the Comparative Study of New Nations, ed. Clifford Geertz, 105–157. Glencoe, Ill: Free Press.

———. 1973. *The Interpretation of Cultures.* New York: Basic.

Gellner, Ernest. 1983. *Nations and Nationalism.* Oxford: Basil Blackwell.

Gerth, H. H., and C. Wright Mills, eds. and trans. 1946. *From Max Weber: Essays in Sociology.* New York: Oxford University Press.

Gibbs, Jewelle Taylor. 1997. "Biracial and Bicultural Children and Adolescents." In *Children of Color: Psychological Interventions with Culturally Diverse Youth,* ed. Jewelle Taylor Gibbs, Larke Nahme Huang, et al., 145–182. San Francisco: Jossey-Bass.

Gilkey, Langdon. 1994. "The Christian Congregation as a Religious Community." In *American Congregations,* ed. James P. Wind and James W. Lewis, vol. 2, pp. 100–132. Chicago: University of Chicago Press.

Glaser, Barney G., and Anselm L. Strauss. 1967. *The Discovery of Grounded Theory: Strategies for Qualitative Research.* Chicago: Aldine.

Glazer, Nathan. 1971. "Blacks and Ethnic Groups: The Difference, and the Political Difference It Makes." *Social Problems* 18:444–461.

Glazer, Nathan, and Daniel P. Moynihan. 1975. Introduction to *Ethnicity: Theory and Experience,* ed. Nathan Glazer and Daniel P. Moynihan, 1–26. Cambridge, Mass.: Harvard University Press.

Gleason, Philip. 1996 [1983]. "Identifying Identity: A Semantic History." In *Theories of Ethnicity: A Classical Reader,* ed. Werner Sollors, 460–487. Washington Square, N.Y.: New York University Press.

Gleick, James. 2000. *Faster: The Acceleration of Just About Everything.* New York: Vintage.

———. 2002. *What Just Happened: A Chronicle from the Information Frontier.* New York: Pantheon.

Glynn, Patrick. 1998. "Racial Reconciliation: Can Religion Work Where Politics Has Failed?" *American Behavioral Scientist* 41:834–841.

Goffman, Erving. 1959. *The Presentation of Self in Everyday Life.* New York: Doubleday/Anchor.

———. 1961. *Asylums: Essays on the Social Situation of Mental Patients and Other Inmates.* Garden City, N.Y.: Doubleday.

———. 1963. *Behavior in Public Places.* Glencoe, Ill.: Free Press.

———. 1967. *Interaction Ritual: Essays on Face-to-Face Behavior.* New York: Doubleday/Anchor.

Gold, Raymond L. 1958. "Roles in Sociological Field Observation." *Social Forces* 36:217–223.

Gordon, Milton M. 1964. *Assimilation in American Life: The Role of Race, Religion, and National Origins.* New York: Oxford University Press.

Griffith, R. Marie. 1997. *God's Daughters: Evangelical Women and the Power of Submission.* Berkeley: University of California Press.

Griswold, Wendy. 1992. "Writing on the Mud Wall: Nigerian Novels and the Imaginary Village." *American Sociological Review* 57:709–724.

Grove, Andrew S. 1996. *Only the Paranoid Survive: How to Exploit the Crisis Points That Challenge Every Company and Career.* New York: Harper-Collins.

Guba, Egon G., and Yvonna S. Lincoln. 1981. *Effective Evaluation.* San Francisco: Jossey-Bass.

———. 1989. *Fourth-Generation Evaluation.* Newbury Park, Calif.: Sage.

Guillaumin, Colette. 1995. *Racism, Sexism, Power, and Ideology.* London: Routledge.

Gundry, Robert H. 1973. *The Church and the Tribulation.* Grand Rapids, Mich.: Zondervan.

Gutiérrez, Gustavo. 1973. *A Theology of Liberation: History, Politics, and Salvation.* Trans. Caridad Inda and John Eagleson. Maryknoll, N.Y.: Orbis.

———. 1996. "Theology, Spirituality, and Historical Praxis." In *The Future of Theology: Essays in Honor of Jürgen Moltmann,* ed. Miroslav Volf, Carmen Krieg, and Thomas Kucharz, 176–184. Grand Rapids, Mich.: Eerdmans.

Haberman, David L. 1994. *Journey through the Twelve Forests: An Encounter with Krishna.* New York: Oxford University Press.

Hage, Jerald, and Charles H. Powers. 1992. *Post-industrial Lives: Roles and Relationships in the 21st Century.* Beverly Hills, Calif.: Sage.

Hammersley, Martyn, and Paul Atkinson. 1983. *Ethnography: Principles in Practice.* London: Tavistock.

Hardiman, Rita. 2001. "Reflections on White Identity Development Theory." In *New Perspectives on Racial Identity Development: A Theoretical and Practical Anthology,* ed. Charmaine L. Wijeyesinghe and Bailey W. Jackson III, 108–128. New York: New York University Press.

Hardin, Bert L., and Guenter Kehrer. 1978. "Identity and Commitment." In *Identity and Religion: International, Cross-Cultural Approaches,* ed. Hans Mol, 34–52. Beverly Hills, Calif.: Sage.

Harms, Richard B. 1999. "Missionary Paradigms from Luke-Acts for the Multicultural Churches in the Twenty-First Century." D.Min. diss., Fuller Theological Seminary.

Hart, Stephen. 1996. "The Cultural Dimension of Social Movements: A Theoretical Reassessment and Literature Review." *Sociology of Religion* 57: 87–100.

Herzog, William A., J. David Stanfield, Gordon C. Whiting, and Lynne Swenning. 1968. *Patterns of Diffusion in Rural Brazil.* Diffusion of Innovations Research Report 10. East Lansing: Department of Communication, Michigan State University.

Hobsbawm, Eric. 1983. "Inventing Traditions." In *The Invention of Tradition,* ed. Eric Hobsbawm and Terence Ranger, 1–14. Cambridge: Cambridge University Press.

Hodge, Charles. 1892. *Systematic Theology.* New York: Charles Scribner's Sons.

Holifield, E. Brooks. 1994. "Toward a History of American Congregations." In *American Congregations,* ed. James P. Wind and James W. Lewis, vol. 2, 23–53. Chicago: University of Chicago Press.

Hunter, James Davison. 1983. *American Evangelicalism: Conservative Religion and the Quandary of Modernity.* New Brunswick, N.J.: Rutgers University Press.

Isajiw, Wsevold. 1974. "Definitions of Ethnicity." *Ethnicity* 1:111–124.

Jackson, Maurice. 1982. "An Analysis of Weber's Theory of Ethnicity." *Humboldt Journal of Social Relations* 10:4–18.

Jacobs, Jane. 1961. *The Death and Life of Great American Cities.* New York: Random House.

James, Janet Wilson, ed. 1989 [1980]. *Women in American Religion.* Philadelphia: University of Pennsylvania Press.

James, William. 1950. *The Principles of Psychology.* London: Macmillan.

Jenkins, Richard. 1997. *Rethinking Ethnicity: Arguments and Explorations.* Thousand Oaks, Calif.: Sage.

Johnson, John M. 1975. *Doing Field Research.* New York: Free Press.

———. 1983. "Trust and Personal Involvements in Fieldwork." In *Contemporary Field Research: A Collection of Readings,* ed. Robert M. Emerson, 253–311. Prospect Heights, Ill.: Waveland.

Jones, E. Stanley. 1970. *The Reconstruction of the Church—On What Pattern?* Nashville: Abingdon.

Jones, Jim. 1998. "Southern Baptists and Blacks: Southern Baptist African American Fellowship, Southern Baptists Deemed Inclusive." *Fort Worth (Texas) Star-Telegram,* June 8, B5.

Jüngel, Eberhard. 1983. *God as the Mystery of the World: On the Foundation of the Theology of the Crucified One in the Dispute between Theism and Atheism.* Trans. Darrell L. Guder. Grand Rapids, Mich.: Eerdmans.

Kaeser, Gigi, and Peggy Gillespie. 1997. *Of Many Colors: Portraits of Multiracial Families.* Amherst, Mass.: University of Massachusetts Press.

Kahn, Jack S., and Jacqueline Denmon. 1992. "An Examination of Social Science Literature Pertaining to Multiracial Identity: A Historical Perspective." In *Racially Mixed People in America,* ed. Maria P. P. Root, 304–317. Newbury Park, Calif.: Sage.

Katz, Jack. 1983. "A Theory of Qualitative Methodology: The Social System of Analytic Fieldwork." In *Contemporary Field Research: A Collection of Readings,* ed. Robert M. Emerson, 127–148. Prospect Heights, Ill.: Waveland.

Kee, Howard Clark. 1995. *Who Are the People of God? Early Christian Models of Community.* New Haven, Conn.: Yale University Press.

Kennedy, Ruby Jo Reeves. 1944. "Single or Triple Melting Pot? Intermarriage Trends in New Haven, 1870–1940." *American Journal of Sociology* 49:331–339.

Kilde, Jeanne Halgren. 2002. *When Church Became Theatre: The Transformation of Evangelical Architecture and Worship in Nineteenth-Century America.* New York: Oxford University Press.

Kimball, Dan. 2003. *The Emerging Church: Vintage Christianity for New Generations.* Nashville: Zondervan.

Kliewer, Stephen. 1987. *How to Live with Diversity in the Local Church*. Washington, D.C.: Alban Institute.

Ladd, George Eldon. 1956. *The Blessed Hope*. Grand Rapids, Mich.: Eerdmans.

LaGrand, James. 1995. *The Earliest Christian Mission to "All Nations": In Light of Matthew's Gospel*. Atlanta: Scholars.

Law, Eric H. F. 1993. *The Wolf Shall Dwell with the Lamb: A Spirituality for Leadership in a Multicultural Community*. St. Louis, Mo.: Chalice.

———. 1996. *The Bush Was Blazing but Not Consumed: Developing a Multicultural Community through Dialogue Liturgy*. St. Louis, Mo.: Chalice.

Lazarsfeld, Paul F., Bernard Berelson, and Hazel Gaudet. 1968 [1944]. *The People's Choice: How the Voter Makes Up His Mind in a Presidential Election*. New York: Columbia University Press.

Lazarsfeld, Paul F., and Herbert Menzel. 1963. "Mass Media and Personal Influence." In *The Science of Human Communication: New Directions and New Findings in Communication Research*, ed. Wilbur Schramm, 94–115. New York: Basic.

Lazarsfeld, Paul F., and Robert K. Merton. 1964. "Friendship as Social Process: A Substantive and Methodological Analysis." In *Freedom and Control in Modern Society*, ed. Morroe Berger et al., 18–66. New York: Octagon.

Lee, Jung Young. 1995. *Marginality: The Key to Multicultural Theology*. Minneapolis: Fortress.

Leonard, Karen Isaksen. 1992. *Making Ethnic Choices: California's Punjabi Mexican Americans*. Philadelphia: Temple University Press.

Lewins, F. W. 1978. "Australia: Religion and Ethnic Identity." In *Identity and Religion: International, Cross-Cultural Approaches*, ed. Hans Mol, 19–38. Beverly Hills, Calif.: Sage.

Lincoln, Yvonna S., and Egon G. Guba. 1985. *Naturalistic Inquiry*. Beverly Hills, Calif.: Sage.

Livingstone, R. B., and T. Dobzhansky. 1962. "On the Non-existence of Human Races." *Current Anthropology* 3:279–281.

Lobdell, William. 2001a. "Differences Aside: At Integrated O.C. Church, Mixed Is a Blessing." *Los Angeles Times*, May 27, B2.

———. 2001b. "Friendships Form as Black and White Churches Integrate." *Los Angeles Times*, May 27, B4.

Lofland, John, and Lyn H. Lofland. 1984. *Analyzing Social Settings: A Guide to Qualitative Observation and Analysis*. 2nd ed. Belmont, Calif.: Wadsworth.

Logan, Sadye L., Edith M. Freeman, and Ruth G. McRoy. 1987. "Racial Identity Problems for Bi-racial Clients: Implications for Social Work Practice." *Journal of Intergroup Relations* 15:11–24.

Lucas, Henry S. 1955. *Netherlanders in America: Dutch Immigration to the United States and Canada, 1789–1950*. Ann Arbor: University of Michigan Press.

Luo, Michael. 1998. "A Church in a Nightclub." *Los Angeles Downtown News*, July 28, 12.

———. 1999. "A Creative Approach to Worship." *Los Angeles Times,* March 16, B3.

Lupton, Robert. 1996. "The Multi-ethnic Church: Unity Inside vs. Community Outside?" *Urban Mission,* June.

Lyman, Stanford M., and William A. Douglass. 1973. "Ethnicity: Strategies of Collective and Individual Impression Management." *Social Research* 40: 344–365.

Lyon, David. 2000. *Jesus in Disneyland: Religion in Postmodern Times.* Malden, Mass.: Polity.

Mallory, Sue. 2001. *The Equipping Church: Serving Together to Transform Lives.* New York: Zondervan.

Mallory, Sue, Brad Smith, Sarah Jane Rehnborg, and Neil Wilson. 2001. *The Equipping Church Guidebook.* New York: Zondervan.

Mamiya, Lawrence H. 1994. "A Social History of the Bethel African Methodist Episcopal Church in Baltimore: The House of God and the Struggle for Freedom." In *American Congregations,* ed. James P. Wind and James W. Lewis, vol. 1, 221–292. Chicago: University of Chicago Press.

Marsden, George M. 1980. *Fundamentalism and American Culture: The Shaping of Twentieth-Century Evangelicalism, 1870–1925.* New York: Oxford University Press.

———. 1991. *Understanding Fundamentalism and Evangelicalism.* Grand Rapids, Mich.: Eerdmans.

Marshall, Catherine, and Gretchen B. Rossman. 1989. *Designing Qualitative Research.* Newbury Park, Calif.: Sage.

Marti, Gerardo. 2003. "Can Lightning Strike Twice? A Comparative Analysis of Two Large, Multi-ethnic Congregations in Los Angeles." Paper presented at the annual meeting of the American Academy of Religion, Salt Lake City, Utah.

———. 2004. "Ethnic Transcendence and Spiritual Kinship in Two Multiethnic Congregations." Paper presented at the annual meeting of the Society for the Scientific Study of Religion, Kansas City, Mo.

Marty, Martin E. 1994. "Public and Private: Congregation as Meeting Place." In *American Congregations,* ed. James P. Wind and James W. Lewis, vol. 2, 133–166. Chicago: University of Chicago Press.

Massey, Douglas S., and Nancy A. Denton. 1993. *American Apartheid: Segregation and the Making of the Underclass.* Cambridge, Mass.: Harvard University Press.

Matsuoka, Fumitaka. 1998. *The Color of Faith: Building Community in a Multiracial Society.* Cleveland: United Church Press.

McAdam, Doug. 1999 [1982]. *Political Process and the Development of Black Insurgency, 1930–1970.* 2nd ed. Chicago: University of Chicago Press.

McAdam, Doug, and David A. Snow. 1997. "Introduction: Social Movements, Conceptual and Theoretical Issues." In *Social Movements: Readings on Their Emergence, Mobilization, and Dynamics,* by Doug McAdam and David A. Snow, xviii–xxvi. Los Angeles: Roxbury.

McCutcheon, Russell T., ed. 1999. *The Insider/Outsider Problem in the Study of Religion: A Reader.* London: Cassell.

McDannell, Colleen. 1995. *Material Christianity: Religion and Popular Culture in America.* New Haven, Conn.: Yale University Press.

McGavran, Donald A. 1990. *Understanding Church Growth.* 3rd ed., revised and edited by C. Peter Wagner. Grand Rapids, Mich.: Eerdmans.

McGavran, Donald A., and Winfield C. Arn. 1977. *Ten Steps for Church Growth.* New York: Harper and Row.

McKay, James. 1982. "An Exploratory Synthesis of Primordial and Mobilisationist Approaches to Ethnic Phenomena." *Ethnic and Racial Studies* 5:395–420.

McKenzie, Steven L. 1997. *All God's Children: A Biblical Critique of Racism.* Louisville, Ky.: Westminster John Knox.

McLaren, Brian D. 2001. *A New Kind of Christian: A Tale of Two Friends on a Spiritual Journey.* San Francisco: Jossey-Bass.

———. 2003. *The Story We Find Ourselves In: Further Adventures of a New Kind of Christian.* San Francisco: Jossey-Bass.

McManus, Erwin Raphael. 2001. *An Unstoppable Force: Daring to Become the Church God Had in Mind.* Loveland, Colo.: Group.

———. 2002. *Seizing Your Divine Moment: Dare to Live a Life of Adventure.* Nashville: Thomas Nelson.

———. 2003. *Uprising: A Revolution of the Soul.* Nashville: Thomas Nelson.

Meeks, Catherine. 1992a. "At the Door of the Church: The Challenge to White and Black People of Faith." In *America's Original Sin: A Study Guide on White Racism,* 79–84. Expanded ed. Washington, D.C.: Sojourners.

———. 1992b. "Rage and Reconciliation: Two Sides of the Same Coin." In *America's Original Sin: A Study Guide on White Racism,* 35–40. Expanded ed. Washington, D.C.: Sojourners.

Miller, Donald E. 1997. *Reinventing American Protestantism: Christianity in the New Millennium.* Berkeley: University of California Press.

———. 1998. "Postdenominational Christianity in the Twenty-First Century." *Annals of the American Academy of Political and Social Science* 558:196–210.

———. 1999. "The Reinvented Church: Styles and Strategies." *Christian Century* 116:1250–1253.

Mittelberg, Mark. 2000. *Building a Contagious Church: Revolutionizing the Way We View and Do Evangelism.* New York: Zondervan.

Mol, Hans. 1976. *Identity and the Sacred: A Sketch for a New Social-Scientific Theory of Religion.* New York: Free Press.

Moltmann, Jürgen. 1974. *The Crucified God: The Cross of Christ as the Foundation and Criticism of Christian Theology.* Trans. R. A. Wilson and John Bowden. New York: Harper and Row.

Moore, R. Laurence. 1994. *Selling God: American Religion in the Marketplace of Culture.* New York: Oxford University Press.

Morgan, Donald W., and Lyle E. Schaller. 2001. *Share the Dream, Build the*

Team: Ten Keys for Revitalizing Your Church. Grand Rapids, Mich.: Baker Book House.

Morris, Aldon D. 1984. *The Origins of the Civil Rights Movement: Black Communities Organizing for Change.* New York: Free Press.

Mosaic People Database. 2003. Maintained by Mosaic, Los Angeles. Data produced by Lucas King by request.

Nagata, Judith A. 1974. "What Is a Malay? Situational Selection of Ethnic Identity in a Plural Society." *American Ethnologist* 1:331–350.

Nagel, Joane. 1994. "Constructing Ethnicity: Creating and Recreating Ethic Identity and Culture." *Social Problems* 41:152–176.

———. 1996. *American Indian Ethnic Renewal: Red Power and the Resurgence of Identity and Culture.* New York: Oxford University Press.

Nees, Thomas G. 1997. *The Changing Face of the Church: From American to Global.* Kansas City, Mo.: Beacon Hill Press of Kansas City.

Neitz, Mary Jo. 1987. *Charisma and Community: A Study of Religious Commitment within the Charismatic Renewal.* New Brunswick, N.J.: Transaction.

Nelson, C. Ellis. 1967. *Where Faith Begins.* Richmond, Va.: John Knox.

Ogden, Greg. 1990. *The New Reformation: Returning the Ministry to the People of God.* New York: Zondervan.

Okamura, Jonathan Y. 1981. "Situational Ethnicity." *Ethnic and Racial Studies* 4, no. 4:452–465.

Okholm, Dennis L., ed. 1997. *The Gospel in Black and White: Theological Resources for Racial Reconciliation.* Downers Grove, Ill.: InterVarsity.

Omi, Michael A. 2001. "The Changing Meaning of Race." In *America Becoming: Racial Trends and Their Consequences,* ed. Neil J. Smelser, William Julius Wilson, and Faith Mitchell, vol. 1, 243–263. Proceedings of the Research Conference on Racial Trends in the United States (Washington, D.C., October 16, 1998). Washington, D.C.: National Academy Press.

Orsi, Robert A. 2002 [1985]. *The Madonna of 115th Street: Faith and Community in Italian Harlem, 1880–1950.* 2nd ed. New Haven, Conn.: Yale University Press.

Ortiz, Manuel. 1996. *One New People: Models for Developing a Multiethnic Church.* Downers Grove, Ill.: InterVarsity.

Papaioannou, George. 1994. "The History of the Greek Orthodox Cathedral of the Annunciation." In *American Congregations,* ed. James P. Wind and James W. Lewis, vol. 1, 520–571. Chicago: University of Chicago Press.

Parker, David, and Miri Song, eds. 2002. *Rethinking "Mixed Race."* New York: Pluto.

Patterson, Orlando. 1975. "Context and Choice in Ethnic Allegiance: A Theoretical Framework and Caribbean Case Study." In *Ethnicity: Theory and Experience,* ed. Nathan Glazer and Daniel P. Moynihan, 305–349. Cambridge, Mass.: Harvard University Press.

———. 1997. *The Ordeal of Integration: Progress and Resentment in American "Racial" Crisis.* Washington, D.C.: Civitas/Counterpoint.

Patton, Michael Quinn. 1990. *Qualitative Evaluation and Research Methods.* Newbury Park, Calif.: Sage.

Payne, J. Barton. 1962. *The Imminent Appearing of Christ.* Grand Rapids, Mich.: Eerdmans.

Pentecost, J. Dwight. 1958. *Things to Come: A Study in Biblical Eschatology.* Findlay, Ohio: Dunham.

Peshkin, Alan. 1986. *God's Choice: The Total World of a Fundamentalist Christian School.* Chicago: University of Chicago Press.

Peters, Tom. 1999. *The Brand You 50: Fifty Ways to Transform Yourself from an "Employee" into a Brand That Shouts Distinction, Commitment, and Passion!* New York: Knopf.

Pettigrew, Thomas F. 1971. *Racially Separate or Together?* New York: McGraw-Hill.

———. 1975. "The Racial Integration of the Schools." In *Racial Discrimination in the United States,* ed. Thomas F. Pettigrew, 224–239. New York: Harper and Row.

———. 1997a. "The Affective Component of Prejudice: Empirical Support for the New View." In *Racial Attitudes in the 1990s: Continuity and Change,* ed. Steven A. Tuch and Jack K. Martin, 76–90. Westport, Conn.: Praeger.

———. 1997b. "Generalized Intergroup Contact Effects on Prejudice." *Personality and Social Psychology Bulletin* 23:173–185.

———. 1998. "Intergroup Contact Theory." *Annual Review of Psychology* 49: 65–85.

Phinney, Jean S. 1992. "The Multigroup Ethnic Identity Measure: A New Scale for Use with Diverse Groups." *Journal of Adolescent Research* 7:156–176.

Pink, Daniel H. 2001. *Free Agent Nation: How America's New Independent Workers Are Transforming the Way We Live.* New York: Warner.

Pinnock, Clark H. 1990. *Tracking the Maze: Finding Our Way through Modern Theology from an Evangelical Perspective.* San Francisco: Harper and Row.

———. 2001. *Most Moved Mover: A Theology of God's Openness.* Grand Rapids, Mich.: Baker Book House.

Plotnikov, Leonard, and M. Silverman. 1978. "Jewish Ethnic Signaling: Social Bonding in Contemporary American Society." *Ethnology* 17:407–423.

Prieto, LaDawn. 2000. "An Urban Mosaic in Shangri-La." In *Gen X Religion,* ed. Richard W. Flory and Donald E Miller, 57–73. New York: Routledge.

Quebedeaux, Richard. 1974. *The Young Evangelicals: Revolution in Orthodoxy.* New York: Harper and Row.

———. 1978. *The Worldly Evangelicals.* San Francisco: Harper and Row.

Quillian, Lincoln, and Mary E. Campbell. 2003. "Beyond Black and White: The Present and Future of Multiracial Friendship Segregation." *American Sociological Review* 68:540–566.

Ramirez, Margaret. 2000. "A Passion Play of Modern Pain." *Los Angeles Times,* April 22, metro section, B1–B2.

Rao, G. Appa, Everett M. Rogers, and S. N. Singh. 1980. "Interpersonal Relations in the Diffusion of an Innovation in Two Indian Villages." *Indian Journal of Extension Education* 16:19–24.

Raymond, Eric S. 1999. *The Cathedral and the Bazaar: Musings on Linux and Open Source by an Accidental Revolutionary.* Sebastopol, Calif.: O'Reilly.

Reason, Peter, ed. 1988. *Human Inquiry in Action: Developments in New Paradigm Research.* London: Sage.

Reese, Alexander. 1975 [1937]. *The Approaching Advent of Christ.* Grand Rapids, Mich.: Grand Rapids International Publications.

Reich, Robert B. 1991. *The Work of Nations: Preparing Ourselves for 21st-Century Capitalism.* New York: Knopf.

———. 2000. *The Future of Success.* New York: Knopf.

Reiter, Richard R., Paul D. Feinberg, Gleason L. Archer, and Douglas J. Moo. 1984. *The Rapture: Pre-, Mid-, or Post-tribulational?* Grand Rapids, Mich.: Zondervan.

Rhoads, David. 1996. *The Challenge of Diversity: The Witness of Paul and the Gospels.* Minneapolis: Fortress.

Rhodes, Stephen A. 1998. *Where the Nations Meet: The Church in a Multicultural World.* Downers Grove, Ill.: InterVarsity.

Rice, Chris P. 2002. *Grace Matters: A True Story of Race, Friendship, and Faith in the Heart of the South.* New York: Jossey-Bass.

Rogers, Everett M. 1995 [1962]. *Diffusion of Innovations.* 4th ed. New York: Free Press.

Romer, Paul. 1993. "Ideas and Things." *Economist,* September 11, 64, 67–68.

Roof, Wade Clark. 1987. *American Mainline Religion: Its Changing Shape and Future.* New Brunswick, N.J.: Rutgers University Press.

———. 1993. *A Generation of Seekers: The Spiritual Journeys of the Baby Boom Generation.* San Francisco: HarperCollins.

———. 1999. *Spiritual Marketplace: Baby Boomers and the Remaking of American Religion.* Princeton, N.J.: Princeton University Press.

Roosens, Eugeen G. 1989. *Creating Ethnicity: The Process of Ethnogenesis.* London: Sage.

Root, Maria P. P., ed. 1992. *Racially Mixed People in America.* Newbury Park, Calif.: Sage.

———. 1996. *The Multiracial Experience: Racial Borders as the New Frontier.* Beverly Hills, Calif.: Sage.

Rosenbaum, James E. 1981. "Careers in a Corporate Hierarchy: A Longitudinal Analysis of Earnings and Level Attainment." In *Research in Social Stratification and Mobility,* ed. Donald J. Treiman and Robert V. Robinson, vol. 1, 95–124. Greenwich, Conn.: Jai.

———. 1984. *Career Mobility in a Corporate Hierarchy.* New York: Academic.

Royce, Anya Peterson. 1982. *Ethnic Identity: Strategies of Diversity.* Bloomington: Indiana University Press.

Sargeant, Kimon Howland. 2000. *Seeker Churches: Promoting Traditional Religion in a Nontraditional Way.* New Brunswick, N.J.: Rutgers University Press.

Schaller, Lyle E. 2000. *The Very Large Church: New Rules for Leaders.* Nashville: Abingdon.

Schatzman, Leonard, and Anselm L. Strauss. 1973. *Field Research: Strategies for a Natural Sociology.* Englewood Cliffs, N.J.: Prentice-Hall.

Schermerhorn, R. A. 1970. *Comparative Ethnic Relations: A Framework for Theory and Research.* New York: Random House.

Schwartz, Gary, and Don Merten. 1971. "Participant Observation and the Discovery of Meaning." *Philosophy of the Social Sciences* 1:279–298.

Schwartz, Howard, and Jerry Jacobs. 1979. *Qualitative Sociology: A Method to the Madness.* New York: Free Press.

Scroggs, Marilee Munger. 1994. "Making a Difference: Fourth Presbyterian Church of Chicago." In *American Congregations,* ed. James P. Wind and James W. Lewis, vol. 1, 464–519. Chicago: University of Chicago Press.

Shaw, Stephen J. 1991. *The Catholic Parish as a Way-Station of Ethnicity and Americanization: Chicago's Germans and Italians, 1903–1939.* Brooklyn, N.Y.: Carlson.

Shearer, Jody Miller. 1995. "Beyond Easy: Building Racial Reconciliation." *Christian Ministry* 26:3.

Shenk, Wilbert R., ed. 1983. *Exploring Church Growth.* Grand Rapids, Mich.: Eerdmans.

Simonton, Dean Keith. 1999. *Origins of Genius: Darwinian Perspectives on Creativity.* New York: Oxford University Press.

Smelser, Neil J., William Julius Wilson, and Faith Mitchell, eds. 2001. *America Becoming: Racial Trends and their Consequences.* 2 vols. Proceedings of the Research Conference on Racial Trends in the United States (Washington, D.C., October 16, 1998). Washington, D.C.: National Academy Press.

Smith, Christian. 1998. *American Evangelicalism: Embattled and Thriving.* Chicago: University of Chicago Press.

Smith, David Norman. 1998. "Faith, Reason, and Charisma: Rudolf Sohm, Max Weber, and the Theology of Grace." *Sociological Inquiry* 68:32–60.

Smith, Ronald A., and David G. Johnson. 1999. "A Leap of Faith: The Merger of Two Churches, One White and One African-American, Is Testing the Ability of Members to Bridge the Racial Divide." *St. Paul Pioneer Press,* April 27, 376.

Snow, David A., E. Burke Rochford, Jr., Steven K. Worden, and Robert D. Benford. 1986. "Frame Alignment Processes, Micromobilization, and Movement Participation." *American Sociological Review* 51:464–481.

Sollors, Werner, ed. 1989. *The Invention of Ethnicity.* New York: Oxford University Press.

"Southern Baptists Attracting More Black Churches." 2000. *Philadelphia Inquirer,* March 25, D1.

Spencer-Byers, Alexis. 1996. "Each According to Its Kind: Do Ethnic Specific Groups Help or Hinder the Cause of Racial Reconciliation." *Reconcilers* (fall).

Spradley, James P. 1979. *The Ethnographic Interview*. New York: Holt, Rinehart and Winston.

———. 1980. *Participant Observation*. New York: Holt, Rinehart and Winston.

Spickard, James V., J. Shawn Landres, and Meredith B. McGuire, eds. 2002. *Personal Knowledge and Beyond: Reshaping the Ethnography of Religion*. New York: New York University Press.

Spickard, Paul R. 1991. *Mixed Blood: Intermarriage and Ethnic Identity in Twentieth-Century America*. Madison: University of Wisconsin Press.

Stake, Robert E. 1996. *The Art of Case Study Research*. Thousand Oaks, Calif.: Sage.

Stark, Rodney, and William Sims Bainbridge. 1987. *A Theory of Religion*. New York: Peter Lang.

Stark, Rodney, and Roger Finke. 2000. *Acts of Faith: Explaining the Human Side of Religion*. Berkeley: University of California Press.

Steinbron, Melvin J. 1997. *The Lay-Driven Church*. New York: Regal.

Stewman, Shelby. 1988. "Organizational Demography." *Annual Review of Sociology* 14:173–202.

Stewman, Shelby, and Suresh L. Konda. 1983. "Careers and Organizational Labor Markets: Demographic Models of Organizational Behavior." *American Journal of Sociology* 88:637–685.

Stockman, Steve. 2001. *Walk On: The Spiritual Journey of U2*. Lake Mary, Fla.: Relevant.

Storper, Michael. 1989. "The Transition to Flexible Specialization in the U.S. Film Industry: External Economies, the Division of Labor, and Crossing Industrial Divides." *Cambridge Journal of Economics* 13:273–305.

Stout, Harry S., and Catherine Brekus. 1994. "A New England Congregation: Center Church, New Haven, 1638–1989." In *American Congregations*, ed. James P. Wind and James W. Lewis, vol. 1, 14–102. Chicago: University of Chicago Press.

Strong, Augustus H. 1907. *Systematic Theology*. Philadelphia: Griffith and Roland.

Stryker, Sheldon. 1981. "Symbolic Interactionism: Themes and Variations." In *Social Psychology: Sociological Perspectives*, ed. Morris Rosenberg and Ralph H. Turner, 3–29. New York: Basic.

Sweet, Leonard. 1999a. *AquaChurch*. Loveland, Colo.: Group.

———. 1999b. *SoulTsunami: Sink or Swim in New Millennium Culture*. Grand Rapids, Mich.: Zondervan.

Swidler, Ann. 1986. "Culture in Action: 'Symbols and Strategies.'" *American Sociological Review* 5:273–286.

Tarde, Gabriel. 1969 [1903]. *The Laws of Imitation*. Trans. Elsie Clews Parsons. Chicago: University of Chicago Press.

Taylor, William C. 1999. "Eric Raymond on Work." *Fast Company,* November, 200.

Thernstrom, Stephan, and Abigail M. Thernstrom. 1997. *America in Black and White: One Nation, Indivisible*. New York: Simon and Schuster.

Thiessen, Henry Clarence. 1979. *Lectures in Systematic Theology*. Grand Rapids, Mich.: Eerdmans.

Thumma, Scott. 1996. "The Kingdom, the Power, and the Glory: The Megachurch in Modern American Society." Ph.D. diss., Emory University.

Thurman, Howard. 1959. *Footprints of a Dream: The Story of the Church for the Fellowship of All Peoples*. New York: Harper and Brothers.

———. 1965. *The Luminous Darkness: A Personal Interpretation of the Anatomy of Segregation and the Ground of Hope*. New York: Harper and Row.

———. 1971. *The Search for Common Ground: An Inquiry into the Basis of Man's Experience of Community*. New York: Harper and Row.

———. 1979. *With Head and Heart: The Autobiography of Howard Thurman*. New York: Harcourt Brace Jovanovich.

Toulis, Nicole Rodriguez. 1997. *Believing Identity: Pentecostalism and the Mediation of Jamaican Ethnicity and Gender in England*. New York: Berg.

Van den Berghe, P. 1967. *Race and Racism: A Comparative Perspective*. New York: Basic.

Volf, Miroslav. 1996. *Exclusion and Embrace: A Theological Exploration of Identity, Otherness, and Reconciliation*. Nashville: Abingdon.

Wagley, Charles. 1952. *Race and Class in Rural Brazil*. Paris: UNESCO.

Wagner, C. Peter. 1976. *Your Church Can Grow*. Ventura, Calif.: Regal.

———. 1979. *Our Kind of People: The Ethical Dimensions of Church Growth in America*. Atlanta: John Knox.

———. 1984. *Leading Your Church to Growth*. Ventura, Calif.: Regal.

———. 1996. *The Healthy Church: Avoiding and Curing the 9 Diseases That Can Afflict Any Church*. Ventura, Calif.: Regal.

Walvoord, John F. 1957. *The Rapture Question*. Findlay, Ohio: Dunham.

———. 1971. *Daniel, the Key to Prophetic Revelation*. Chicago: Moody.

———. 1976. *The Blessed Hope and the Tribulation: A Biblical and Historical Study of Posttribulationism*. Grand Rapids, Mich.: Zondervan.

Warner, R. Stephen. 1988. *New Wine in Old Wineskins: Evanglicals and Liberals in a Small-Town Church*. Berkeley: University of California Press.

———. 1993. "Work in Progress toward a New Paradigm for the Sociological Study of Religion in the United States." *American Journal of Sociology* 98: 1044–1093.

———. 1994. "The Place of the Congregation in the Contemporary American Religious Configuration." In *American Congregations*, ed. James P. Wind and James W. Lewis, vol. 2, 54–99. Chicago: University of Chicago Press.

Warner, W. Lloyd, and Leo Srole. 1945. *The Social System of American Ethnic Groups*. New Haven, Conn.: Yale University Press.

Warren, Rick. 1995. *The Purpose-Driven Church: Growth without Compromising Your Message and Mission*. New York: Zondervan.

———. 1997. *The Purpose-Driven Life: 7 Steps for Discovering and Fulfilling Your Life Mission*. New York: Zondervan.

Waters, Mary C. 1990. *Ethnic Options: Choosing Identities in America*. Berkeley: University of California Press.

Webber, George W. 1964. *The Congregation in Mission: Emerging Structures for the Church in an Urban Society.* Nashville: Abingdon.

Webber, Robert E. 2002. *The Younger Evangelicals: Facing the Challenges of the New World.* Grand Rapids, Mich.: Baker Book House.

Weber, Max. 1976 [1930]. *The Protestant Ethic and the Spirit of Capitalism.* Trans. Talcott Parsons. New York: Charles Scribner's Sons.

———. 1978 [1968]. *Economy and Society: An Outline of Interpretive Sociology.* Ed. Guenther Roth and Claus Wittich. Trans. Ephraim Fischoff et al. Berkeley: University of California Press.

Weber, Timothy P. 1979. *Living in the Shadow of the Second Coming: American Premillenialism, 1875–1925.* New York: Oxford University Press.

Welch, Mary Jane. 2002. "Mosaic." *Commission* 63:28–37.

Welker, Michael. 1996. "Christian Theology at the End of the Second Millennium." In *The Future of Theology: Essays in Honor of Jürgen Moltmann,* ed. Miroslav Volf, Carmen Krieg, and Thomas Kucharz, 73–88. Grand Rapids, Mich.: Eerdmans.

Wells, David F. 1994. *No Place for Truth: Or, Whatever Happened to Evanglical Theology?* Grand Rapids, Mich.: Eerdmans.

Wheeler, Barbara G. 1990. "Uncharted Territory: Congregational Identity and Mainline Protestantism." In *The Presbyterian Predicament: Six Perspectives,* ed. Milton J. Coalter, John M. Mulder, and Louis B. Weeks, 222–245. Louisville, Ky.: Westminster John Knox.

Wheeler, David L. 1995. "A Growing Number of Scientists Reject the Concept of Race." *Chronicle of Higher Education,* February 17, A8–A10, A15.

White, Harrison C. 1970. *Chains of Opportunity: System Models of Mobility in Organizations.* Cambridge, Mass.: Harvard University Press.

Whyte, William H., Jr. 1956. *The Organization Man.* New York: Simon and Schuster.

Wijeyesinghe, Charmaine L. 2001. "Racial Identity in Multiracial People: An Alternative Paradigm." In *New Perspectives on Racial Identity Development: A Theoretical and Practical Anthology,* ed. Charmaine L. Wijeyesinghe and Bailey W. Jackson III, 129–152. New York: New York University Press.

Wilcox, Melissa M. 2003. *Coming Out in Christianity: Religion, Identity, and Community.* Bloomington: Indiana University Press.

Williams, Melvin D. 1974. *Community in a Black Pentecostal Church: An Anthropological Study.* Pittsburgh: University of Pittsburgh Press.

Wilson, Thomas P. 1970. "Conceptions of the Interaction and Forms of Sociological Explanation." *American Sociological Review* 35:697–710.

Wind, James P. 1990. *Places of Worship: Exploring Their History.* Nashville: American Association for State and Local History.

Wind, James P., and James W. Lewis, eds. 1994. *American Congregations.* 2 vols. Chicago: University of Chicago Press.

Winter, Gibson. 1961. *The Suburban Captivity of the Churches: An Analysis of Protestant Responsibility in the Expanding Metropolis.* New York: Doubleday.

Wolfe, Alan. 2003. *The Transformation of American Religion: How We Actually Live Our Faith.* New York: Free Press.

Wuthnow, Robert. 1993. *Christianity in the Twenty-First Century: Reflections on the Challenges Ahead.* New York: Oxford University Press.

———. 1994. *Sharing the Journey: Support Groups and America's New Quest for Community.* New York: Free Press.

———. 2003. *All in Sync: How Music and Art Are Revitalizing American Religion.* Berkeley: University of California Press.

Yancey, George. 1996. *Beyond Black and White: Reflections on Racial Reconciliation.* Grand Rapids, Mich.: Baker.

———. 1998. "Reconciliation Theology: Results of a Multiracial Evangelical Community." Paper presented at the Color Lines in the Twenty-First Century conference, Chicago.

———. 1999. "An Examination of the Effects of Residential and Church Integration on Racial Attitudes of Whites." *Sociological Perspectives* 42:279–305.

———. 2003. *Who Is White? Latinos, Asians, and the New Black/Nonblack Divide.* Boulder, Colo.: Lynne Rienner.

Young, Lawrence A., ed. 1997. *Rational Choice Theory and Religion: Summary and Assessment.* New York: Routledge.

INDEX

GERARDO MARTI is a Cuban American who earned his Ph.D. in Sociology from the University of Southern California. He is now the L. Richardson King Assistant Professor of Sociology at Davidson College. A trained sociologist and an ordained pastor, Marti has studied multiethnic and multiracial churches and congregational responses to social change. His latest book is *Hollywood Faith: Holiness, Prosperity, and Ambition in a Los Angeles Church.*